JOEL BARLOW:
A CONNECTICUT YANKEE IN AN AGE OF REVOLUTION

JOEL BARLOW:
A CONNECTICUT YANKEE IN AN AGE OF REVOLUTION

By Dr. Samuel Bernstein

The Ultima Thule Press
Cliff Island, Maine

To Rose

Copyright © 1985 by
The Ultima Thule Press
Box 93
Cliff Island, via Portland, Maine 04019
All rights reserved. No part of the work may be reproduced or transmitted in any form or by any means without written permission from the publisher, Sammis Publishing Corp., 122 East Twenty-fifth Street, New York, NY 10010

Library of Congress Cataloging in Publication Data

Bernstein, Samuel, 1898-
  A Connecticut Yankee in an age of revolution.

  Includes index.
  1. Barlow, Joel, 1754–1812—Biography. 2. Authors, American—18th century—Biography. 3. Diplomats—United States—Biography. I. Title.
PS705.B47   1984   811'.2 [B]   84-9971
ISBN 0-87469-045-5

CONTENTS

	Page
Preface	1
Introduction	3
Chapter I: In the Spirit of the Enlightenment	12
Chapter II: An Intellectual in Search of a Calling	21
Chapter III: A Noble Vision	33
Chapter IV: The Scioto Business	44
Chapter V: The Big Debate	56
Chapter VI: An Urge to Reform the World	72
Chapter VII: Propagating Revolution	85
Chapter VIII: Conservatism versus Reform	98
Chapter IX: French Revolution Historiography	110
Chapter X: Mission to Algiers	121
Chapter XI: The Conquests of Science	134
Chapter XII: The Cold War Between the United States and France	146
Chapter XIII: Voices of Peace	156
Chapter XIV: Looking at Tomorrow	168
Chapter XV: Proposed Roads to Tomorrow	179
Chapter XVI: Mission to Napoleon	192
Chapter XVII: Failure of a Mission	205
Notes	213
Index	227

Preface

This book is about the Connecticut Yankee, Joel Barlow. He was a many-sided Yankee, a poet and a master of prose, a diplomat and a political philosopher who figured in the revolutionary movements of the last quarter of the eighteenth century. To place our story in a fitting framework, it becomes necessary to take account of these movements and their disquieting aims.

Barlow was a spirited maker of history. He served in the American Revolution, promoted the ends of the British reform societies, penned one of the best among the many polemics against Burke's *Reflections on the Revolution in France*, submitted a set of constitutional revisions to the French National Convention, which earned its praise, and furthered the propaganda of the French Republic.

This is not to say that he put the good of France above that of America. For in the body of his thought the French Revolution was the sequel of the American. Rooted in him was the conviction that by advancing the principles of France he was fortifying those of the United States. His was the belief that the two nations' community of ideas held the prospect of international fraternity. That was why he fought stubbornly against Francophobia in his own country.

Among the Americans in France in the 1790s, Barlow had the reputation of being an astute negotiator. This quality was so strong that James Monroe, American Minister to France, chose him for the trying assignment of bringing round the irascible ruler of Algiers. Back in his own country, Barlow was the confidential consultant to Jefferson and Madison on matters of political and foreign policy.

This invites a bit of comparison between him and the two statesmen. To be sure, he lacked Jefferson's versatility and critical acumen, and he was inferior to Madison in erudition and the power of penetrating historical questions to their depths. But he was at least their equal in probing the political and international questions. According to good authority, no important political issue of either administration was decided without his considered opinion.

Barlow's imagination was captivated by his country's promise. His vision was of an America with vast territory united by roads and internal waterways, untapped resources awaiting the labor of settlers, people instructed and enlightened by a national system of education, potential productivity that would obviate want and poverty, and finally, the leveling of barriers to a democratic way of life—such was his prospectus for the young nation. In his overall view, moreover, America was the exemplar for the subjected peoples after Bonaparte's seizure of power.

A salient feature of Barlow's thought is its unity and continuity. From his early poem "The Prospect of Peace," which he read upon graduating from Yale, to his final composition, "Advice to a Raven in Russia," written in Vilna, runs the invincible hope of the union of peoples.

While collecting material for this book, I visited many research centers and requested microfilms of manuscripts from institutions I was unable to visit. I extend my gratitude to the staffs of all of them for the time and service they gave so ungrudgingly. Especially helpful were the staffs of the Houghton Library, Harvard University; the Pequot Library, Southport, Connecticut; the American Antiquarian Society; the New York Historical Society; the Massachusetts Historical Society; and the Portland, Maine, Public Library. My warmest thanks go to Miss Mary Brown of the American Antiquarian Society and to Mr. Edward Chenevert, director of the Portland Public Library, and his assistant, Mrs. Barbara Smith.

It is difficult to find the proper words that would best express my debt to Rose who has been with this book from the start.

Introduction

Our story spans approximately seven decades. It begins in the middle of the eighteenth century and ends in the second decade of the nineteenth, revolving around events that gave history a push, such as the American War of Independence, the French Revolution and the contemporaneous British agitation for democracy. America, after casting off the colonial straitjacket, confronted the European powers with an equal sense of national pride and determination to defend its rights. In terms of the overriding developments, the period may well be described as the Age of Revolution.

1

Intellectual ferment was evident in America during the second half of the eighteenth century. Benjamin Franklin, John Bartram, David Rittenhouse and Cadwallader Colden were glittering stars in American science and esteemed internationally. Colleges like Harvard and Yale showed a surprising capacity to train teachers of mathematics and science, a number of whom corresponded with learned societies abroad. With Philadelphia as a model, Charleston, South Carolina, established a Library Society which in time expanded beyond early expectations to include a museum and scientific equipment. But Philadelphia was pre-eminent, thanks to the initiative of Franklin and James Logan, and the Library Company they were instrumental in founding possessed before long the best American collection of scientific publications and natural history specimens.

Symptomatic of a growing culture were the scientific societies. In this respect, America was a late-comer. Academies and scientific organizations had been long in existence in Italy and Germany, England and France. In England and France they had been fostering experimental science.[1] America's lag is explainable, if account is taken of the struggle to subdue nature. Even so, scientists and intellectuals established societies in nearly every colony and drafted plans for the collaboration of scientific talent.

The foundation of the American Philosophical Society dates from the 1740s. But its early history was short. Its revival in 1769 was stimulated by Great Britain's aggression against the colonies. The Society aimed at assembling and applying useful knowledge "to common purposes of life." The program was ambitious: to advance agriculture, enlarge trade, reduce domestic drudgery and, in the broad sense, to promote man's happiness.

Two years after its restoration, the Society issued the first volume of its transactions. The enthusiastic reception it received exceeded all anticipation and made the Society known to Europeans before the outbreak of the American Revolution.[2]

The objectives of the Philosophical Society were consistent with Enlightenment opinion that science could level obstacles to improve material conditions. Science and humanitarianism were seen in intimate relation, and scientists were ranked citizens of the world. According to current belief, science and art thrived best in an atmosphere of freedom, for without it the human mind could neither penetrate the mysteries of the universe nor discover the laws governing politics, economics and society as a whole. Accordingly, American scientists gave their services to the Revolution, for they saw a cause-and-effect relationship between the Revolution and the Enlightenment. They believed, as did many French *philosophes*, that America held the key to human perfectibility.

This is not to suggest that American scientists of the revolutionary age were trail-blazers. On the contrary, save for Bartram, Rittenhouse and Franklin, they were harnessed to Europe, to England in particular, and remained so well into the nineteenth century. The frontier mentality and inexorable necessity bred a spirit of anti-intellectualism, so that, in fact, the American climate was inhospitable to scientific theory. An emphasis on applied research characterized science in America for quite a long time.

In literature, as in science, Americans depended on importations or reprints of English classics. The literary explosion during and after the Revolution offered only a hope. American literary talent turned to politics or to law or to what Parrington termed, "the arid realm of theology."

"Revolution," said a Spanish writer, "creates the conditions of a true cultural mutation,"[3] and the American Revolution was no exception. Some of the best prose of the revolutionary generation was reserved for political polemics. Among the cultivators of this style of writing were the aristocratically minded John Dickinson, the democrat Samuel Adams, the humanitarian-cosmopolitan Thomas Paine and the strategist-statesman Thomas Jefferson. Paine's *Common Sense*, the controversial bestseller in its day[4] continues to have a reading public. So does Jefferson's Declaration of Independence.

The agrarian democrat, Benjamin Franklin, was unique for many reasons. Witty, learned and sophisticated, astute and worldly, he was America's gem, respected internationally for his contribution to science. His style was distinguishable—masculine, clear, deliberate and classic in the eighteenth-century manner. He was direct, never pedestrian like John Adams, or verbose like Burke.

There were also minds with a bent for political philosophy, including James Madison, Alexander Hamilton and John Adams. The first was an erudite democrat whose theory on the economic roots of politics had indelibly marked American historical and political thinking. The second, an advocate of the rich, propertied classes, countenanced government by the wealthy and anticipated a booming industrial America. John Adams argued the case of the well-born and educated. Their individual interests could be best fortified, he reasoned, by a balance of interests, which James Harrington had prefigured in the seventeenth century.

Literati and political philosophers, though versed in the legacies of earlier writers, were creators in their own way. Ideas they borrowed from Hobbes, Harrington and Locke, Defoe and Petty, or from Montesquieu, Voltaire and Beccaria, blended with their experience to form principles that were applicable at home. They were removed from the mysticism and stern Calvinism of the Mathers and Jonathan Edwards.

The poetry of the revolutionary age bespoke the youth of America. The style was imitative, but the verses had sincerity and spontaneity. The volume of versification was immense, but only a small portion had enough intrinsic merit to earn it an honored place in American letters. In this surviving body are such anonymous songs as "Yankee Doodle's Simplicity," "The American Patriot's Prayer" and "The Volunteer Boys." By the standards of literary criticism, the mass of songs and ballads falls short of the criterion of good poetry. But it came from the guts and the heart and was a tocsin calling the nation to arms.[5]

Thomas Paine and Philip Freneau belong with the best poets of the Revolution. To Paine we are in debt for "The Liberty Tree" and "The Boston Patriotic Song";[6] to Freneau, justly acclaimed the "Poet of the American Revolution," for his political satires. They were razor-edged, as trenchant as Juvenal's or Churchill's. Freneau was at once an artist and social philospher, cast into the turmoil of history. Art was his weapon, as it was William Blake's. But unlike Blake, he neither hated empiricism nor rejected the Enlightenment.[7]

2

An account of the development of American culture requires some consideration of its debt to French thought. For as Alfred N. Whitehead remarked, "In the eighteenth century France carried the 'White Man's Burden' of intellectual advance."[8] The infiltration of French ideas, noticeable after the Seven Years' War, left its imprint on the pamphlet literature at the start of the American Revolution.[9] Howard Mumford Jones once showed that nearly every prominent French man of letters was more or less frequently advertised by book dealers in New York and Philadelphia. Voltaire's historical works sold better than his philosophical writings.[10] Whatever popularity Rousseau had in America derived from his novels and *Emile* rather than from his political discourses. These were in little demand, including the *Social Contract*, which had but a limited sale even in France before 1789.[11] His discourse on the origin of inequality and the essay on political economy seem to have escaped notice in America.

Montesquieu had an honored place in the American political milieu. His *Spirit of Laws* was featured in advertisements and respectfully referred to at the Continental Congress. Madison's notes on the Constitutional Convention tell us that Montesquieu was cited oftener than Locke. According to a specialist on Montesquieu in America, his classic "was used as an authoritative handbook of political information." Gazettes reprinted lengthy extracts, even entire chapters, to such an extent that had the work become extinct, "a goodly portion of it, certainly the most important parts, could be reconstructed accurately from American newspapers of the eighteenth century."[12]

Americans could find a great variety of French writings in the better bookshops. Fenelon's *Telemachus* was a favorite, probably more so than Marmontel's *Incas*, although *Incas* was set in the Western hemisphere. Diderot, D'Alembert and Helvetius were less frequently listed. Diderot's plays, however, were noticed in the 1790s as was Holbach's violently anti-religious *Christianity Unmasked*.

Howard Mumford Jones observed that, "In no case are thinkers of a conservative stamp much read. Bossuet and Massillon do not appear. We have instead Fontenelle, Pluche, Vertot—liberals and rationalists—in the seventeenth century; and a heavy representation of rationalist thought in the eighteenth century."[13]

American legal theory had native roots, but like literature, philosophy and science it was grafted with scions from Europe. William Blackstone's *Commentaries on the Law of England* was the American lawyers' source book and final authority. His method was exposition, that is, teaching law as it was. The great part of it was common law, which meant that its binding power stemmed from long usage. The fact that history had made it obsolete was less important than its imposing existence and continuity. As a collection of age-old decisions, the law obviously required the services of knowledgeable men who could interpret as well as apply it to immediate situations. Clearly the *Commentaries* sanctioned conservatism.

We are not ruling out other legal authorities to whom students of the law were referred. Vattel, for example, was read for his principles of international law. Scholars also studied Hooker, Sidney and Bolingbroke, Grotius and Puffendorf, Beccaria and Burlamaqui.

Jean Jacques Burlamaqui was long considered a minor authority in American legal history and political science. This viewpoint has since been revised. New evidence has proved that Burlamaqui's *Principles of Natural and Politic Law*[14] was well known. It was popular with lawyers, teachers of the law and ministers who preached election sermons. Its essential doctrines, applicable to the United States, were as follows: A basic law was distinct from the law of nature; all political power resided in the body politic; government had to be restrained by the fundamental law, specifically by the separation of authority; the body politic had the right of revolution as a final sanction; the constitution was the source of governmental power; it stemmed from the people and could be changed in the same way it was established.[15]

Burlamaqui was cited by the creators of the American constitution and conservatives. He held "that the best governments are those which are so tempered, as to secure the happiness of the subjects, by avoiding tyranny and licentiousness"; or as he further phrased it, "an aristocracy tempered with democracy, by some privileges in favor of the body of the people."[16]

3

European ideas are recognizable in eighteenth-century American thought. There is, for instance, a faith in progress, which Americans liked to believe was best exemplified by their own country. The effect was to animate national pride and to inculcate a sense of history, which Voltaire and Chastellux had laid out in broad vistas. The Revolution sharpened this sense. Looking into the past, Americans learned that separation from England had been long in coming; the Revolution was the culmination. What they found out from European soldiers, the French especially, also brightened their prospects. For they were informed of the esteem in which their country was held abroad and of the infectious example of their free institutions.

Noticeable, too, in American thinking was the compact theory Hobbes had made into a prop of absolutism. But Americans leaned on Locke who justified revolution and the sovereignty of the people.

A capital issue which divided the best minds in America and Europe alike was the type of political order that would ensure the greatest stability. Hamilton's stand upon a strong government that could keep the multitude in line bespoke the interests of the wealthy. According to John Adams, the best equipped to govern were a "natural aristocracy," by which he meant those well-born and well-endowed with a morally binding sense. It was government by an elite that would secure property and act as an umpire between the wealthy oligarchy and the disadvantaged masses. To this purpose he would curb the excessive concentration of wealth, limit the franchise and promote the diffusion of land ownership.[17]

Neither Hamilton's nor Adams's scheme of government made any concession to the popular judgment in which Jefferson's faith lay. Power exercised by a privileged minority, Jefferson said, meant tyranny. His antidote was that all authority belonged to the people. The threat to social peace arose not from them, he claimed, but from a rising financial and capitalist class and an urban proletariat. The remedy was an expanded class of small farmers. They made the best citizens.

The trend to unfettered trade relations, accelerated by the American Revolution, was impelled by liberals and reformers. Monopoly, they said, was an abuse of power. It deadened talent, impeded the fair exchange of values, benefitted a tiny minority and aggravated class strife. Extending the reasoning to politics, anti-monopolists opposed a strong government, believing that it would inevitably encroach on the people's rights. Government should be invested merely with policing powers.

Jefferson was one of the most articulate foes of monopoly. He drew his arguments from several sources, principally from Adam Smith and less so from the Physiocrats, as has been shown.[18] Jefferson would employ bold measures to contain monopolies, such as preventing the concentration of wealth, taxing the rich and promoting the division of large estates.

Anti-monopoly also inspired Benjamin Franklin, perhaps the acutest economic mind of his generation in America. Reflecting the interests of the American middle class, he opposed tariffs and argued for a paper currency. Though he hobnobbed with Physiocrats and for a time subscribed to their cardinal tenet that agriculture was the source of all value, he never accepted either their doctrine of legal despotism or the economic table of their master, Quesnay. Instead, he considered labor the measure of value and spelled out the necessary virtues of an individual whose ambition was to succeed in an acquisitive society. Unlike Jefferson, Franklin prefigured the American capitalistic mind.

With the growth of a national culture arose a sense of unity, though it was slow in taking hold. The most important attempt at confederating the colonies before the Revolution was the Albany Convention in 1754, where seven colonies were represented.[19] After 1763 Americans were shedding their colonial point of view and, under the stress of events, were seeing America in broader, even worldwide, perspective. Expression of national consciousness at times had a rude, strident tone. Yet it conveyed a pervading and increasingly persuasive sentiment that Americans were special, that their country was called upon to fulfill the promise of a happy society.

This image of the country was in character with its idealization by contemporary European minds, a number of which regarded America as a bucolic Eden. Philosophers, such as Turgot and Diderot, Chastellux, Mably and Condorcet, foresaw America reaching a state in which man would achieve the noblest creations in art, science and politics.[20] Those with a steadfast faith believed that Providence had assigned America a glorious future.

There were also voices of dissent. Buffon and Raynal, for example, shared the thesis of Cornelius de Paw, which maintained that instead of being the paradise of the noble savage, America was decadent and Europeans had nothing to learn from her.[21]

Americans themselves disproved the thesis. During the French and Indian War, Frenchmen discovered that Americans were not only excellent marksmen and valiant soldiers, but were also resourceful people with an untapped potential. Then came the stormy years, beginning with the Stamp Act and culminating in the Revolution. Certainly, no observer of events, however blinded by prejudice, could possibly connect decadence with such militancy. The Revolution not only conclusively refuted the thesis, it sounded a loud alarm in Europe and hastened the attack on the old order. Americans could be justly proud of having been, if not a model, at least in the vanguard of the war against feudalism and despotism.

Consistent with America's pioneering in the struggle for freedom was a rising anti-slavery sentiment. The slave trade was the principal target of pamphleteers as they assaulted the entire institution of slavery. Anthony Benezet was the most prolific,[22] and Tom Paine the most forthright, going as far as abolitionism.[23] In 1775 was founded the Society for the Relief of Free Negroes Unlawfully Held in Bondage.

4

America was growing up rapidly in the second half of the eighteenth century. Its population was increasing and spreading westward. Its trade was reaching out and bringing wealth into the country. Much of the trade was with southern Europe and the West Indies, where the necessary specie was obtained for paying balances to British creditors. By wiping out foreign controls, the Revolution set America on a course of free development.

The event unshackled minds and excited the leveling spirit. But it did not send crashing into ruins the foundations of existing institutions, as did the French and Russian revolutions, nor did it radically disorder class relations. Socially and politically, Americans continued to be divided. Although class lines were far from hardened, the mass of the society rested in the bottom rungs of the social ladder. Only slaves, indentured servants, apprentices and a large number of debtors were below them. Like many others, they were disfranchised for want of the necessary property qualifications. At the top was the ruling gentry guarding its privileges and vigorously opposing pressures for reform. Only he could vote who had a free hold of at least twenty-five to fifty acres. If land was cheap, many could meet the requirement. But if land values rose, especially in established communities, artisans and laborers were disqualified. Also deprived of the voting right were religious dissenters. The Revolution broadened the franchise, not because property qualifications ceased to be the rule, but because many individuals acquired portions of the confiscated loyalist properties. Entails were abolished in all but two states in the decade after the Declaration of Independence. The religious barrier to voting was, however, only gradually removed in several states.[24]

Class divisions and economic inequality were everywhere in America. A considered estimate has it that a high degree of concentrated wealth existed in the southern as well as in the northern states. Approximately one-third of the population, if Negro slaves were included, was in the poor class.[25] Many were debtors, rotting in prisons. Social dichotomies like these may explain the anxieties and policies of the well-to-do in pre- and post-revolutionary years.

Resentment against privilege and monopoly was prevalent. Only three years after the signing of the peace treaty, insurrections erupted in Massachusetts and New Hampshire. Similar reasons accounted, in the 1790s, for the spread of democratic republicanism, the popularity of Jefferson and the wave of enthusiasm for the French Revolution.

Irreconcilable were the differences between aristocratic and democratic views of the social order. Those who subscribed to the principles of the former, equated democracy with anarchy. The people were unfit to govern, they said, for they were corruptible and controlled by demagogues. The argument was in line with the Puritan doctrine that the different orders of society had to remain in the stations God had assigned them. Attempts to climb to a higher order would subvert the Providential plan.

The Revolution shook the old order without toppling it. Returning soldiers could scarcely share the old notion that the plain people were incapable of participating in lawmaking. Nor were they passive onlookers of constitutions and measures that protected the rich and left the poor in distress. A sense of having been wronged and an urge to correct injustices gripped many Americans. Criticism of property relations in America did not extend as far as common ownership, as it did with the Diggers in England or with the Babouvists in France. The comparable movement in America, led by Daniel Shays, was an uprising against foreclosures, imprisonment for debt and harassing legislation. Its final aim, as the physician and magistrate William Whiting proposed, was equal ownership, that is, a society of small property owners.[26] The aim was also that of the Jeffersonian republican innkeeper, William Manning of Massachusetts, as he postulated in *The Key of Liberty*.[27] In other words, Shays' movement was not a threat to the existing order founded on private property. But the well-to-do regarded it as a gloomy foreboding and called for its suppression. It is common knowledge that the constitution makers of 1787 looked upon the outbreak as good ground for setting up a strong central government.

This was their answer to a deeply disturbed situation. Trade was nearly paralyzed; foreign payments were halted for want of specie; paper money was abundant and falling in value; the volume of private and public debts impaired credit; and land speculators conspired to plunder the public domain. Most everyone doubted the security of existing institutions. Churchgoing declined. The spread of rationalism caused many either to question age-old dogmas or to become sceptics and scoffers. Strayers from the accepted faith were charged with irreligion or atheism. The accusation was, of course, exaggerated. Deviators from orthodoxy migrated either to dissident sects or to deists who viewed the Great Artificer merely as the First Cause. In either case, it was a far cry from atheism.

The struggle between orthodoxy and dissent was especially bitter in New England. In three of the states, Congregationalism was the established faith, which even dissenters long supported with tithes. Church attendance was obligatory. It was also an escape from the tedium of a daily, shut-in existence. Life in the community revolved around the church. It was the social and intellectual center, rivaled only by the tavern as a meeting place. In fact, the tavern was often located close to the church "for the express purpose of Sunday refreshment during the noon period."[28]

Connecticut, where Joel Barlow grew up, held out against reform for quite sometime. Here the social hierarchy remained entrenched. It had overcome the challenge of ambitious men from below, and had resisted the corrosive effects of trade. Prosperity came to Connecticut in the middle of the eighteenth century. Population rose, as did the standard of living. But prosperity also weakened the grip of orthodoxy, so that Congregationalism had to grant legal status to Anglicans and Baptists. By 1765, according to a recent study, the Establishment could not set the intellectual and moral tone of the colony, for the reason that "no single authorized intellectual system overreached all of society."[29]

Tradition, nevertheless, had a firm grip in Connecticut. Old families continued to stay at the helm of power. A code of Blue Laws forbade the use of dice, cards, shuffleboards, billiards and kites. They were all regarded as shams, vice-breeding joys.[30]

Authority died hard in Connecticut. The colonial charter served as a scheme of government up to 1818. Also disestablishment was stalled until the same year. In other words, Connecticut was long a stronghold of conservatism.

Chapter I:
In the Spirit of the Enlightenment

1

Two delegates from the Society for Constitutional Information in London were admitted to the bar of the French National Convention on November 28, 1792. Applause hailed their declaration that the French example had animated the spirit of inquiry and reform in England. With profuse optimism, they foresaw the day when the French would in turn congratulate a British convention.

The address conveyed the Society's confidence that the new French constitution would be grounded on reason and nature. The French should not be misguided by the noisy opposition abroad, for their friends were very numerous. The conclusion said grandiloquently that neither English liberties nor the American example could have stirred people into action without the impulse of the French Revolution.

The delegates then announced that their Society had donated 1,000 pairs of shoes to the soldiers of France and had promised to send the same number for six consecutive weeks. The hall resounded with prolonged acclamation. It was interrupted by the chairman, the priest, Henri Grégoire, a defender of the rights of Negroes and Jews. The opening words of his reply epitomized the fraternalism of the deputies. "The defenders of our liberty will one day be the supporters of your own. You command our esteem, you will accept our gratitude. The sons of liberty through the world will never forget their obligations to the English nation. The shades of Pym, of Hampden and of Sidney, are hovering over our heads; and the moment cannot be distant when the people of France will offer their congratulations to a national convention in England."[1] (The rest of the answer was a variation on the theme. Both address and answer were ordered to be printed and distributed.)

The two delegates reported to their Society the cordial reception of the Convention. "The scene," they wrote, "gave rise to reflections, which can scarcely be conceived by men in any other circumstances of life; it was the reconciliation of brothers, who had long been excited to a mortal enmity of misunderstanding and mutual imposition."[2]

One of the delegates was the reformer, John Frost, who at forty-two had the effective energy of a younger man. He had been trained for the bar, but his attention to the practice of law had been sidetracked. Converted to the principles of the French Revolution, he endeavored to seed them in England. Early in 1793 he was charged with sedition and sentenced to six months in prison, but poor health secured his release. Meanwhile, his name had been struck off the roll of attorneys.[3]

The other delegate, Frost's junior by four years, was Joel Barlow, a Connecticut-bred Yankee. He was well-known among British radicals for his reply to Burke's *Reflections on the Revolution in France* and for a reasoned inquiry into the defects of the French Constitution of 1791. Copies of the two publications were sent to the London reform societies.[4] Barlow was also an active member of the Society for Constitutional Information and apparently a member in high standing, for when the Society resolved to send an address to the French Convention, Barlow was appointed to the drafting committee. The address, adopted on November 2, 1792, was from his pen, which is most likely the reason for his choice as delegate.[5]

Barlow's name had become popular in English democratic circles.[6] His reputation might have landed him in Newgate. So he decided to stay in Paris where he had many friends. Among them were Brissot, a journalist and a top Girondist; the influential Mme. Roland; Paine, whom he had known in the United States; American businessmen; and British residents, one of them Helen Maria Williams, a blue-stocking spinster and a poetess of sorts. Besides, the French capital was exciting, the one spot in Europe where Barlow could see revolution in the making. Paris was a caldron of dreams, the kind that would move heaven to earth. Here were assembled the nation's best minds; Paris was a nursery of seminal ideas.

Barlow supported the Revolution heart and soul. Shortly after he and Frost had submitted the address to the convention, he was invited to join a commission to recently annexed Savoy. Apparently he had already won the confidence of the deputies. A further token of their esteem was their honoring him with the title of French citizen.

Barlow felt that he was on the threshold of a radiant tomorrow. His head was full of ideas that had sprouted from the Enlightenment and the American Revolution. His ideas gave no peace to those vested with power, insofar as they stemmed from the conviction that liberty could be achieved only through victory over decadent institutions and antiquated practices.

Suggested in the address to the Convention was his pride in the American Revolution, which developed during his long stay abroad into an image of America's future greatness.

2

Barlow's view of life had lost its parochialism since his boarding the boat to France some five years earlier. He was then a homespun littérateur, a confessed poet and the author of a mediocre epic. Yet his purpose in going abroad was quite prosaic. He was to serve as a real estate agent for American land speculators. This employment, it hardly needs stressing, mixed poorly with the profession of letters. Nearly a decade earlier, Barlow had written to Ruth Baldwin, his fiancée, that the commercial occupation narrowed the mind, made pedants of people and hindered the "exertion of genius."[7] Why then did he enter upon the business of land salesman? The most obvious answer was that he needed a source of livelihood. He had tried teaching, publishing, printing, bookselling, law practice, even the chaplaincy, but they were either unrewarding or wearisome. Only literature intrigued him, poetry in particular, the most precarious of all bread-earning pursuits.

But poetry was his love. He had been playing with rhymes since adolescence. The older he grew the deeper went his passion for versifying. He read Milton, Dryden and Pope, Thomson, Gray and Goldsmith, perhaps also the many ballads and songs composed during the American Revolution.

Reasons other than employment impelled Barlow to journey to France. He was as restless as a pioneer, on the move at every occasion, as if in pursuit of some receding goal. He imagined himself roaming over an open world. He had heard much about France and met Frenchmen during the American Revolution. He might have read translations of French writings, for who among literati did not know the names of Voltaire and Rousseau? And who in America did not hear of Lafayette and Rochambeau? Notable Americans such as Franklin, esteemed in France as always, and Jefferson, serving as his country's minister, had already been or were still in France. Over and above dreams and allurements, selling land held the hope of eventual success. Land-hungry Frenchmen in their overpopulated country of large estates would be likely purchasers. Barlow had visions of fortune and of the longed-for leisure to luxuriate on Mount Parnassus. With this expectation, he sailed from New York on May 25, 1788.

3

Let us go back more than three decades to Barlow's beginning. He was born March 24, 1754, in the village of Redding, Connecticut, sixty miles southwest of Hartford. In 1767 part of Fairfield, Redding, was incorporated as a town.[8] Its population had increased as had that of the colony, for Connecticut was sharing in the general prosperity. If a consequence was to amplify dissent, it was still unable to weaken the power of the aristocracy.

The Barlows had a long history. By the time Joel was born, the family was in its fourth generation and raising a fifth. The father, Samuel Barlow, an industrious farmer, had nine children by two wives. The second, a Redding girl, was the mother of five children, of whom Joel was the fourth.[9] During the Revolution, Aaron, the second son, served as a colonel and subsequently died of yellow fever in Norfolk, Virginia. Thomas, the youngest of his large family, was later adopted by Joel Barlow.

Samuel Barlow was reckoned prosperous in his day. With his seven sons he could work his farm of 170 acres, maintain the family and show a profit. Joel had the usual jobs of a farm boy: chopping wood, following the plow, feeding and milking the cows, hoeing and harvesting. The farming season left little time for diversion, save compulsory Sunday attendance at the Congregational Church. It is impossible to say whether Joel's attention survived the long, droning sermons. But he probably looked forward to the weekly visit, when he met boys of his age living miles away, or exchanged furtive glances with long-gowned, guarded maidens. Joel did not shun the corn field.

When the pledged roasting-ears invite the maid
To meet her swain beneath the new-formed shade,

nor did he miss the husking-bee in the corn house. In a spell of homesickness years later, Barlow recreated the joyous scene which a Breughel might have immortalized.

The dry husks rustle, and the corncobs crack;
The song, the laugh, alternate notes resound,
And the sweet cider trips in silence round.[10]

We have no way of knowing when Joel began to learn reading and writing. Probably, as in other rural communities, he was taught by the pastor. Books seem to have held his interest. What he read can only be conjectured. The library of a typical New England village of the eighteenth century had no more than one hundred books, not including works on religion. A young bibliophile might have found on the shelves a Josephus, Rollin's *Ancient History*, Cowper's *A Pilgrim's Progress* and lives of distinguished preachers. Perhaps there were also Dryden, Pope and even Shakespeare, although Shakespeare's dramas were proscribed. Of the more than four hundred titles by Cotton Mather, a number would surely have been in the local library.[11]

His love of books made Joel the pastor's favorite and convinced his father that he was meant for higher learning. At nineteen he was enrolled in an academy in Hanover, New Hampshire, to prepare him for

Dartmouth. An agreement was reached whereby his board and tuition would be covered provided he perform sundry chores at school. (The duties might have been quite time-consuming for one with a bent for reading.) Upon the death of his father three months after his enrollment, Joel Barlow tranferred to Yale.

The reasons for the move escape us. Perhaps his widowed mother wanted him closer to home. Perhaps it was his own decision, for a backwoods community like Hanover must have been an extremely dull place. He loved people, and at the age of twenty he longed for some excitement. So he went to New Haven and was admitted to the freshman class.[12]

The intellectual climate at the college had begun to change before his arrival. The refreshing air of science was penetrating the stuffy stronghold of Calvinism. The founding of a chair in mathematics was regarded as a successful encounter with superstition. There was a call, too, for the teaching of chemistry and botany.[13] In fact, the whole curriculum was in the process of revision. Student societies performed plays, even as die-hards complained that the stage was an idle amusement and a straying from Godliness.

A tendency to question accepted dogmas was popular. Ezra Stiles, who became president of Yale in 1777, observed that during the French and Indian War, American army officers in New England had been sufficiently corrupted by infidelity to deny basic Calvinist principles. And this, he predicted, "will have an unhappy effect of a sudden to spread Deism or at least Scepticism thro' these colonies." The way to withstand the heresy, said Stiles, was not to keep the deistical writings from readers, but to meet them in open discussion.[14] The Revolution spread scepticism among Yale's undergraduates. By the time Barlow was admitted, doubts about Calvinist doctrine had already been seeded there.

The course of study at Yale was designed to produce orthodoxists. During four long years, students lived with the New Testament, the catechism, the Westminster Confession and basic books, among them *The Freedom of the Will* by Jonathan Edwards. Equally prescribed was Locke's *Essay Concerning Human Understanding*. Its sensational psychology was looked upon as inconsequential for conduct. What mattered was the author's view that the Christian belief was necessary for human guidance. Translating from Latin and Greek was considered good exercise to discipline the mind. It probably left many with an incurable distaste for the classics.

Everyone had to abide by the college rules or risk punishment. Every morning and evening students had to be at Chapel to hear the president or a tutor read a portion of the Scriptures. They were also required to attend worship on the Lord's Day, on Days of Fasting and Thanksgiving. They dare not be absent without permission, save at specified hours. The grounds for fines and expulsion were many, from profanity and denial of the divine authority of the Scriptures to gambling, drunkenness and fornication.[15]

During Barlow's four years at Yale, the colonies were incited to revolution. Parliament's order to close the Boston harbor in retaliation for the tea dumping in December 1773 brought into existence the first Continental Congress. Several days before its opening, General Gage seized the Massachusetts powder stock. The colony responded by summoning a provincial congress and calling into action an organization of minutemen.

A pamphlet war arose between champions of imperial unity and defenders of colonial rights. Men like James Wilson, Joseph Galloway and Daniel Leonard wrote in behalf of the British Empire. The cause of America was upheld by such advocates as Franklin, Jefferson and Hamilton. Before very long, they were joined by Paine who had arrived from England in November 1774.

After Lexington and Bunker Hill, an adjustment of differences became difficult, though it continued to be the hope of many. But the sizable number of casualties drained the force of their arguments. The fact was the American Revolution had begun and there was no turning back. The Second Continental Congress met in May 1775, appointed George Washington commander-in-chief of the Continental Army, issued paper money, created a Committee on Foreign Affairs and initiated an American navy. In other words, a dual power had been created that could act with sovereign authority.

Efforts at reconciliation proved ineffectual. The landing of British troops and George III's Proclamation of Rebellion only frayed the ties with the empire. Committees of Correspondence speeded communications from North to South; volunteers filled the ranks of the revolutionary army; and, if Americans still doubted the necessity of separation from Great Britain, Paine's *Common Sense* brought them around. Published January 10, 1776, it sold 120,000 copies in the first three months. The idea of American independence was taking hold. The Declaration of Independence made it a fact.

The Revolution disordered studies at Yale as it did in other colleges. Before Barlow finished his freshman year, the first battles of the Revolution had been fought. "The students," Barlow wrote to his mother on July 6, 1775, "are sensably [sic] affected with the unhappy situation of publick affairs, which is a great hindrance to their studies; and for that reason, there has been talk of dismissing college; but whether they will tis uncertin."[16]

Feeding the students became such an overriding problem that the college authorities had to move them to three separate communities. Classes were dispersed but not suspended. A professor and a tutor were in charge of each division. Barlow was housed in Glastonbury, close to Hartford. His class was directed by Nathanial Strong, Professor of Natural and Experimental Philosophy, and the Reverend Joseph Buckminster,[17] with whom Barlow became friendly.

But let us regress just a bit before continuing. Tragedy cast a shadow over Barlow's first year at Yale. His mother died at the end of August 1775, at the age of fifty-four. As executor of the estate, he had to stay in Redding until the will was settled. The old house seemed desolate. Only a fourteen-year-old sister remained at home. Three brothers were with General Montgomery's army in Canada. A mood of loneliness brought forth these early lines:

Pale want appears and sickening hope is fled.
In early life of every aid bereft;
Alone, untaught, an orphan stripling left
While the small hope my faithless fortune gave
Sinks with my parents to the untimely grave![18]

Joel probably welcomed the return to college. Classmates and friends must have exchanged news of the spreading war. The siege of the British in Boston, the American capture of Ticonderoga and Crown Point, the raising of ten companies of riflemen by the Continental Congress, the British burning of Falmouth—fighting had broken out on many fronts. Early in 1776 Barlow learned that his favorite brother had died in Poughkeepsie while returning from the battle of Quebec.

The Revolution required the service of all devoted Americans. The Declaration of Independence had animated the students. The British were counting on the capture of New York City, and with that achieved, they planned to move northward to sever New England from the other states. A call to arms was answered in Connecticut. Yale students volunteered, Barlow among them, and were immediately marched to New York. By the end of August the Americans were badly beaten in Long Island, and Washington retreated to Harlem Heights. We do not know Barlow's part in the battle. Illness soon compelled him to return to New Haven.

His two last years at college were comparatively calm. After more than a twelve-month's stay at Glastonbury, under trying conditions, and a disciplinary action by the college corporation, Joel resumed the normal course of studies. By the time he went back to classes, the college was headed by a new president, Ezra Stiles, a fine human being and a friend of the students. An understanding developed between Stiles and Barlow that would ripen in later years.

The graduating class of 1778 was exceptional. Of its twenty-three members, many rose to distinction. Among them were Oliver Wolcott, Secretary of the Treasury under President John Adams; Zaphaniah Swift, Secretary to Oliver Ellsworth, envoy to France in 1800, and the author of the first American law text; and Uriah Tracy, senator from Connecticut;

Noah Webster; Josiah Meigs, professor of mathematics and natural philosophy at Yale and later president of the University of Georgia; and of course Barlow, littérateur and diplomat.

Joel Barlow never excelled in his studies, but he was amiable and well-liked. His classmates considered him to be the coming American poet. Oliver Wolcott, who fought wearisome battles with rhymes, sang his praises. Barlow belonged to a literary society of which Webster and the cousins Oliver and Alexander Wolcott were members. Apparently he had a penchant for debating. Ezra Stiles recorded in his diary on July 14, 1778, "The Seniors disputed forensically this day a two fold Question, 'Whether the Destruction of the Alexandrine Library, and the Ignorance of the Middle Ages, caused by the Inunda of the Goths and Vandals, were Events unfortunate to Literature.' They disputed inimatably well, particularly Barlow, Swift, Webster, Gilbert, Meigs, Sage etc."[19]

Barlow had two tutors who turned out to be life-long friends, Joseph Buckminster and Abraham Baldwin. Buckminster was later called to the pastorate of the First Congregational Church in Portsmouth, New Hampshire. The Marquis de Chastellux, who heard him preach in November 1782, made the following notation:

"Mr. Buckminster, a young minister, spoke with a great deal of grace, and reasonably enough for a preacher. I especially noted the skillful manner in which he introduced politics into his sermon by comparing Christians redeemed by the blood of Jesus Christ, but still compelled to fight against the flesh and sin, to the thirteen United States who have acquired liberty and independence, but are still obliged to employ all their strength to combat a formidable power and preserve the treasure they have gained."[20]

Buckminster was one of those clergymen who encouraged freedom of inquiry. An exchange of letters ensued between him and his former pupil, the one urging the other to cultivate his taste for poetry, preferably with religious themes, and to enter the ministry because it would give him the leisure to write.

Baldwin became Barlow's brother-in-law and intimate friend. His public career was distinguished: He assisted in drafting the Federal Constitution, served several terms as senator from Georgia and drew up the charter of its university.

Timothy Dwight was another tutor at Yale, Barlow's senior by two years. Graduating from Yale at seventeen, Dwight was a tutor at nineteen. In 1779 Barlow was employed at Dwight's school at Northampton, Massachusetts, where he wrote a draft of what later evolved into *The Vision of Columbus*.

By the time Barlow graduated in July 1778, the Revolution was making giant strides. States were setting up governments and adopting constitutions. The previous November, Congress had adopted the Articles, of Confederation, which twelve states signed within the next six months.

French aid, which Burgoyne's surrender had assured, was secured by two Franco-American treaties, a Treaty of Commerce and a Treaty of Alliance. Nearly a fortnight before the commencement exercises at Yale, France declared war against Great Britain.

The commencement was without academic pageantry. Barlow had been programmed to read "The Prospect of Peace."[21] The poem was not a masterpiece. Though Barlow was twenty-four, he was still writing in the form of the heroic couplet. If his first poetry, dating from 1775, was a sample,[22] it showed little creative talent.

"The Prospect of Peace" marked an advance. It had, to be sure, the metrical monotony of his earlier verses. Yet it oozed optimism. It voiced a national feeling the Revolution had unbridled, and it glorified America's future. With the coming of peace would flourish agriculture, industry and commerce. Cities would arise, freed slaves would take their rightful places as equals, and science would advance all of mankind. Franklin and Rittenhouse were extolled as enlighteners of the two hemispheres.

The poem revealed strains of thought that entered into the author's later body of ideas. Though it made religion a partner of science, and saw:

th'imperial GUIDE from heaven descend,
Whose beams are peace, whose kingdom knows no end,

It was secular nevertheless. Progress was the theme, science the means, peace the end, and freedom the universal climate. Barlow closed his stay at Yale on a note that sounded the spirit of the Enlightenment.

He left New Haven without knowing what to turn to for a livelihood. He had neither a trade nor a profession nor an estate. He had, of course, the formal academic training had only by a tiny minority in those days. But he also had two serious impediments to fortune: he was a would-be poet and an intellectual, both of which suffered when he finally attained a measure of affluence. Still he wrote some of the best prose of the day and composed at least two enduring poems.

Chapter II
An Intellectual in Search of a Calling

Philip Freneau once cautioned those who aspired to live by their pen:

Of all the fools that haunt our coast
The scribbling tribe I pity most;
Their's is a standing scene of woes,
And their's no prospect of repose.[1]

Barlow, in the 1780s, lacked the experience to appreciate such advice. For these were the years he worshipped the arts. The thought possessed him that he might rise to eminence as the poet of the new nation. "The Prospect of Peace" had been rushed into print as though it were the product of an illustrious littérateur. Buckminster and Oliver Wolcott eulogized it and his lady-friends in New Haven were flattered by the company of a celebrity. Barlow was simply elated.

But Barlow was also in want of security. He had neither funds nor a place he could call his own. "I have been very unsteady since I broke loose from college," he wrote in 1778 to his equally impecunious classmate, Noah Webster. "I have been sometimes at N. Haven, sometimes at Redding and sometimes in the army, or *at* the army."[2] And to the same friend a few months later:

> You and I are not the first men in the world that have broken loose from college without friends and without fortune to push us into public notice. Let us show the world a few more examples of men standing upon their own merit, and rising in spite of opposition. I have too much confidence in your merit, both as to greatness of genius and goodness of heart to suppose that your actions are not to be conspicuous; and I hope you have too much confidence in my friendship to suppose that I do not speak from the heart. . . . I am yet at a loss for an employment for life, and unhappy in this state of suspense.[3]

The learned professions had little attraction for him. He had studied enough theology to know that he was not cut out to preach. Teaching might be a way to eke out a living, but it extinguished the spark of creative talent. Literary merit, he trusted, might be rewarding in the young republic, once it gained independence. However, he must have been a bit disheartened when he read in one of Buckminster's letters "that neither our country nor our countrymen are sufficiently refined, enriched, and improved to give a sufficient support to works of genius merely, and had you the genius of a Pope or a Milton, nay, as much superior as you wish, you might starve upon the pittance that a few persons capable of relishing your productions would give."[4]

The letter condensed a wealth of understanding. A revolutionary period, generally speaking, is inhospitable to creative writers, for the revolution itself is immensely creative and engrosses the best talents. Nor is a post-revolutionary era congenial to the flourishing of the arts, even where they have had a long history. In the years following the Revolution in America, there was an epidemic of verse, but only second-rate poets held the public eye. The one exception was Philip Freneau, a writer with an uncommon, perceptive faculty. Like Buckminster, he discerned the efficient hindrance of the country's literary flowering.[5]

1

Barlow flitted from one calling to another. He was first employed as a school teacher in New Haven. But after nearly six months of confinement, he borrowed money for another year's study at Yale for his master's degree. In the back of his mind lurked Buckminster's advice to turn to the ministry. It at least provided a living and time for writing.[6] Barlow hesitated. He was poorly equipped for saving souls. In the middle of March 1779 he wrote Wolcott that he was thinking of quitting New Haven, "bidding adieu to literature, to taste and elegance of every kind. As soon as this takes place I care not how soon I bid adieu to the world. . . . I'll go to preaching if not to plowing."[7]

What would he write about? Of the religious themes Buckminster had suggested only Daniel held his fancy. It was dramatic; it was epic. "This would involve the great action of Cyrus. His battle with Crassus and his siege of Babylon would figure well in Poetry." But others had already drawn on the Scriptures for topics. The exploits of Columbus also interested Barlow. "The discovery of America," he explained to Buckminster, "made an important revolution in the history of mankind. It served the purpose of displaying knowledge, liberty, and religion in the world perhaps as much as any human transaction that ever took place."[8] Did he know that the subject had already inspired poems by Freneau, for example? At any rate he worked at it and sent the pastor several verses.

From Dwight's school in Northampton, Massachusetts, where he served as usher, Barlow confided to Webster that he was "as eagerly employed in building poetical air castles as ever I was when a boy in building cob-houses, and they are about as important." He planned to return to Connecticut "where the air must serve me for diet as well as castle-building."[9] Before leaving Northampton, he completed a plan of *The Vision of Columbus*.[10]

He was still on the ragged edge. On September 26, 1779, he wrote to Ruth Baldwin, his wife-to-be: "I rose this morning about eight o'clock and all the shades of uncertainty and disappointment fell upon my mind at once and I trembled upon the borders of despair. I have now got to the end of my line. I am here at Hartford without a single project or resource of any kind. I have not a plan that will carry me an inch out of this town, and know not which way to ride. I have nothing to go after, nobody to go to see and nothing to do. . . . I don't know which way or when I shall go out of town or where I shall be or when I shall see you again."[11] The same tone of despair ran through a letter to Wolcott two months later.[12]

Friends tried to find a Maecenas for the struggling poet. Judge Titus Hosmer was sympathetic, but that was all. A trip to New London to see some rich merchants was thoroughly disappointing. Their brains, he wrote to Ruth, were "too fat for the play of genius or refinement of taste."[13]

Barlow was at a loss where to turn. He could not depend on his family, and he was loath to look to friends for help. They "are wearied with my complaints and I sometimes determin [sic] that they shall hear no more of me. . . ."[14]

The poet was forced to compromise his taste. In May 1779 he heard from Abraham Baldwin, who had given up his tutorship to be a chaplain in the American army. He recollected, "with a kind of melancholy pleasure," their happiness at the college. He then referred to chaplain vacancies in his brigade, which General Putnam wanted to fill.[15] The suggestion was plain. Barlow was not enthusiastic, for a chaplaincy was little removed from the ministry. Knowing his friend's state of mind, Baldwin was forthright. "The plan is for you to come and be chaplain in our other brigade, for I have them both to preach to." And here was the attraction: The situation would be "agreeable to your turn, you would be happy in it, you could get matter and work it up, and do just as you pleased; if you won't believe me come and see. I will engage to make you happy a little while at least." Barlow still vacillated. Two months later another letter arrived, this time with the forethought of a happy reunion. "If you were here we should have as good times as anybodies [sic] folks. . . . Joel we should show them chaplaincy in true stile."[16] But the strong argument was gainful employment with ample leisure.

Baldwin's objective was furthered by the Connecticut-born David Humphreys, aide to General Putnam with the rank of major, and later aide-de-camp to the commander-in-chief. Humphreys spent many free hours writing elegaic verses and patriotic ballads.[17] He admired Barlow, calling him "one of the most considerable genius's in Poetry, which we have ever had amongst us."[18] He wrote to General Greene that a reading of the first book of *The Vision of Columbus* gave him "an exceeding high idea of the performance." The poet needed means of support to finish it. He could be helped "by having him appointed a Chaplain to some vacant Brigade; for tho he is not in orders at present, he would I am well assured from his character and other circumstances, qualify himself for the office immediately, accept the appointment with cheerfulness, perform the duty with dignity and have leisure enough to prosecute his favorite pursuits."[19]

Barlow entered upon the study of theology to prepare for an oral examination before the Association of Ministers of New Haven, which was sceptical of his orthodoxy. But words from influential men had the desired result. On August 15, 1780, the Association licensed him after a brief test. In about a fortnight Barlow was the chaplain of the Fourth Massachusetts Brigade.

2

Barlow was a ladies' man. The younger set of women regarded him as handsome, and several even thought him interesting. He was hardly a good choice for a *mariage de convenance*. He was a dreamer in a way, and almost habitually poor.

Three belles vied for his attention, and all three were desirable companions. Betsy Stiles, daughter of Yale's president, was an attractive society girl; Elizabeth Whitman,[20] a blue-blood and bluestocking, was a poetess in her own way and gushingly affectionate; and there was Ruth Baldwin, a woman of commoner stock. She was charming, gay and gifted with practical sense.

Ruth finally took possession of his heart. Boarding with the Baldwins after graduation, Barlow saw much of her. Friendship blossomed into love, much to her father's displeasure. The would-be son-in-law was an unknown, save in a small circle of literary friends. Still worse, in the eyes of the anxious father, he was without a competence, a sort of school-bred ne'er-do-well who was cleverer at writing jingles than at finding employment. Consequently, he separated the lovers. Joel went to room with Abraham at Yale, while Ruth was sent to visit friends. Letters spanned the distance between them.

Their early correspondence metered their deepening tenderness. She longs for his presence, wants to be sure of him; she is haunted "by a thousand doubts and fears" that he will forget her. She is jealous and lovesick.[21] He in turn thinks of his "lovely Ruthy," rereads her letters a dozen times, and contemplates her perfections, "till I grow sick of myself and despair of my merit unless it can be derived from my connection with you."[22]

He was "acting upon a large scale of happiness" for both. "I am determined to make you happy," Ruth read in one of his letters. "Our good fortune is yet to come. Be cheerful my dear girl." While he was in the army, she should employ her time forming connections and improving her mind. Like Daniel Defoe, he disdained the conventional opinion that women were meant to be "only stewards of our houses, cooks, and slaves."[23] Or, as he elaborated later: "It is telling you that you are not fitted to improve in the Fine Arts, which in other words is telling you that you were not capable of any embellishments of life. . . . But my Ruthy would never have me give up the opinion that the Ladies are best calculated to advance the progress of the Fine Arts." His definition of them was comprehensive and it included gardening, architecture, painting, statuary, music, history, eloquence and poetry, and such accomplishments as dress, dancing and horsemanship. It is doubtful whether Barlow expected his wife to gain proficiency in all of them. He very likely aimed at directing her toward a fuller life than one of domestic routine. Behind this educational program for women was a set of principles he had outlined in his plan of *The Vision of Columbus*.[24] Here was implied the thought that social institutions would be inconsequential if the problems of women were not solved. Like Mary Wollstonecraft and Charles Fourier, he related it to human well-being. Women's liberation would eventually result from the advance of science. And his understanding of science was that of eighteenth-century Americans. It was an aspect of social history as well as of natural science.[25] Barlow hoped that Ruth would understand and actively share his dedication to the arts.

Circumstances seconded their union. Ruth was unhappy living at home with a stepmother. Joel felt that marriage would stabilize his life. On January 26, 1781, they were secretly wed in the small town of Kensington near Hartford. We do not know the father's reaction when he learned the secret. Before long, however, he had reason to respect his son-in-law. Barlow preached at the Yale chapel on September 8, 1781, and at the commencement three days later, he received a Master's Degree. Also, at the request of President Stiles, he read "A Poem Spoken at the Public Commencement" that was published in Hartford the same year. It was a paean to the triumph of peace. He received a further honor of being elected tutor, a post he refused because the chaplaincy paid better.

Joel saw Ruth frequently when the army went into winter quarters. These were months of honeymooning and dreaming of their future. The return to camp dejected them. But he kept her informed of his doings.

His letters assured her that camp life made fewer demands on him than he had expected. Practice taught him the art of preaching, so much so that he was complimented on his sermons. He met "gentlemen of the first cut," among them General Greene who invited her Joel "to dine with him." As he confessed to Ruth, "After all my bad feelings I have certainly done right in coming into the Army. My duty is extremely easy and it is not disagreeable; they certainly treat me with attention, and I believe they mean pretty well toward me." His "flaming, political" sermon on the treason of Benedict Arnold, he learned, had done him "great honor." There was talk of having it printed. But he would oppose its publication. "For tho it would be a sweet mortification to my Rev Fathers, the Association, to see their heretic son gain such applause, yet I have no ambition of appearing to the world in the character of a declaimer."[26]

Barlow was tremendously impressed by Major André's dignity at the time of his execution and much affected by it. He tells of a "grand entertainment" he had at West Point on July 4th, and of several weeks' illness that the doctor had pronounced "extremely critical." Fortunately, Abraham came to visit and nursed him back to health. As a token of his recovery, he sent her lyric stanzas that revealed a mark of originality. Breaking away from the heroic couplet, he sang out:

Cease Fidelia cease complaining
Why should worth and beauty grieve,
Why that tear thy cheek destaining?
Yet oh! yet behold him live.
See he lives again to view thee
Sings and sighs for thee alone
Every wish devoted to thee
Sooths and softens every groan.[27]

He also had moods of despondency which might have been brought on when he reached a plateau with his writing. In one of these moods he wrote to Webster, "We are all a pack of poor dogs and I have half worn out my life in buffeting my destiny, and all I have got for it is the knack of keeping up my spirits, letting the world slide, and hoping for better days."[28]

On August 12, 1782, he sent Ruth the glad news of preliminary peace talks proposed by Great Britain. Should the negotiations go on, "furloughs will then become fashionable." That would also advance his schedule of visits with regard to *The Vision of Columbus* and further their setting up housekeeping.[29]

One of the visits was to Philadelphia to collect subscriptions for the poem, for publication by subscription was popular in the eighteenth century. Travelling in the company of General Lincoln, the secretary of war, Barlow indulged himself thoroughly in long philosophical dialogues. "The worst of it was we got into several very learned disputes which are yet unsettled, but which we are to adjust before I return." The city "agreeably disappointed" him. "There don't appear to be that extravagance, that haughtiness or idleness which I have had represented," he wrote to Ruth. "Here is a mixture of all nations & all creatures, they serve to correct each other. The polite circles are easy, thotless & agreeable. I don't think there is that affectation by any means which we find in Boston & many places of less report. They have a strange nack of turning day to night & the contrary. It is common in splendid entertainments not to sit down to dinner till candle lighting."

These observations undoubtedly pleased Ruth. Especially gratifying must have been the account of his reception by eminent men. They gave him "the warmest encouragement." They said "that they & their country will be more endebted to me than I can be to them. This you see depends upon my judgment which is not unbiased by vanity." [30] He left Philadelphia elated. He had letters of introduction to influential men farther north.[31]

He reported progress on the poem. In January 1782 he penned more than 1500 lines.[32] Eight days of steady work in February produced 600 lines "of the most excellent quality." He had set himself a schedule. "To sit eight weeks at this table . . . write 3600 lines . . . which will finish my poem, bring it along in the scratch-copy to N. Haven where I can spend a week with my Ruthy." He wrote on March 2 that in two and a half weeks he had finished two books, "containing near 1300 lines." But he still had twice that number to write. "I see no body, say but little & think a great deal. All this my situation and business require."[33] He recorded astonishing progress on March 16: nearly 2400 lines in approximately four and a half weeks.[34]

The figures were evidence of diligence, if not inspiration. He had been at the work since 1779, planning, reading, correcting. Finished late in 1784, the poem was published less than three years later.

The chaplaincy had been a godsend. It is doubtful that it made him a savior of souls, but it certainly saved him from impending distress and gave him freedom for his labor of love. Preaching aside, he spent much time writing songs, by which he set great store. "One good song is worth a thousand addresses and proclamations" he is reported to have said. [35] But there is no record of the number he wrote. They were anonymous like many others of the revolutionary years. "The Burning of Charlestown" revealed a state of disturbed emotions. [36] In an eruption of anger, he called on Jehovah to avenge the "ghastly" deed of Lord North,/ "And faithless Gage, who gave the dread command."

His principal objective was stimulated by the death of Judge Titus Hosmer who had encouraged him in his dark days. As a tribute, he wrote "An Elegy on the Late Honorable Titus Hosmer, Esq." [37] It reveals Barlow's effervescent confidence in the nation. The poet saw it as a beacon, and its revolution as an alarm for other people.

He sees our rising, all-involving cause,
Spread like the morn to every distant clime,
Awake the mild magnificence of laws,
And roll down blessings on the stream of time.

An internal force links the "Elegy" to "The Prospect of Peace" and "A Poem at the Public Commencement." It was also in character with the philosophic temper of *The Vision of Columbus*. Upon reading the "Elegy," Abraham wrote to his sister that it was "one of the best in that kind of writing . . . not inferior to Gray's or any of the rest of those who are already consigned to immortality."[38] The opinion was, of course, subjective. Abram, as he was known to intimates, was perhaps unaware that Barlow's model had been the "Elegy Written in a Country Churchyard."

The verses written for the fourth anniversary of Burgoyne's surrender belong to the same minor category. They had been commissioned in an indirect way, for the soldiers looked upon Barlow as their bard. The observance of the event was made all the more appropriate by the news from the commander-in-chief that Cornwallis was "closely besieged,"[39] to cite Joel's words to Ruth. Attuned to the unison of triumphant joy, the poet intoned the burden of his song.

Hail the day & mark it well,
Then the scourge of Freedom fell,
Then your dawning glory shone,
Mark it, Freemen, 'tis your own.[40]

Barlow apparently had an aptitude for lyric poetry. Had he pursued it, he might have achieved literary fame. But he seems to have had a preference for the heroic couplet, perhaps because he believed it was better adapted to the epic form.

3

Months before the Paris peace treaty was signed, the Barlows had started housekeeping in Hartford, a growing town that was incorporated as a city almost a year and a half later. In the previous 25 years, the population of Hartford had risen from over 3,000 to nearly 5,500. The number of shops kept increasing with the residents. But prosperity ended with the Revolution. Prices dropped as did wages; debtors were hard pressed; a demand arose for the cancellation of debts and the issue of paper money. Convinced that the prime cause of the crisis was luxury spending, comfortable Hartford women formed an association that pledged to abstain from using such articles as ribbons, feathers, muslins and silks, save for weddings.[41]

The Barlows were probably hard put to make ends meet. The prospect of living on the royalties of *The Vision of Columbus* was still distant. The word had gotten out that it was near completion. Parts of it had already been read and praised by men of letters. Ezra Stiles was so impressed that he wrote in his diary six lines from the second book.[42] But compliments never substituted for food and drink.

Dim days were brightened by social life. In Hartford lived the effusive Elizabeth Whitman[43] and two of Barlow's classmates, Noah Webster and Oliver Wolcott. (Webster was already occupied with his grammar and spelling books that would be so instrumental in formalizing the American language.) Also an acquaintanceship developed between Barlow and John Trumbull, a successful lawyer who belonged to the Connecticut elite and had won a name for his burlesque poetry. In 1784, arrived Dr. Lemuel Hopkins, a tuberculosis specialist, with an incurable itch for writing satirical verse. When he and his wife moved to Hartford, they stayed with the Barlows. David Humphreys joined them before long.

The need to earn a living impelled Barlow to look for some business enterprise. He first planned to go into printing, publishing and bookselling with a relation of General Greene. "That business," he wrote to the general, on March 21, 1784, "has long been my object." On the list of early publications were the works of Trumbull, Dwight and his own.[44] One of Barlow's primary concerns was to bring *The Vision of Columbus* before the public. But the contemplated partnership fell through.

His chance came when he met Elisha Babcock, a printer, who had arrived from Springfield, Massachusetts. Together they set up a business issuing a weekly paper, publishing and selling books and dealing in stationery, groceries and imported merchandise. Babcock provided his printing and business experience; Barlow, his literary reputation and social connections. Thus, through his friendship with Oliver Wolcott, the firm sold stationery to the government of Connecticut.

Barlow remained in the business less than a year and a half. Perhaps the profits failed to meet his expectations, for he was impatient to rise to affluence. Another problem might have been his artist's temperament. Painting word pictures held more fascination than keeping ledgers. In November 1785 the partnership dissolved.

By that time *The American Mercury,* the firm's weekly, had been appearing for nearly sixteen months. It was a four-page sheet with nothing to distinguish it from other papers. It carried news from American and foreign cities, letters from readers, advertisements and items from the Congressional Journal. It also serialized books of general interest, such as Captain Cook's last voyage and Richard Price's *Observations on the Importance of the American Revolution.* For Barlow it was a medium for getting some of his minor writings into print, works that were unsigned. Starting in September 1784, the paper ran a series on the Articles of

Confederation. But they cast little light on the subject. An acute reader summed them up with the word, "rubbish."[45] A letter from Noah Webster answered critics of his *Grammatical Institute of the English Language* that the firm had published.[46]

Early in September 1784 Barlow notified the readers of *The American Mercury* that he was preparing a new version of Dr. Watts' Psalms. How he happened to have entered upon the project was told by him in a letter the paper reprinted many times.

> Application has been made to the subscriber by the General Association of the State of Connecticut, to make alterations in a number of Psalms in Doctor Watts' Version, that are locally applied to Great Britain. The Committee of said Association have likewise recommended giving a Version of sundry Psalms that are omitted by Doctor Watts; and have directed that the whole be applied to the state of the Christian Religion in general, and not to any particular Country. The subscriber, with the assistance of several other Gentlemen, is now preparing for the press a Psalm-Book upon the plan, and hopes to have it ready for publication in a few weeks.
> Joel Barlow.[47]

The new version of the Psalms was profitable to the firm of Babcock and Barlow. For Barlow it proved to be a challenge to his talent.

The question arises why the Connecticut clergy entrusted the revision to one they suspected of heresy. Three plausible answers may be offered. First, he was a licensed minister who, by all reports, had developed while in the army into a successful preacher; second, Timothy Dwight, John Trumbull, and perhaps Ezra Stiles might have spoken in his behalf; and finally, he was hailed as a leading American poet. (The gentlemen he referred to as his assistants can only be inferred. They may have been Hopkins, Trumbull and Dwight.)

The Association's committee was pleased with the revision and officially approved it. It was published in March 1785. Barlow had considerably changed six Psalms, refined others, and added twelve as well as five hymns that had been omitted.[48]

Ezra Stiles was critical. Comparing the old and new texts, he concluded that "Mr. Barlow has *corrected* so much as to assume the *place* of the Author, as if he was the Author. I think he has corrected too much and unnecessarily mutilated the Book and sometimes hurt the poetry." It should have been indicated "what is Wattsian & what is Barlowan; for as the matter is now Barlow has mounted up at one leap to all the Glory of Watts. This is a new way of Elevation of Genius & Acquest of Honor. . . . Mr. Barlow is an excellent poet; yet he cannot retouch Watts to advantage."[49]

The revision was accepted as standard in New England until news spread that the reviser was vindicating French revolutionary heresies. It was replaced with a version by Timothy Dwight.

Barlow was full of projects. Since the edition of Watts's Psalms was selling briskly, it occurred to him that an anthology of poetry by living Americans might have similar success. He very likely had in mind works by Trumbull, Dwight, perhaps by his friend Hopkins and his own, of course. It seems he also thought of including lesser known poetry, for example, by Governor Livingston of New York, whose social standing might win the anthology a better market.[50] But the idea was abandoned.

Barlow's hopes were fastened to his longer work. It still needed retouching and it especially needed more subscribers. Meanwhile, friends urged him to study law. Wolcott and Trumbull were successful lawyers, as was his other friend, Chauncey Goodrich, a tutor at Yale during Barlow's graduate days. He might have been motivated, too, by political ambition. Already in 1786 he was elected to Hartford's Common Council.

Barlow studied Blackstone's *Commentaries* which stressed the authority of common law. He also read Beccaria's *Essay on Crimes and Punishments*,[51] Voltaire's *Essay on the Manners and Spirit of Nations* and Montesquieu's *Spirit of Laws*, which disputed Blackstone. In Barlow's mind the teachings of men of the Enlightenment prevailed over those of Blackstone. This may be observed in the dissertation he read at Fairfield in April 1786 on being admitted to the bar.[52] Let us briefly consider its guiding ideas. The changeless character of natural law, he maintained, was a false dogma, defended by a metaphysical distinction between a state of nature and a state of society, "without any foundation in reason and common sense." Actually, modifications of the laws of nature varied according to the subject to which they applied. Very few of them relating to man "can remain in full force through all the variety of changes that society is capable of producing in his nature." That was just as true of the common law. It "was common sense at the time it became law, but it does not follow that it *is* common sense at a subsequent period." Its very antiquity made it unsuitable. For instance, the laws concerning debtors, inheritance and primogeniture were no longer applicable because they had been outdated.

Several conclusions may be drawn from the dissertation. Barlow was departing from the Calvinist belief that the nature of law and society had been made eternal by the great Artificer. Implied was a questioning of the doctrine of man's total depravity which served as the rationale of social caste and aristocratic rule. He believed that man was going forward, shaping institutions to his needs, replacing the petrified and detrimental with the living and beneficial. Institutions had to conform to the evidence of science and reason. For that was the way of Enlightenment. It was a process of change, a way of liberation.

Barlow's social philosophy befitted the buoyant heartedness brought on by the Revolution. Americans believed that things American were good or were becoming so. People spoke of improvement and expansion, and they dreamed of making the country the exemplar of the globe. If equality was their objective, they did not wish to eradicate the system of private ownership. Contemporaneous writings were singularly free of that aim. They had in mind instead an equal right to vote, a reform of the penal and inheritance laws, the circulation of paper money for the benefit of debtors and an end to servitude.

Reform was a consequence of the Revolution. In 1784 Connecticut and Rhode Island voted laws for gradual slave emancipation. Virginia abolished primogeniture in 1785. The legislation was imitated by other states during the next six years.

Barlow practiced law for over a year, but with indifferent success. The reason is hard to find. It was not an inability to speak publicly, for we saw that President Stiles had named him among the best debaters in college. Preaching in the army had in fact improved his manner of delivery. Was it then ennui, the weariness of consulting precedent or pleading causes with which he had no sympathy? Was it, as in the business partnership, a temperamental rebellion against petty details? Or a want of bluff and self-assertiveness, described by an unnamed friend as "that *happy impudence* which is so essential to the success of an advocate"?[53] Whatever the reason, he discovered before very long that the law was not his calling.

He turned his interest to selling land. Before recounting the perplexities it caused him, we must look at *The Vision of Columbus*, which was already in the hands of subscribers.

Chapter III
A Noble Vision

The years 1787 to 1789 were momentous in the histories of America and France. The American Constitutional Convention, opening in May 1787, produced after nearly four months of debate and compromise a framework of government with a strong executive and a check and balance system, calculated to give the fullest protection to the rights of property.

The American Constitution went into effect just as France was galloping into revolution. An Assembly of Notables, summoned in 1787 in the midst of a serious national crisis, dissolved without proposing any changes inconsistent with the establishment. That task was left, by default, to the representatives of the bourgeoisie.

Famine spread throughout the land. Riots broke out and public opinion grew progressively irate. Unable to quell the one and silence the other, faced also with the frightening forecast of bankruptcy, the king reluctantly convened the Estates General. Its meeting in 1789 initiated one of the great revolutions in history.

The two nations went their separate ways. The United States settled down to test its new political machinery. France entered upon a revolution which by force of circumstances grew into a general war that rocked the European political and social systems.

The years 1787-1789 were also consequential to Barlow. The publication of *The Vision of Columbus* elevated his standing among American poets. But poetry as a means of livelihood, he soon discovered, was like a will'-o'the-wisp.

1

The eighteenth century seems to have hosted a revival of interest in epics both in Europe and in America. This might have been due, first, to Dryden's translation of the *Aeneid* and Pope's and Cowper's of the *Iliad* and the *Odyssey*, secondly to scores of narratives of journeys to new or imaginary lands and to strange peoples,[1] and finally to historical works on early America. In 1775 William Hubbard of Boston published *A Narrative of the Indian Wars in New England*. Handled more expertly was William Robertson's *History of America*, in 1777, which provided data on the native people of Latin America. [2]

Littérateurs varied in their estimates of the epic. Edward Gibbon thought that it beautified the heroic centuries without disguising them. It was like a grand tableau in which one espied the history and culture of a people.[3] Voltaire was critical of any set rules for it. They were the surest way to its oblivion. Its only requisite was genius, and that was inimitable. The epic was a form through which an age vented its emotions and ideas.[4] In Dr. Johnson's opinion Homer was the only great epic poet. The others did "little more than diversify the incidents, and new-name the characters of their great original."[5] The judgment took no account of Camoëns, for instance, or of Milton. But it was well-founded with regard to the eighteenth-century poets, whose imitations of Homer and Virgil evoked the savage satire of Pope and Freneau.[6]

For epic poetry was long past its summit. Though its spirit still hung over countries like Portugal and Spain, it had little to say to an age that had repudiated mythology and avowed skepticism and rationalism. The epic as a literary pattern was abandoned in England and France. Said the contemporary Scottish historian, John Millar: "In reality, considering the state of society at present, both in France and England, it may be doubted, whether an epic poem, of great length, and highly finished in all its parts, embellished with the harmony of versification, and the splendor of diction, and enriched with metaphors and figures of all sorts, be an entertainment suited to the general taste of the people." [7]

Yet, the notion was prevalent that the epic was adaptable, at least circumstantially. This idea was given fresh vitality by the American Revolution. For here was a perfect theme for heroic poetry. It had neither a Helen nor a Dido, to be sure. But it had a shining hero, with noble qualities, whose travails symbolized a nation at its moment of birth. The Italian historian, Carlo Botta, heard it said in a Paris salon that the American Revolution was the only modern subject with ample material for a heroic poem. [8] Botta was not a poet. But he was so involved in its events that he sat down to write one of the first important histories of the American Revolution. [9]

The epic tradition seems to have held on in America. However, as it turned out, its devotees were better at aspiration than at creation. They were a group of Connecticut poets among whom were John Trumbull, David Humphreys, Timothy Dwight and Joel Barlow.

Freneau was the exception in the American literary setting and the most gifted. His poems from 1771 to 1779 explored the theme that America would owe her greatness to the spread of her liberty and not to the piling up of wealth. The "Pictures of Columbus" was a development of "The Rising Glory of America"; "The Hermit of Saba" enlarged upon a theme of the "Pictures" and "Columbus to Ferdinand" heralded the other three. "The Hermit of Saba" reminds us of Diderot's "Supplément au voyage de Bougainville." Freneau's calling down "Perdition on those friends from Europe . . . whose thirst for gold lays the world in ruins" brings to mind the indignant words spoken by the Tahitian elder to the departing European brigands.

A word about the versifying of three of these Connecticut bards. Trumbull's "Prospect of the Future Glory of America" (1770) was followed six years later by the first two cantos of "M'Fingal," which he regarded as a "modern Epic Poem." It was written at the request of friends in Congress in the hope of raising confidence in the American cause. Whether it achieved its objective cannot be said. Though the most successful of his poems, it was not original, but modeled on the Latin classics and imitative of Samuel Butler's *Hudibras*. [10]

"A Poem on the Future Glory of the United States" by Humphreys was equally uncreative. The tone was as monotonous as a chant, and the lines were labored. He painted the dawning of America's golden age, when its citizens would achieve domestic bliss and carry the torch of freedom to the world. [11]

Dwight's "Conquest of Canaan," though based on a biblical theme, resounded with national overtones. Readers said that it was allegorical. The Israelites were meant to be Americans and Egypt the British government. The author's claim that he had begun the poem and finished it before the start of the Revolution [12] did not negate the fact that he had revised parts and added episodes in the light of later experience. A critic observed that "Dwight's poem was full of eighteenth-century Americans with Hebrew names who talked like Milton's angels and fought like prehistoric Greeks." [13] Anna Barbauld asked, "What had he to do to make Joshua his hero, when he had Washington of his own growth?" [14]

"The Conquest of Canaan" was more ostentatious than elegant. Vernon Parrington's judgment of his writings as a whole is applicable to the poem. It is the work of a man "wanting humor, wit, playfulness, artistry, grace, lacking subtlety and suggestiveness." [15]

The three poets were slaves of rules and copiers of models. They were versifiers, wanting in spontaneity. A few little pieces of Freneau, concluded a literary historian, "are worth all the epic and Pindaric strains of the Connecticut bards." [16] And Freneau's acid pen put them down as "a set of heavy moulded pedants." [17] Still their verses had a certain popularity.

2

Among the Connecticut poets, Barlow stood near the top. Humphreys called him a "child of genius"; [18] others, "the American Homer." But a later judgment by a newspaper editor declared him deficient in "that versatility of genius which is so peculiar to Mr. Freneau." Barlow had "one style, one measure, one subject, and one solemn tone." Freneau accommodated his talent "to any subject, any measure, or any style."[19]

The editor had in mind Barlow's "Columbiad," a revised version of *The Vision of Columbus*. The defects were more apparent in the earlier poem which, but for its faith in the immense strides of mankind, one is tempted to put aside. During the seven years he devoted to this piece, his reading was neither wide nor deep. He probably had access to translations of Homer and Virgil; he might have pondered *Paradise Lost*, and perhaps sat with compassion over the fate of Satan and his legions of angels. But he needed further study of the epic form before adapting it to his introduction that the poem "will be rather of the philosophic than of the epic kind" and confined his plan "to the train of events which might be represented to the hero in vision." This was as much as he could do, considering his limitations.

Barlow's yawn-inducing verses bring to mind James Thomson's "Liberty." Here its guardian deity is in the van of man's progress from the pastoral age to early organized society and finally to Great Britain. Everywhere it elevated art, science and philosophy. Its destiny was to culminate in a peaceful world, one free of distress and bigotry. The dream was also Barlow's, a dream of America in the course of becoming.

We have referred to records of travel and discovery that might have served him in shaping his poem. The claim that he leaned on *The Royal Commentaries of Peru* by Garcilasso de la Vega [20] is worthy of notice. He undoubtedly also relied on Marmontel's story of the Incas and Robertson's history. [21] For all that, the poem showed but a limited reserve of learning. In other words, *The Vision of Columbus* represents the green fruits of his intellectual rising.

The poem aimed at depicting the advance of America from strife and discord to peace and harmony. A dialogue between a disconsolate Columbus in prison and a radiant seraph unfolds the grand pageant of civilization. If one wished to exalt the poem, he might liken it to a frieze on a Greek temple. Unfortunately the lines are rude, drawn with a blunting sameness. Columbus and the seraph together ascend a mountain from which they survey the distinguishing features of the North and South American continents. They then turn to the people and their primitive way of life. Asked by Columbus if they ever enjoyed civilization, the seraph answers that in Mexico a happy social order had existed until the arrival of Cortez and his "murdering band" destroyed it and reduced the natives to their primitive state. This vision of cruel and bloody deeds is offset by the story of Manco Capac, founder of the civilizing institutions in Peru. His legendary achievements are compared to those of Moses, Lycurgus and Mohammed. Gloom overtakes Columbus after hearing the seraph prophesy the destruction of the Incan Empire, but he is comforted by the sights of settlements in North America, the growth of commerce, the spread of enlightenment and the American Revolution. These are the final visions of Book Six.

Book Seven opens with a hymn to peace:

Bring, bounteous Peace, in thy celestial throng,
Life to my soul, and rapture to my song;
Give me to trace with pure unclouded ray,
The arts and virtues that attend thy sway;
To see thy blissful charms, that here descend,
Through distant realms and endless years extend.

Then follows a set of tableaux of America's ascent to independence. The progress extends to many regions, reaching into useful crafts and education, into invention, science and the fine arts. American inventors, painters and poets pass before the reader. Finally, there is the prophecy of science spreading its beneficence to all mankind and augmenting knowledge in medicine, technology and politics. Man is drawn to man in "universal love." It was also the dream of Francis Bacon as well as of eighteenth-century *philosophes*. The poet sings of "fair science, of celestial birth," but its divine luster somehow fails to dim the progressive plan:

That draws, for mutual succor, man to man,
From friends to tribes, from tribes to realms ascend,
Their powers, their interests and their passions blend;
Adorn their manners, social virtues spread,
Enlarge their compacts and extend their trade.
[Commerce] triumphs o'er the rage of war. [Peace will reign supreme.]
No more the noble patriotic mind,
To narrow views and local laws confined,
'Gainst neighbouring lands directs the public rage,
Plods for a realm or counsels for an age;
But lifts a larger thought, and reaches far,
Beyond the power, beyond the wish of war;
For realms and ages forms the general aim,
Makes patriot views and moral views the same,
Sees with prophetic eye in peace combined,
The strength and happiness of human-kind.

Languages will blend until one, "a single, universal sound," was the common tongue of all peoples.

The rage of war shall sweep the plains no more;
Nor give distress these strange events foredoom,
But give the marks of nobler joys to come;

Nations will unite in

> *. . . one great empire, with extensive sway*
> *Spread with the sun and bound the walks of day.*
> *One centred system, one all-ruling soul,*
> *Live thro' the parts, and regulate the whole.*

A golden age of universal brotherhood—this was the goal of civilization. The millenium, foretold in Scripture, might be introduced "without a miracle," Barlow said in a long footnote. It would be attained in three stages. In the first, all parts of the world would be "considerably peopled." In the second, the nations would become known to one another. In the third, man's increased wants would stimulate communication and international trade. The first stage, he said, had been reached in a fairly late period. The second, though greatly accelerated, was still far from completion. The third would be the result of the first two. For it was the Providential plan that the "spirit of commerce" should bring about world amity and "assimilate the manners, feelings and languages of all nations." Among the remoter consequences would be improved government and legislation and the eradication of superstition. [22]

Since man's advance was deplorably slow, much time would pass before the goal was reached. But progress could be hastened by revolutions. Barlow had in mind, of course, the Revolution he had served. Significant was the implication that revolutions were the motors of history, which raised a contradiction. For if progress was Providentially determined, as Barlow tells us, why did he count on revolutions to accelerate it? Revolutions are after all man-made, and that is the impression conveyed by Books Five and Six. Obviously Barlow had to contend with a confrontation between spiritually predestined progress and man's intervention to expedite it. He resolved the difference in the course of time by assigning man the role of making history. In *The Vision of Columbus*, however, Providence was the unchallenged maker.

It is possible to point to examples of a deistic tendency. For Barlow, like many Americans of his and earlier generations, had been exposed to deism. But it would be to little avail to hold that the poet deviated from formal orthodoxy. He still shared with his Hartford friends the stock of conservative dogmas. Webster and Dwight, both pious churchmen who had read the poem in manuscript, commended it.

Barlow, however, was already going in another direction. His law dissertation, we saw, had ascribed to man a capacity for replacing obsolete with vital institutions and affirmed the need of delivering the individual from a wilderness of prescriptions. We can share the judgment of a biographer that the intellectual content of the poem "represents an end of Barlow's youth rather than the beginning of his mature career." [23] Yet it already signifies a groping for an exit from the conventional frame and an inclination to reach out beyond America's borders. In line with this tendency, the poem manifested the national temper of the post-revolutionary years, a faith in the young republic and an expectation that it might be an exemplar to the western world.

On the personal side, the poem was a fulfillment of an ambition that had possessed Barlow for a number of years. The subject was alluring indeed, and it had a latent fire to inflame the imagination. What it needed was a poet who would set the emotions in flight and paint the social landscape in arresting colors. Barlow lacked the gift to do so.

He had unbounded confidence in the "spirit of commerce" to foster peace, believing strongly, as did classical economists, that unshackled trade would bring about the best of all possible worlds.

The poem was dedicated to Louis XVI, for two reasons. The first was patriotic, and expressed the prevalent feeling of gratitude for French aid. The second was opportunistic. "What is said in it of the French king & nation," he confided to Jefferson, "may perhaps occasion it to be translated into that language." [24]

The final pages carried an incomplete list of subscribers, including Louis XVI, George Washington, Franklin, Lafayette and Generals Knox and Lincoln, Hamilton and Livingston, Paine, Ezra Stiles, Oliver Wolcott and Aaron Burr. The French king subscribed for twenty-five copies, Washington for twenty, Lafayette for ten, and Franklin and Knox for six each. The final number of subscribers was eleven hundred and fifty-two. How many of them read the poem is a question that will never be answered. It is safe to say that the great majority either laid it aside or could not go beyond the first few books.

Financially the poem was a success for its time. Barlow netted over fifteen hundred dollars. Yet, considered in the light of the time he labored on it, the return for his work was comparatively small.

The first edition, published in May 1787, quickly sold out, and in October plans were made for the second, published in spring of the following year. [25] Meanwhile, it was put out in England, but without the dedication. In 1793 a radically revised edition, which Barlow called the fifth, appeared in Paris. The revision showed how profoundly his ideas had changed. Traditional theological dogma gave way to deism; man replaced God as the prime force of progress; the improvement of mankind was no longer ascribed to Providence but to nature; and credit for French aid to the Americans was transferred from the king to the *philosophes*. [26] For all the changes, *The Vision of Columbus* did not raise Barlow to the rank of great American poets. Its merit is of the minor sort, which Howard Mumford Jones assessed in these words: "Together with the widely read histories of the Scotchman, William Robertson, *The Vision of Columbus* may be said to inaugurate in the United States the literature of the 'great subject,' that is, "the discovery, exploration and conquest of the New World. . . ." [27]

The poem was well-received in the United States. The author was praised for his style, imagery and vivid painting, for his correct versification and novelty of ideas. One critic thought it deserved to rank "with some of the first English poems." [28]

English critics were friendly, but not fervent. One said, "Mr. Barlow thinks with freedom, and expresses himself with spirit"; a second, that the poem was grand in design, "extensive, and well adapted for the display of the author's descriptive and reflective powers." A third described it as "a narrative of real facts in a poetical dress." [29] And a fourth, writing in 1798, concluded that "after every deduction, *The Vision of Columbus* must be considered as a specimen of talents highly honourable to a young man." Despite the absence "of those bold and original flights of genius, the poem may be repeatedly perused with pleasure. . . ." [30]

Barlow sent a copy of the manuscript to Dr. Price with the hope that he might be instrumental in having it published in England. The clergyman answered "that the Dedication to the King of France, the encomiums on France and the American army, and the censures of this country in your Poem render it improper to be published in this country."[31] In back of the answer was the sharp criticism of American poetry by the doctor's friend, Thomas Day, a poet, an author of tracts and children's books, a defender of American independence and a political reformer. [32]

Through an indirect source, Barlow might have been informed of the strictures Day prescribed for American poetry. This is suggested in a brief letter Barlow sent him, in which he conceded that the art of poetry had been cultivated with little success in his country. The cause was peculiarly American, he said, only he could not decide whether it lay in "a defect in native genius," or in the want of an intellectual climate. [33] Awareness of such endemic obstacles might have eventually disabused him of the prospect of riding to fortune in the company of the Muse.

3

The *New Haven Gazette* and the *Connecticut Magazine* of October 26, 1786, carried under the heading, "American Antiquities," the first number of a series, entitled, *The Anarchiad: a Poem on the Restoration of Chaos and Substantial Night*. Its twelve numbers appeared irregularly for almost a full year. They were unsigned, but according to a letter from Humphreys to Washington, Trumbull, Barlow and he were the authors. [34] He might have added the name of Dr. Hopkins. The literary team was nicknamed "the wicked wits" of Hartford. Later, when others hovered around them, the group became known as "The Connecticut Wits" or "The Hartford Wits." Apart from their fabulous story of the discovery of the *Anarchiad*, the authors introduced it as "a pre-eminently New England Poem" that appeared while New England was confronted by evils, such as Shays' movement, paper money, "the debtor crew" and "The giddy rage of democratic States."

The familiar "prophetic bard" was employed. From his vantage ground on a lofty mountain, he beheld the demons of America—namely mob-rule and chaos, both products of Shays' insurrection. The consequences were as follows: the majority ignored the requisitions of Congress; the report of America defaulted on interest payments and there was the threat of disunion. The asylum of liberty was in imminent danger of destruction. Paper money was also indicted as it was necessarily accompanied by misrule and dishonesty. Its rapid depreciation in Rhode Island caused the "wits" to write:

Hail! realm of rogues, renown'd for fraud and guile,
All hail! ye knav'ries of yon little isle.
There prowls the rascal, cloth'd with legal pow'r,
To snare the orphan, and the poor devour;
. . . .
Bankrupts their creditors with rage pursue,
No stop, no mercy from the debtor crew.

The scene turns gloomy as Anarch depicts America's future:

Here shall my best and brightest empire rise,
Wild riot reign, and discord greet the skies.
Awake, my chosen sons, in folly brave
Stab Independence! dance o'er Freedom's grave!
Sing choral songs, while conquering mobs advance,
And blot the debts to Holland, Spain and France—
Till ruin come, with fire, and sword, and blood,
And men shall ask where your republic stood.

Hesper, America's guardian angel, appears to give battle to Anarch. Before doing so he makes a rousing appeal to all lovers of country to stand by its hard-won rights. In the climactic conflict between order and chaos, Anarch is at first victorious, with the result that desolation spreads and mobs demolish courts of law. Discord and disunion are everywhere, but Hesper finally triumphs. America is then extolled as the land of freedom, where neither tyrants rule, nor tinsel guards and titled knaves parade.

Numbers XI and XII picture the Land of Annihilation, similar to the infernal regions of Virgil. To this abode of everlasting pain the authors banished all their foes—paper money, Indian wars, Wronghead and Blackleg. There, too, went the spirits of de Paw, Raynal and Buffon, for having represented American natives as degenerate; the historian Robertson who shared their opinions; Robert Morris, follower of Mammon; Mably and Turgot, critics of American politics. [35]

Literary historians have pointed to similarities between the awkward yet venomous satire of "the wicked wits" and their archetypes.

Pope's *Dunciad* was a likely model, perhaps also *The Rolliad* by a group of English poets. Satan's soliloquy in *Paradise Lost* might have been a pattern for Anarch's monologues.

More relevant to the purpose was the political objective of the satire. It appeared at a time of a big, nationwide debate over the type of American government and the nature of the forthcoming federal constitution. The *Anarchiad*, irrespective of its trivialities and woodenness, was part of this controversy. Its motivating prejudice was conservative in the full sense. The "wicked wits" stood for hard against soft money, for creditors against debtors, for strong against weak government, and for the rule of the wealthy and well-born against the sovereignty of the people. In Farrington's words they "embodied a conception of life and society that had taken form during nearly two hundred years of provincial experience, and they phrased that conception at a moment when vast changes were impending and the traditional New England was on the point of being caught in the grasp of forces that were to destroy the most native in her life." To that extent they were "the literary old guard of eighteenth-century Toryism." [36]

The "wicked wits" stood firmly by the mores and beliefs of Connecticut's ruling oligarchy. With the exception of Barlow, they were comparatively well-off and well-connected. And Barlow, too, for all the changes of fortune, was at the point of being absorbed by them. His law dissertation was, of course, at odds with the principles of the ruling class, but the deviation had not yet affected his social relations. He moved in the highest circles of Hartford. And friends and former army associates had brought him in contact with a land company from which he expected to draw substantial gains.

Symptomatic of the high regard he was held in was an invitation to address the Connecticut Society of the Cincinnati on July 4, 1787. The speech was compatible with the *Anarchiad*, at least in one respect. It argued the case for a unified federal government as the *sine qua non* of the country's even development. The American Revolution, he said, marked "a distinguished era in the history of mankind." Of its two objectives one had been completed, namely, independence. The other, "the establishment of a permanent federal system," was still to be achieved or the Revolution would remain half finished.

Novel in the address was a theme that recurred in Barlow's later writings. Political unity, he declared, was the key to a growing, prosperous America and to an improved world order. "The natural resources of the country are inconceivably various and great; the enterprising genius of the people promises a most rapid improvement in all the arts that embellish human nature; the blessings of a national government will invite emigrations from the rest of the world, and fill the empire with the worthiest and happiest of mankind; while the example of political wisdom and felicity here to be displayed will excite emulation through the kingdoms of the earth, and meliorate the condition of the human race." [37]

The *Oration* rose above the *Anarchiad* both in tone and breadth of view. Barlow focused attention on the epoch-making character of the Revolution and the innovating example of the nation's independence. His perspective stretched beyond his own period, for he foresaw other nations striving to equal his own. Love of country blended with love of humanity, and peaceful competition superseded international rivalry. A world outlook was replacing his provincialism even before his departure for Europe.

Chapter IV
The Scioto Business

America before the Revolution was comparatively free of stock-jobbing and speculation. The quantity of money in circulation was small, and credit facilities were meager. Colonial governments had to fill fiscal deficiencies with paper money. In 1764 Parliament forbade its further issue, but the Revolution annulled the decision. The states and the Continental Congress printed almost $210 million of paper currency to finance the war. The sum circulated by Congress surpassed that of the states by some $30 million. Thus currency depreciation set in, [1] which even legal tender laws failed to prevent. The effects were spiraling inflation, distressed wage earners and active speculation.

Conditions turned for the worse with the end of the war. Prices fell almost precipitously; debtors were numerous; hawkeyed men were quick to see a connection between the public debt and the public domain. Dealings in securities reached a frightening point. The army debt, sold again and again according to a New York newspaper, finally went into the hands of speculators. Rich men held the greater part of the public debt, for who could better await the appreciation of the bonds and their accumulated interest? [2] A gale of speculation swept through Philadelphia, Boston and New York. Traders gulled one another without the least sting of conscience. That had become the state of common business practice.

1

In this climate were born the Ohio and Scioto Land Companies. The first was public, organized by former army officers, with the object of acquiring large tracts in exchange for bonds or continental certificates. The second was secret, in which the top men of the first company had a principal interest. The Ohio Company, according to one of its directors, the Reverend Manasseh Cutler, obtained a grant of nearly five million acres, of which one and a half million belonged to the company. The other three and a half million were to go to the clandestine body, serving as a front for a number of plunderers. [3] The area of the Ohio Company, north of the Ohio River, was an outright purchase. The larger portion lying between the Ohio and Scioto Rivers, was an option, to be paid for in six installments. The condition of this long-term credit was the prompt payment by the Ohio associates for their one and a half million acres. In other words, the option on the Scioto property hinged on the fulfillment of the Ohio Land Company's agreement. [4]

During the negotiations between Cutler and Congress, the suave and well-connected Colonel William Duer appeared. He had acquired an interest, often the principal one, in many enterprises, so that he was truly one of the few commanding *condottieri* of the American business community. His activities were surreptitious; his dealings direct and personal. He wrote few letters, and destroyed records that might incriminate him.

Duer was of English descent. Arriving in New York in 1768 to buy lumber for the British navy, he saw vast opportunities in the young nation. He bought property along the Hudson and became an American citizen. During the Revolution, he held a number of important posts and even served on the committee to draft a constitution for New York State. He became so effectively involved in the contract system that at the close of the Revolution he was a wealthy man.

Prominent speculators were among his associates, but his was the guiding hand. He entertained lavishly, surrounded himself with politicos and had access to key committees. Besides, he was the Secretary of the Treasury Board. "Indeed," wrote a student of his career, "his private interests and official responsibilities were in some instances so interwoven that one is inclined to account him grimly prophetic when, in 1777, he expressed to Jay the fear 'that we shall not increase in virtue as we may in years.' " [5] He was charged with having paid off earlier debts in depreciated currency. Before the refunding of the national debt, he had managed to acquire quantities of specie certificates and securities. [6]

Duer's association with the Scioto Land Company was in character with his other adventures. Hearing of Cutler's difficulties in negotiating the Ohio Company's contract, he offered his help. The historian of the Scioto speculation tells us that the price of his intervention was "an extension of the original contract for land and the taking in of a new company," made up of a number of principal men in New York. Under the cover of the legitimate Ohio Company, they would obtain a vast tract of public land for speculation. In return, Duer and his friends promised to persuade Congress to concede Cutler's terms.

At the end of October 1787 Cutler and Winthrop Sargent, acting for the Ohio Company's directors, signed two contracts. One was with the Treasury Board, to which Cutler handed over $500,000 in public securities that had been advanced by Duer and his friends. The second was a private agreement signed by the two directors for the Ohio Company and by Duer for himself and his colleagues. It concerned the much larger part of the grant and was a plot to defraud the nation of a good portion of its domain. The property was divided into thirty shares, of which twenty-six were broken up equally between the two parties. The remaining four were to be sold abroad.

This arrangement was the basis of the Scioto Company. It had no charter and no articles of incorporation. It was a scheme devised by two sets of partners, each of whom distributed its shares among other persons. Barlow was assigned part of a share by the Ohio associates, [7] possibly to reward him for his exemplary initiative in selling their shares, possibly, too, to gain his interest in the venture. But he was ignorant of its stealthy nature. Other assignees were General Rufus Putnam, Benjamin Tupper and Royal Flint, a close business friend of Duer. Among the beneficiaries of the New York group were Andrew Craigie, a crafty wholesale merchant well-known in the business world, and James Jarvis, a contractor and speculator. But Duer probably had the largest single interest.

The Scioto principals counted on realizing big gains before making any cash payments. Their intention was to dispose of the property in France and Holland, primarily to holders of large blocks of American securities. Thus they hoped to act as middlemen in reducing the national debt. Failing that, they anticipated borrowing abroad with the unpaid-for tract as security. To this end, Daniel Parker, a friend of Duer, had already gone abroad to negotiate with foreign bankers. [8] The only investment was the trifling cost of getting purchasers.[9]

2

Duer's was the controlling hand in the Scioto speculation. He could negotiate loans and sales, and he was empowered to send an agent to Europe, subject to his instructions. His choice was Royal Flint, who had been paymaster of the Connecticut army during the Revolution. But Flint became ill. To expedite matters, he and Cutler proposed the appointment of Barlow [10] who had been a successful salesman for the Ohio Company. His other qualification, or so it was thought, was his literary reputation, which might be a passport to influential circles abroad. Flint had already assigned him an interest in a contemplated purchase of two million acres on the Wabash River and of another million on the Mississippi. [11] Moreover, General Samuel Parsons, an Ohio director, had a high opinion of Barlow's competence. [12]

Duer was reluctant, perhaps because the nominee lacked sufficient business knowledge. But he yielded to pressure and advised Barlow to make the preliminary arrangements and report to New York for instructions. [13] Duer gave him power of attorney for the Scioto associates "to undertake and conclude such arrangements with such bodies or such individuals as he shall judge the most suitable for the interest of the company in disposing of the territory they have acquired of the United

States altogether or to bond it for whatever sum he shall judge suitable."[14] Barlow was thus vested with extensive authority.

What induced him to go abroad? We know that his source of income was uncertain. He could no longer rely on poetry, and his business ventures either had been failures or had brought him only small returns. The legal profession had shown little promise. In fact, while practicing law he had to supplement his income by selling real estate. Like many of his contemporaries, he had been infected with the speculative virus. The slow, tedious way to success was at odds with his restless nature. He was curious to know what lay on the other side of the mountain.

The trust placed in him by the Ohio associates might have puffed up his vanity. They had ranked high in the army. Many were wealthy, familiar with the best and *en rapport* with government committees. Among financiers, William Duer, or "Billy" as intimates called him, was considered on a par with Robert Morris.

Barlow was elated. He believed that fortune had befallen him, and he anticipated great triumph. Success in the Scioto business might link him with financiers in matters relating to the national debt. [15]

It was undoubtedly trying to say goodby to his brothers and especially to Ruth. It eased his mind somewhat to know that she would stay with her brother Dudley, a lawyer at Greenfield Hill, a rustic and refined place, near enough to her pastor and friend, Dr. Timothy Dwight.

A parenthesis is appropriate at this point. While Barlow was on his way to France, a Frenchman named J. P. Brissot de Warville was coming to the United States as a representative of five European bankers. His voyage had a twofold object: first, to learn the extent of the state and federal debts and the nation's capacity to meet its obligations; and second, to study the feasibility of selling western lands to French settlers. In this connection he met Duer and Craigie, with whom he considered developing an international project involving the Scioto property and the foreign-held American securities. [16] Before sailing home, Brissot seems to have acquired interests in land companies, the Scioto among them. [17] Back in France, he and the Swiss banker, Etienne Clavière, wrote a book portraying America as a new paradise.[18] The purpose was to encourage French emigration to the United States. It should be observed that they assured foreign holders of American securities of the government's good faith. Significantly, the revised version of the book, published in 1791, lauded Duer as a financier and held up the Scioto heads as "reputable men" whose title to the land was "incontestable." [19] This was, of course, a gross misrepresentation.

3

Barlow's departure was a turning-point in his life. He remained abroad more than seventeen years, during which his ideas matured. The provincial, impecunious Connecticut Yankee came back worldly and with a comfortable estate; the companion of the conservative Hartford wits returned a liberal democrat.

The French ship Barlow boarded took a full month to reach Le Havre. Ocean-going vessels of the eighteenth century were without any of the modern comforts. They were small, and the cabins were dark, narrow, usually dirty, and infested with fleas and bedbugs. The dining room was small, and still worse, the food was stale and unappetizing. The French cuisine, moreover, was intolerable to an unsophisticated palate. Food, however, had no attraction for Barlow, for the crossing was a harrowing experience. In his diary, he put it in a nutshell, "thirty days of more keen distress could not be numbered in any part of my life, & God has given my share of pain." The torture continued from Sandy Hook to Le Havre with little abatement. To top it all, they ran into a storm in the English Channel which tossed the vessel "from heaven to hell." But a stay on shore restored him. [20]

We need not dwell on his journey from Le Havre to Paris. His most interesting observations were the good condition of the roads and the small fruit trees. Of course, the trees in America were larger and their fruits more flavored. But there was nothing in America like the Rouen Cathedral. The Gothic style and majestic structure filled him with a sense of gravity. He spent much time there measuring the dimensions of its huge bell.

Barlow's first visit to Paris was brief and uneventful. Among his papers were letters of recommendation from George Washington to Comte de Rochambeau, Marquis de la Luserne and Marquis de Lafayette. All three letters spoke of him as a gentleman of literary accomplishments, as the author of a celebrated poem and "a genius of the first magnitude." [21] The most important occurrence during this sojourn was his acquaintance with Jefferson, then minister to France, at whose residence he and other Americans spent July 4th.

Meeting Daniel Parker was more material. In 1788 Parker was a key man in the Scioto speculation. His role was trying to involve European bankers in a plan linking the American debt to the western lands. He and Barlow traveled to London and Amsterdam, but without success. The bankers were reluctant to commit themselves. Before long, Parker lost interest in the Scioto enterprise.

The winter of 1788-1789 passed with little or no progress. [22] Barlow's diary of travel with Parker showed that he was more absorbed in men and things than in the negotiations. In England he visited museums, Windsor Castle and the London Tower. St. Paul's Cathedral appeared to him "vastly more magnificent than Notre Dame." The character of the second, as of Gothic cathedrals in general, *"is solemnity;"* that of the first "is pure *sublimity*." "It is like a distant mountain seen in company with nearer hills, where you have nothing to distinguish distance but the colour thro' the atmosphere." Barlow was reaching out to grasp at imagery, for at heart he was more the man of letters than the man of business.

A by-election in Westminister was a singular experience. The contest was between Whigs, led by Charles James Fox, and Tories, led by the king. Neither side spared money to buy voters and hire thugs. The bustle, the clamor and the casualties went on for fifteen days. The Whig candidate was finally declared the winner.

A number of shocking facts met Barlow's notice. One duke sent sixteen members to Parliament; the buyer of a borough had the right to choose two members; and to secure a parliamentary majority, a prime minister could dip into the national treasury. Barlow was led to conclude that, "The business of legislating by parliament is little more than a farce."

He was eager to see new things and new faces. Mechanical improvements, of which there were many in England in this period, won his admiration principally because they were labor saving. The practical-minded Yankee at once saw the value of a recently invented gun for throwing the harpoon in whaling, of a mangle for smoothing linen, of Rumsey's steam-propelled boat, of Thomas Paine's iron bridge which contradicted the age-old principle of arches. Paine was in England and dined with him and Horne Tooke, the famous philologist. All three met later in the British political reform movement. In London Barlow dined out at least six days a week, often with literary men. A businessman, he remarked, would consider this "a bad economy of time. But for me it is the best way of collecting information, and does not interfere with other business." He might have added that the company of literary men agreed with his propensity.

Flanders aroused the tourist's curiosity. He roamed through Ghent, Bruges, Brussels and Ostend, inspecting harbors and rivers, lace and linen factories. His spirit was depressed as he walked through the elegant streets of Antwerp and compared its tomblike silence with the brisk life it enjoyed in the sixteenth century. The contrast drew from him four stanzas in hexameter verse. The third has the mood of all four:

How must thy present base dejected state
Gloom in sad contrast to the smiles you bore,
And show, amid the shifting scenes of fate,
The wrecks of war & impotence of power.

He returned to Paris wiser perhaps, certainly better informed. Here he stayed, with few interruptions, burdened with Scioto affairs. But business never stifled his love of ideas and letters.

Fortune had it that he came to France when one of America's great men was her minister. At Jefferson's Paris home he made the acquaintance of scientists, economists, reformers and literary critics. For anybody in the capital who had standing in the republic of letters had visited there one time or another. It was a kind of salon where current subjects, recent publications and scientific theories were examined candidly and freely. Here one might have met La Rochefoucauld, Condorcet, Lavoisier and other distinguished Frenchmen. Discussions pivoted on big issues. For example, did indigenous America exemplify decadence, as Raynal and Buffon had been saying? Jefferson refuted this hypothesis by having specimens of skeletons and skins and horns of fauna sent from America, which showed that her animals were in fact bigger and stronger than those in Europe. His *Notes on Virginia*, translated by the *philosophe* and critic, the abbe André Morellet, inevitably turned the conversation to the American Revolution and the Constitutional Convention at Philadelphia, [23] noteworthy events that had earned the admiration of Europeans and negated the assumption of American degeneration. It was rather France and the Continent that were decadent, came the retort, considering their despotism, clericalism, feudalism and serfdom.

Among the many guests were former disciples of Dr. Quesnay, the founder of the school of economists known as Physiocrats. Their teachings are not of primary interest here. Suffice it to say that they argued for the substitution of the mercantilist policy by one based primarily on a single tax paid by the farmers, in the belief that they alone were the productive class, and secondarily on the doctrine that economic freedom was the best course to national welfare. Whether Barlow's subsequent leaning to free enterprise was traceable to the Physiocrats remains unanswerable. Long before his arrival in France their school had fallen apart. But its principles were still taught in a modified form by such adherents as Mercier de la Rivière and Du Pont de Nemours. A friendship developed between Barlow and Du Pont. Perhaps it was at Du Pont's suggestion that he wrote down the names and books of foremost Physiocrats. [24] Also recorded by him was the name of Turgot and his famous essay on the formation and distribution of wealth. [25]

Among the guests were the versatile Tuscan and friend of Jefferson, Philip Mazzei. He had been Virginia's agent in Europe and a stout defender of the American Revolution. [26] To correct misconceptions of America, he wrote a documented account in four volumes of the origins and development of the new nation. [27] It was published about the time that Barlow came to Paris.

Barlow was acutely responsive to facts and opinions. This may explain his rapid intellectual growth in the first few years of residence abroad. One would find it difficult to trace any of his ideas to particular individuals. But the total effect was exceptional. He turned Francophile and defender of the reform movement.

Deteriorating conditions in France furnished impressive lessons to an American who was proud of his country's republican institutions.

Equally, if not more instructive were the numerous plans demanding renovation of the social order. The programs, taken as a whole, called for the suppression of feudal dues, the confiscation of church property, the establishment of public workshops for the unemployed and granaries for famine emergencies, the containment of concentrated wealth and the removal of impediments to trade and industry. A number of them even proposed collective ownership. [28] We are at a loss to know which of the programs won Barlow's attention.

The panoplied grandeur of absolutism and feudalism had worn so thin that it ceased to hide the sores of the body politic. The great mass of the people had grown irritable under the heavy strain of class privilege, a large and venal bureaucracy and oppressive taxation. Barlow wrote in his diary that almost every town had its customs barrier and that the inspectors were living on bribes. He noticed a constant struggle over taxes. "For this purpose," he observed, "every considerable town in France is honoured with a regiment of soldiers, whose business is not so much to keep the peace, as to assist in collecting duties." Everything had its impost, including bread, wine and salt. In the spirit of a reformer, he remarked that had the expenditures on tax gathering been diverted to useful needs "they might have levelled mountains & prepared the way of the Lord."

Distress made the strain harder to bear. Cyclical crop failures had depleted availability of bread, so that by 1789 the situation became ominous. Moreover, a depression had set in, following the commercial treaty with England, that favored the agricultural interests. The country was plagued with unemployment, hunger and vagrancy. Out of a total population of 600,000 in Paris, 120,000 were paupers and beggars. [29]

France was on the eve of revolution. But the portentous symptoms escaped notice among the socially élite. At a dinner party at Lafayette's Barlow heard guests say that the true solution lay in a "free constitution" and the meeting of the Estates General. All agreed that a measure of liberty should be conceded. But what did they mean by liberty and how far would they go? Barlow had some doubt about their appreciation of it. And he wrote in his diary, "I presume there not to be found five men in Europe who understand the nature of liberty & the theory of government as well as they are understood by five hundred men in America. . . . They are as intemperate in their idea of liberty as we were in the year seventy-five."

Events ripened the public mind. Frivolous conversation yielded to consideration of political problems, Jefferson reported, and all talked of nothing else. [30] A press, rich in political diversity, appeared from the underground. Approximately three months after Jefferson's observation, the Parisians captured the Bastille. The big assault on French despotism might have reminded Barlow of Lexington and Bunker Hill. For here was an armed challenge to authority that could develop into a sweeping renunciation of political and social bonds, as it had happened in his own country. In a state of excitement, he wrote to Ruth: "The sudden & glorious revolution that has taken place in Paris within the last fortnight has prevented my completing the business which I had promised myself should be done before now. You will get ten thousand lies & a great deal of truth about these affairs in the American papers, before they would reach you in my letter." He had sent Abraham a mass of publications about the important news. "Therefore," he continued, "I shall only say, that all the true things which you see published there, however horrible, however cruel, however just, however noble, memorable & important in their consequences, have passed under my eye; & it is really no small gratification to me to have seen two complete revolutions in favor of liberty." [31]

And again to Ruth, nearly six months later: "The french [sic] are beginning to come to their senses. They have been fools for many centuries." [32]

Barlow was intoxicated with the spirit of the Revolution. In common with others, he looked to its peaceful solution. For few could yet apprehend the bitter conflict that would ensue between its friends and foes.

4

The Revolution brightened the prospects of the Scioto Land Company. Those who were alarmed by events and dreaded the future looked to America for a haven. Many spoke of emigration, but Barlow was unable to turn it to his advantage. As he wrote to Winthrop Sargent, he was without money and without a word of advice from his employers at home. [33] He had furthermore learned that the persons he had been sent to meet were cool to the Company's enterprise. For as dealers in American funds, they were averse "to the sale of any lands which were to be paid for to the United States in those funds." [34]

He had also discovered that selling land in small lots was slow and unremunerative. Besides, it did not fit in with the plan of the Scioto speculators. Consequently, he chose the more expedient method and established a company to take over the entire tract. The project was in thorough keeping with the power of attorney Duer had given him in New York. A company would inspire more confidence, and it divided responsibility. Thus, on August 3, 1789, was established in Paris the Compagnie de Scioto, whose eight members agreed to purchase the Scioto Company's acres. The attorneys of the new company, Jean Soisson, William Playfair and Barlow, were empowered to resell part or all of the property. [35]

The entire transaction, regarding the French company, "was largely a paper proceeding." [36] Given the nature of the Scioto claim, any attempt to retail its option would be but to operate on slight ground. [37]

Of Barlow's associates in the Compagnie de Scioto, Playfair alone merits comment here. He had a bent for technology, but was diverted by an ambition to write. He was uncommonly prolific, with more than three dozen titles to his credit. There was scarcely a subject of public interest that failed to elicit his remarks. His favorite topics were politics and political economy—specifically, the French Revolution and questions raised by Adam Smith. He was a bitter foe of the Revolution and a tireless advocate of the new economics. Capital, he wrote, "is the accumulation of previous labour"; the value of a commodity "consists of the labour employed in making it"; and the difference between productive and unproductive labor is that "the one admits of being accumulated, the other does not." [38]

These ideas on political economy dated from Playfair's twenty-sixth year. Gibbon's classic work on the *Decline and Fall of the Roman Empire* might have motivated him to seek the reasons for the decline of wealthy nations. More pernicious than any external causes, it seemed to him, were the internal problems, such as excessive taxation, which induced people to migrate; conflicts of vested interests that brought forth swarms of attorneys; the concentration of wealth, which led to violent disturbances; the disappearance of the middle class, in which resided the intelligence and industry of a country; and finally, the degradation of the working class. The net result was the severance of the social bonds. Of all the causes the most baneful was this: "The great lose sight of the origin of their wealth, and cease to consider, that all wealth originated in labour, and that, therefore, the industrious and productive classes are the sinews of riches and power." [39] It may be said in passing that he anticipated Max Weber's thesis by arguing the relationship between the Protestant ethic and the rise of capitalism. [40]

So much for Playfair the economist. But what about Playfair the unscrupulous businessman? Barlow might have been attracted by his bold, enterprising nature, his knowledge of economic affairs, his literary penchant, his wide acquaintance with businessmen, and his fluency in French, which Barlow still lacked. Unfortunately, the agreement that set up the Compagnie de Scioto put Playfair in a position to embezzle funds.

The Company was formed at a propitious time. Many Frenchmen sought an escape from the Revolution, and in what better place could they seek a new life than in the American West? The Company's prospectus that advertised the lands bore the stamp of Playfair's imagination. The climate, it said, was wholesome, the country beautiful, the rivers teeming with fish, the forests filled with sugar-producing trees and overrun with deer, the plant life copious for raising hogs. And there was neither taxation nor military service. [41] Brissot's revised book on America completed the rosy picture. Enthusiasm ran high. The prospect of paradise regained was opened for Frenchmen.

Buyers were imposed upon. They had not been told that they were buying only preempted land, that it was yet unfit for habitation, that settlers would first have to clear it and secure themselves against hostile natives. The deeds they received, drawn by Playfair and Soisson, were worthless.

Business was brisk. The biggest purchaser was the Society of the Twenty-Four, with which Barlow had entered into an elaborate agreement stipulating that the American company would provide the immigrants transportation and supplies, hire workmen to survey and clear the land and build houses. The obligations Barlow threw into the laps of the Scioto speculators astonished them, even though the agreement was not inconsistent with the terms of his power of attorney. Duer, for one, had never had the slightest intention of developing the option by sponsoring its occupancy, and accordingly shunned responsibility. Nevertheless, the Scioto associates were faced with the vexing burden of expenditures to make the land habitable. As might have been expected, little was spent on the project, with the result that the settlers found themselves in insufferable circumstances. The reports they sent home made heart-rending reading. [42]

Barlow was in serious difficulty. Trusting the exaggerated accounts of sales and receipts given him by Playfair and Soisson, he had authorized Duer to draw on him notes totalling 220,000 livres. But they were returned unpaid. Those who had bought on credit defaulted. It may also be noted that the Scioto agent had American competitors in Paris, among them Gouveneur Morris, who were better situated because they could at least give title to the properties they sold.

In February 1790 Barlow's optimism began to desert him. Sales were continuing, but he saw nothing of the proceeds. He could not even draw his expenses. Buying soon declined, distrust arose, the public was inflamed against the Company and he was threatened with assassination. The Compagnie de Scioto deteriorated. Barlow carried on sales in his own name with a group, of which Playfair was a member, in an effort to salvage the Company's assets. But alarming reports from settlers hastened the collapse of the Scioto business.

Barlow never seemed really to understand that he represented speculators rather than rightful landowners. He had utmost faith in the colonization scheme he had worked out for the French. For should the first immigrants "find themselves happy," he wrote to a merchant in Alexandria, Virginia, in 1790, "the business may be carried to almost any extent." [43] And to Benjamin Walker he said toward the end of the year, "I believed that the United States might be much benefited by turning this tide of emigration to that country and that the interest of the Scioto concern required that I should try for a while what could be done in Paris." [44]

Barlow was also wanting in caution and expertise. He had not inquired closely into the bookkeeping of Playfair and Soisson. And he discovered too late that the "enterprise in its origin was perhaps of too hazardous a nature for a prudent man to have engaged in." [45]

Scioto associates were in a fury. Duer, whose practice it was to write few letters, nevertheless sent one to Barlow, bristling with charges. The agent, he said, had concealed information; he had not reported sales, receipts and disbursements; he had issued bills that could not be honored; he had misrepresented the real state of affairs; and he had placed him, i.e. Duer, on the brink of ruin. [46] But Duer was not the man to turn accuser. He had neglected Barlow, ignored his letters, failed to send instructions and left him to his own discretion. The Revolution had furthermore created monetary conditions beyond the control of even the most knowledgeable businessman. Specie was scarce; purchasers of land could not make payments. Barlow's notes were thus rendered worthless. But Duer was oblivious to these facts. True, he and his associates had been unexpectedly confronted with the problem of settling the immigrants. But he had managed to evade it. Only General Rufus Putnam had gone to Marietta to face the new arrivals. Duer was interested only in speculation, not in the occupation of the land.

Partners of Duer differed with him. Barlow might have been inadequate for the task, they held, but he was not without integrity. They sent Duer's friend, Benjamin Walker, to investigate matters. Reaching Paris in December 1790, he found the Company too far gone to be salvaged. He exonerated Barlow of the charge of fraudulence and ascribed his difficulties to lack of practical wisdom in business. The true culprit was Playfair, Walker believed, and he publicly warned prospective buyers against any dealings with him. Playfair, however, cast all the blame on Barlow. [47] Walker planned to form another company that would take over the contract with the Ohio group. But the revolutionary events made it impossible to do so. His return to America marked the end of the Scioto speculation.

Playfair spread the word that Walker's public statement against him was libelous and announced that the Company's business would be carried on as usual. No one but he had the authority to sell the land. [48] But it was mere ostentation to mask deceit.

Barlow found himself in a distressing situation. He had nothing of the Company's money and even less of his own. He notified Walker that he was "very considerably in debt for my personal expenses." [49] The letter to him of April 10, 1791, ended on a despairing note. The whole business had mortified him, wrote Barlow. He even faced possible prosecution by Duer upon his return to America. But life in prison, he concluded, would be happier "than the one I have led for the last three years in his service." [50]

Chapter V
The Big Debate

1

Barlow's first year abroad was an unhappy one. He had suffered business misfortune and he longed for Ruth.[1] Early in 1789 he had mentioned her coming to Europe, but she hesitated. She felt snug in her rustic environment. Except for Joel's absence, even her social life seemed complete. Besides, an ocean voyage was something hazardous. But he kept on urging. She would be away but a short time; the stay would be quite pleasant. Knowing her conventional ways, he tried to prepare her for the revolutionary climate. "I am more afraid you will be disgusted with the folly than awed at the splendor of the decripped [sic] world."[2] When she at last agreed to make the voyage, he sent her detailed instructions including the address in London where he would meet her. In the event that he was detained, he directed her to write to John Paradise, his good friend in London, or to Henry Bromfield, his subagent.

It was as he had foreseen. The Scioto business prevented him from leaving Paris. Ruth, alone in the English metropolis, was ill at ease, worrying and wondering why he lingered in France, even though he had informed her of the tormenting obstacles. They were finally reunited the last week of July 1790.

The country-bred woman did not feel at home in the large English city. The crowds bewildered her; the brick walls confined her. Paris was no better, in fact worse. She was a stranger in a strange land, not knowing its language. Things were happening that alarmed her: street meetings that foreshadowed misfortune; the Scioto business going under; Joel in straits. Adding to his anxieties was the news of the distressing state of the immigrants in Ohio.

The Barlows were living in Paris in constant turmoil. There was an endless coming and going, visits of Americans, business calls, political appointments. Barlow was being pulled into the revolutionary movement.

Ruth was bewildered and disconcerted. After a month's stay in Paris, she wrote to Mrs. Dwight: "O! it is altogether disagreeable to me. It is only existing. I have not an hour to call my own except when I sleep. Must at all times be dressed to see company, which you know, my dear

Madam, is not to my taste. We are pent up in a narrow dirty street surrounded with high brick walls and scarcely see the light of the sun. We have no Sabbath; it is looked upon as a day of amusement entirely. O! how ardently I do wish to return to America, and to Greenfield, that dear delightful village."[4]

Barlow felt despondent. The colonization project on which he had set his heart was reported a failure. His integrity had been assailed. After wearing himself out to give the preemition a semblance of respectability, he had but insult and a threat of prosecution for his reward. He was deep in debt. And he faced the prospect of being looked upon as a bankrupt in his own country.

Fortunately, he had in Paris a number of American friends who were on good terms with French political leaders. There were Colonel Blackden and John Paradise, John Paul Jones, Thomas Appleton and Benjamin Jarvis, William Henry Vernon from Rhode Island and James Swan from Boston. Both Vernon and Swan were friends of Lafayette. And all of them were in sympathy with the French revolutionary cause.

On July 4, 1789, Barlow and five Americans presented Thomas Jefferson with a testimonial of his services as American minister. Barlow apparently had a hand in drafting it. Gouverneur Morris declined to sign it.[5]

The Barlows had to count their pennies. They lived in what a friend described as an attic prison" of the Palais Royal. The big inner quadrangle was nearly always crowded and buzzing. People came to hear some platform orator or to learn the latest news. Tramps and beggars, pickpockets and prostitutes were about; gamblers were drawn to the gaming dens. To reach Barlow's quarters, a friend recalled, "I was obliged to pass through the door of a great gambling establishment that occupied the floor below his. This door was attended by a porter, who kept it locked, so that to get admittance, I had to announce myself as a visitor of Mr. Barlow. A man ought to be cheaply lodged to be induced to reside behind such a barrier. The poet's poverty consented rather than his will."[6]

The future looked gloomy. They could, of course, return home. Abram, the bachelor brother-in-law and a United States Senator from Georgia, had invited them to live with him even before he knew of the Scioto fiasco.[7] By May 1791, they had almost made up their minds to sail home. But Joel delayed going. He was still hopeful that he might retrieve the Scioto speculation, or perhaps sell other American properties in Europe. The question also arose: What would Joel do in America? He might go West and start anew as Abram had done in Georgia. He might practice law in Hartford or seek an appointment to a public office.[8] One more thought lodged in his brain. He might write the history of America, as Jefferson had suggested. The project was forever contemplated but never executed.

Finding a livelihood was of secondary interest, according to Abram. The first step was to return. He was fairly gratified that Joel had missed making a fortune. Many fools and "goose heads" had made it, but it did not bring them respect. Abram feared that the "anxiety for money getting" might make Joel "less useful and less pleasing" to his friends.[9] At any rate, he was lonely and wanted them back.

Things took a turn for the better, Joel had made a business connection with the prospect of recovering "in some measure from my heavy losses and disappointments."[10] But it is not known what the business was. At the same time, the French Revolution was claiming more of his attention. In October 1791, he wrote to Abram from England that he was meditating a piece of writing in its defense, the tentative title of which was a program in capsule form, "The Renovation of Society, or an Essay on the Necessity & Propriety of a Revolution in the Governments of Europe." He gave notice that neither impartiality nor prudence would restrain him. "I have such a flood of indignation," he confided to his friend, & such a store of argument accumulated in my guts on this subject, that I can hold it no longer; & I think the nurselings of abuses may be stung more to the quick than they have yet been by all discussions to which the French Revolution has given occasion." Then, with an admirable economy of words, he announced the plan of his work. On the assumption that the revolution in France would set off a general revolution in Europe, he proposed to examine the extent of its desirability and the nature of its consequences with regard to feudal rights, established churches, military organizations, revenue and public expenditure, administration of justice, and the economic, social and cultural aspects of society. With these as chapter headings, he gave a preview of his *Advice to the Privileged Orders* which he expected to complete while he was winding up his affairs abroad.[11]

2

The French Revolution was a keynote in Barlow's letters beginning in 1789. Having seen it from the beginning, he followed its course with the passion of one who had already served a world-shaking revolution. So absorbing were the French events that at times they deflected him from business.

The first stage of the Revolution was drawing to a close in the summer of 1791. The National Assembly had voted many fundamental changes. It had cleared out much of the feudal rubbish, confiscated the church properties, abolished serfdom, guaranteed the people's liberties and set up a framework of government that resembled the British, save that it provided for a unicameral system. Louis XVI's acceptance of the reforms gave the impression that the nation would peacefully adjust to the new order.

But eruptions were brewing. Peasant risings, begun in 1789 and fueled by poverty and famine, were still unabated. In urban centers, escpecially in the capital, factions and parties rivaled for ascendancy. Clubs had sprung up—the Jacobin, the Cordelier, the Feuillant—each seeking to make its views sovereign. Simultaneously, a court junto was plotting the restoration of absolutism. Princes and nobles had already emigrated and were pressing upon the King to flee the country. The French monarchy in exile, they reasoned, would be an attractive focal point for all foes of the Revolution. On June 20, 1791, the royal family quietly drove off to the northeastern frontier. But they were intercepted and brought back to Paris. A small republican party came into being, and the question arose whether the King's attempted flight did not signalize a design to restore the *ancien régime* with foreign aid. But the monarchists rallied their strength and restored him to the throne. Constitutional monarchy, provided for by the Constitution of 1791, was put to the test in France.

Barlow, along with others, was of the opinion that the Revolution would achieve its end without the need of force. As in America, so in France. The Constitution would be accepted as the law of the land. The emigrés, instead of wandering over Europe, would come back and adapt to the new regime. "If they don't chuse [sic] to return," he wrote to Abram, "they may go to the devil. France can do without them."[12]

Barlow presumed that revolutions followed a given pattern, as exemplified by the American. But before much time elapsed, he learned that history does not repeat itself. It has parallels but no recapitulations, for the circumstances and traditions of peoples vary. In America, for instance, classes were fluid; in France they had become stratified. The feudal aristocracy was freighted with privileges. Beneath it on the social ladder was the rich middle class that aped it and aspired to climb to its ranks by purchasing land and titles. The great mass of the nation consisted of artisans, shopkeepers, small peasants, landless farmhands and serfs. Social demarcations were clear and difficult to cross. The abolition of privileges and the confiscation of church properties turned their former owners into enemies of the Revolution. Unlike the Loyalists in America, they had the support of foreign governments.

The contrast brings to mind other differences between the two Revolutions. The American divided the crowned heads of Europe; the French united them. The struggle over the partition of the confiscated properties was sharp in densely populated France; it was far less so in sparsely settled America where unoccupied western land tended to cushion contentions. Finally, the American Revolution, unlike the French, neither disrupted the foundations of society nor signalized the perturbing question of inequality.

3

The essay Barlow mentioned to his brother-in-law was completed at the end of 1791 and published anonymously in February 1792 under a long title, of which the press gave only the first part, *Advice to the Privileged Orders in the Several European States*.[13] It was a reply to Edmund Burke's *Reflections on the Revolution in France*.

Barlow had already professed his support for the French Revolution. On July 10, 1790, he was one of a dozen Americans in Paris who petitioned the National Assembly for the privilege of participating in observing the first anniversary of Bastille Day. He had apparently been the author of the petition.[14] In lofty eloquence it spoke of the gratitude and respect due to the French benefactors of humanity by those whose liberty they had helped attain. The power of truth was irresistible. The blessings of liberty would one day be cherished universally. Nations would demand the rights of man in a voice that could not be stifled. Class distinctions and religious fanaticism would recede like phantoms before the light of fraternity. The First King of the French would then be glorified as the First King of Men.[15]

The petition was received with acclaim. The motion to have it printed was introduced by Robespierre.[16] Barlow had caught the spirit of the brotherhood of man with which Paris was saturated. Only those who had escaped infection could discern the signs of rising reaction. Already, it had such champions as Antoine Rivarol and Charles Alexandre de Calonne, the first in his political journal,[17] the second in a work published in England.[18] But Edmund Burke's *Reflections on the Revolution in France* sounded the loudest alarm against the Revolution. Thereafter he was regarded as the most resolute advocate of conservatism and the prophet of counterrevolution.

It may be noted that conservatism arose in the eighteenth century as a philosophy of negation—directed against the principles of the Enlightenment, and it scorned the facile optimism of the *philosophes* about progress and human perfectibility. Instead it postulated tradition and the sanctity of age-old institutions. In contrast to the Enlightenment that rejected the Middle Ages, it venerated their values.

Burke had shown the trend of his views on the Revolution before writing his *Reflections*. As early as February 9, 1790, he warned the members of Parliament of the dangers implicit in the spread of French principles. It was the danger from "an imitation of the excesses of an irrational, unprincipled, proscribing, confiscating, plundering, ferocious, bloody and tyrannical democracy;" and it was the danger "from atheism." He announced that he would resist "all violent exertions of the spirit of innovation." He was moreover disturbed by the likeness distinguished men in England saw between 1688 and 1789. For the first was "a revolution, not made, but prevented," he answered. It repaired and strengthened the monarchy; it did not impair it. Institutions, social orders and the Church remained the same. But 1789 commenced with ruin instead of reparation. Its convulsive movements exposed the nation "to the derision of the world."[19]

These remarks were parenthetical in a speech on a national issue. But the whole of the *Reflections* was from beginning to end a denunciation of the Revolution. It became the manual of European reaction. It was translated into French, German and Italian; it inspired such political philosophers of the status quo as Friedrich von Gentz in Germany, Joseph de Maistre in Italy, Viscount de Bonald in France and Nikolai Karamzin in Russia; it set off a controversy on change and conservation that has not yet come to a close.

Appearing early in November 1790, the *Reflections* almost at once opened a bitter debate. "It may be doubted," wrote Sir James Prior, "whether any previous political production ever excited so much attention and discussion, so much praise from one party and animadversion from another."[20] In the first year 19,000 copies sold in England and 13,000 in France; and more than 30,000 English copies were disposed of within a few years. No less than thirty-eight answers came out within a year or two, we are told, "but were all the letters, essays, fragments, and invectives of every denomination collected, which appeared then and since, in magazines, reviews, newspapers, and every form of publication, periodical and otherwise on this prolific theme they would amount to many hundreds"[21] Siding with Burke in England were such eminent men as Edward Gibbon, Arthur Young and George Canning. Against him gathered an imposing number that included the legal minds, Sir Samuel Romilly and Sir James Mackintosh, the scientist John Priestley and the dramatist Richard Brinsley Sheridan.

Englishmen, by and large, at first rejoiced in the French Revolution. Wordsworth wrote in retrospect:

Europe at the time was thrilled with joy,
France standing at the top of golden hours
And human nature seeming born again.

• • • • • • • • • • • • • • •

What temper at the prospect did not wake
To happiness unthought of? The inert
Were roused, and lively natures rapt away!

The Prelude

The dream of nearby better days may account in part for the plethora of replies to Burke's book. Their greatest number fell on the accumulating heap of ephemera. Those that best captured the public mind were Paine's *Rights of Man,* Godwin's *Enquiry Concerning Political Justice* and Barlow's *Advice to the Privileged Orders.* Paine's book was the most eloquent and Godwin's the most philosophical. The calm and solid reasoning of the *Advice* helps to explain its three editions in little more than a year.

At least seven women entered the lists against Burke, of whom the best known in their day were Helen Maria Williams, Mary Hays, Catherine Macaulay and Mary Wollstonecraft. Wollstonecraft alone has escaped oblivion, not for her polemic against Burke, but for her pioneering in the defense of women's rights.

A reader of the *Reflections* cannot avoid the impression that its invective and unmannerly insinuations were but camouflage for a dearth of evidence. Presumption, specious chivalry and effusive sentiment over royal frivolities were invested with authority over fact and argument. As James Mackintosh put it, "it was hard to have supposed that he should have exhausted against it [French Revolution] every epithet of contumely and opprobium that language can furnish to indignation; that the rage of his indignation should not for one moment have been suspended; that his heart should not betray one faint glow of triumph at the splendid and glorious delivery of so great a people." Burke was frightened by "the homely miseries of the vulgar," [22] whom he denominated the "swinish multitude." He conceded that the Revolution was "the most astonishing that has hitherto happened in the world," and "the most important of all revolutions which may be dated from that day." [23] But he was unable to penetrate its taproots. He could see it only as "a strange chaos of levity and ferocity."

Burke's fundamental idea was the much considered doctrine of prescription. It was his answer to the theory of natural rights from which had stemmed the revolutionary rights of man. A constitution, he held, had a history. It was something organic, developed through the centuries, which could not be scrapped by a popular revolution. Its existence through time was an assumption in its favor and proof of its utility. The rights of man, on the other hand, were but the creation of bold metaphysicians. A state was a partnership of the dead, the living and those to be born; it had continuity and traditions that commanded veneration and had a claim on men's minds. Governments and institutions of long duration represented the accumulated experience of generations. They could only be repaired, not obliterated. Mingling social orders, abolishing the rule of an aristocracy, confiscating property and disestablishing the Church were the undoing of all political and social bonds.

By lingering amid the relics of the past, Burke lost sight of the misery and pain of the present. He shut his eyes to the social and economic changes that were transforming England in his day. Prescription sanctioned the saying, "whatever is, is right." It made little or no concession to the fact that, while tradition has a strong grip on men's minds, it can and has been loosened by circumstances. Historical change cannot otherwise be explained.

Implied in prescription was the assumption that the common man was incapable of attaining political competence and of improving his condition. Its aim was a status quo, braced by an impregnable faith in the Creator's Chain of Being, a widely held doctrine of eighteenth-century England. Burke shared with Robert Malthus the conviction that religion and the rule of an aristocracy were the essential supports of a state. And his infallible authority was precedent which one historian defined as "the dry bones of the past." [24] In spite of all that, his book gave a mighty impulse to an inquiry into the ruling ideas of the time.

Burke justified armed intervention to stamp out the Revolution. The sovereigns, he said, had the obligation to preserve Europe from anarchy. No government was safe as long as the French were free to disseminate subversion, for their aim was universal revolution. It was an affliction that had to be blotted out, he wrote to Catherine II of Russia. [25] Copies of the *Reflections* were sent by the courts of London and Paris to the other courts of Europe. Men of letters read it as did men of state. Barlow charged in 1793, "That the present war with all its train of calamities must be attributed almost exclusively to the pen of Mr. Burke." [26] The charge needed proof. At the utmost, the book rationalized the European coalition that was bound to come, even if he had not written it.

4

In the mass of replies to Burke's *Reflections* Paine's *Rights of Man* was unique. To Washington, to whom it was dedicated, he wrote from London on July 21, 1791, "The work has had a run beyond anything that has been published in this country on the subject of Government, and the demand continues. In Ireland it has had a much greater." [27] Paine was referring to the first part of his work; the second was published in Paris in 1792. French and German translations increased its audience on the continent, and its reprint in the United States enlivened the dispute between democrats and monocrats. If to the approximate forty answers to his book that came to his notice by June 1792, we add those appearing subsequently, the total number would be exceedingly high and must be counted apart from the sale of 200,000 copies of the book. [28] Evidently the debate Paine aroused was both far-reaching and intense.

The excitement Paine's book caused in Great Britain was in a measure due to its welfare program. Artisans and small shop owners saw it as the statement of their grievances and aspirations. An English correspondent wrote at the end of November 1792 that the *Rights of Man* "is now made as much a Standard book in this country as *Robinson Crusoe* & the *Pilgrim's Progress.*" [29]

Burke and Paine saw things and men from opposite points of view.

The one extolled the existing British political and social system based on privilege; the other disclosed its dead weight on the English nation and the irrationality of privilege. The first acclaimed the rule of an aristocracy; the second, the sovereignty of the people. Burke rested his case on precedent; Paine, on the freedom of each generation to act for itself. The former praised the compromise of 1688 as the summit of political wisdom; the latter glorified the birth of the United States as the herald of revolution. Finally, Burke was passionately attached to monarchical government, of which the British was his model; Paine was just as intensely devoted to a democratic republic.

Paine epitomized the popular wishes. He recommended a graduated income tax, care of the poor and aged, limitation of armaments and international peace. His originality, however, lay less in his principles than in the vigor of their presentation, in his simple style and deep compassion for the distressed.

Let us take a rapid look at the effect of his book in the United States. To begin with, the *Daily Advertiser* ran it serially[30] and the *National Gazette* printed extracts from it. [31] Then as an antidote to two works by John Adams, Jefferson had it reprinted, prefaced, through error, by brief remarks involving him as Secretary of State. The result was a polemic which Jefferson pictures to Paine in these words:

"Indeed I am glad you did not come away till you had written your *Rights of Man*. That has been much read here with avidity and pleasure. A writer under the signature of Publicola has attacked it. A host of champions entered the arena immediately in your defense. The discussion excited the public attention, recalled it to the 'Defence of the American Constitutions' and the 'Discourses on Davila,' [both by John Adams] which it had kindly passed over without censure in the moment, and very general expressions of their sense have been now drawn forth; and I thank God that they appear firm in their republicanism, notwithstanding the contrary hopes and assertions of a sect here, high in name but small in numbers. These had flattered themselves that the silence of the people under 'Defence' and 'Davila' was a symptom of their conversion to the doctrine of king, lords and commons. They are checked at least by your pamphlet and the people confirmed in the good old faith." [32]

The Publicola Jefferson referred to was John Quincy Adams, son of the vice president. His reply consisted of eight letters in the Boston *Columbian Centinel* that were subsequently collected in a pamphlet. [33] Its major themes were of a piece with Burke's. It stood by the doctrine of prescription, and it repudiated the right of revolution. In Paine's sense this right meant that the people made their own history. The younger Adams, however, like contemporary romantic writers, appealed to "the eternal and immutable laws of justice and morality," thereby shifting the question of revolution from the realm of history to the realm of mysticism. The transfer was consistent with his philosophical outlook. Philosophy which does not rest on God, he once wrote, "is but a cobweb of the brain." [34]

5

Shortly before the second part of *The Rights of Man* was brought out, Barlow's publisher, Joseph Johnson, put on the market the first part of *Advice to the Privileged Orders*. It appeared in an agitated atmosphere. Other replies to Burke were steadily coming out; French events were the talk on streets and in taverns, and political clubs were arising. The Society for Promoting Constitutional Information that had been near death in 1790 revived toward the end of 1791. At the same time, a shoemaker by the name of Thomas Hardy was organizing The London Corresponding Society for the Reform of Parliamentary Representation. [35] With a small membership and even smaller funds, he started the first political labor movement in England.

Barlow, accompanied by his wife, had been in London since the fall of 1791. Whether the reason for the visit was business or a desire to find a publisher for his translation of Brissot's *Travels* is not known. Anyhow he could not have chosen a more exciting time to be in the English capital. Nor could he have been in more stimulating company. He saw the publishers, Joseph Johnson and J. S. Jordan; the women's rights advocate, Mary Wollstonecraft; the novelists, Mary Hays and Charlotte Smith; and the poetess, Helen Maria Williams. [36] The circle also included Thomas Christie, a friend of Dr. Price and a writer on politics and natural history; Thomas Holcroft, a self-taught cobbler who turned into a novelist and dramatist; Capell Lofft, a founding member of the Society for Constitutional Information and the author of a polemic against Burke; the poet William Hayley; James Mackintosh, the author of one of the best reasoned replies to Burke; John Thelwall, an English pioneer of social reform; John Oswald, a republican and the author of a critique of the British system, *Review of the Constitution of Great Britain*, and the painters, George Romney, John Trumbull, John Copley and Benjamin West. Barlow's relations with Godwin dated from 1792. The latter noted in his diary that at the "occasional meetings," at which both were present, "the principles of my work were discussed." One entry records: "Tea at Barlow's with Jardine, Stuart, Wollstonecraft and Holcroft; talk of self-love, sympathy and perfectibility, individual and general." [37]

Compared with *Rights of Man*, the *Advice* was moderate save for some satirical shafts at the adversary. Burke's vocabulary in the *Reflections* was as scorching as his epithets were copious. Barlow had little use for such outbursts of passion; his method was reason and argument. He appealed to man's intelligence, in the belief that concurrence would follow conviction. He set out to prove two cardinal points: first, that the French Revolution was as ineradicable as it was unrestrainable; and second, "that the establishment of general liberty will be less injurious to those who now live by abuses, than is commonly imagined." [38]

He took his stand on the principle of self-interest that *philosophes* like Holbach and Helvetius had considered the motivation of progress. The ruling classes could choose between two courses, he said. They could yield to right thinking or be guided by their personal advantages. The first choice was of course the wiser, for the reformers had two powerful weapons, "the force of reason and the force of numbers." Since reform was unavoidable, any effort to retain the existing order would be futile.

The purpose of the first four chapters was to exhibit the decadence and mischief of the old system. Among the author's aversions were the laws of entail and primogeniture that had been early casualties of the American Revolution. They were calculated "to perpetuate family distinctions, and to temper the minds of men to an aristocratical subordination." [39]

Barlow examined feudalism with the test of history and found it detrimental to the social organism. Its original purpose, "the preservation of turbulent societies," was effected by uniting the personal interest of the head of each family with the security of the state. In the course of time, however, motives of family and nation came into conflict. Military tenures, titles and privileges were eventually tied up with the functioning of the church and the continuance of despotism. Feudalism became an impediment to economic growth. It made idleness a criterion of *noblesse*. But the French broke the charm. [40]

Barlow likened the Church to an engine forged with the object of preventing a confrontation between the privileged minority and the majority of the nation. The engine assumed different forms with different peoples. But its character remained the same. It was only a question of where it had done the most mischief. [41]

He differentiated between religion and church. The first, he said, was in man's nature; the second was a means of oppression. The distinction concealed but superficially the effect of French deism and materialism on his thinking. Not only his reasoning, his vocabulary, too, bore the marks of such critics as Fréret, Boulanger and Holbach.

His principal target was the Catholic Church. Here Joseph Priestley's *History of the Corruptions of Christianity* and Gibbon's *Decline and Fall of the Roman Empire* served him well. Barlow laid to the Christian Church the loss of as many lives as existed in Europe in his day. It had hunted down the Druids, overturned the temples of polytheists and drenched the plains with the blood of Arians. It had incited wars to convert Huns, Lombards and Moors. The crusades alone, he estimated, had accounted for the death of at least four million. Spain had been depopulated by the expulsion of the Moors and ruined by the Inquisition. Thousands upon thousands had been slain by the struggle to reconvert the Eastern Empire and by the wars following the Reformation. He concluded that the enjoyment of any liberty was irreconcilable with the existence of any kind of church. [42]

The list of artful stratagems Barlow ascribed to the priests brings to mind the *Essay on Prejudices* by Du Marsais and such works by Holbach as *The Priests Unmasked* and *The Spirit of the Clergy*. To delude people the priest resorted to incantations. The imposition was made easy by the increasing wealth of the Church and "the authority of precedent." For people "believe by prescription," he wrote, "and orthodoxy is hereditary." The priest inculcated the idea of inequality, rendered men "cruel and savage in a preternatural degree." The conclusion was "that nations are cruel in proportion as they are guided by priests." The priest invested himself with the cloak of infallibility the better to deceive and pervert minds. [43]

The Church and its priests were like a standing army. Everywhere they were the most dependable supporters of arbitrary power "both for internal oppression and external violence."

Despotism also needed another instrument of power, that is, a military system. Just as the Church relied on "the principle of religion, so the military relied on "the principle of honour." The profession of arms was both honorable and enviable. The lowest orders were prevented from practicing it. The body of the noblesse stood detached from the nation and grew into an indispensable arm of the sovereign as the spirit of enlightenment sapped the power of the Church. Standing armies and wars were means of maintaining the political order. Wars were political in character and offensive, for despots could not fight a defensive war. That was a task for the armed people alone.

Barlow would change the political order by introducing the equality of rights. Representative government would replace despotism and privilege, and an armed citizenry would convert the weapons of war into means of security. In that respect, he observed, the French National Assembly had not been consequential. It had maintained a military establishment which, if allowed to continue, might be destructive of the end. [44] Barlow was uncommonly prophetic.

Most devastating in the first part of the *Advice* was the chapter on the judicial system. It was an exposé of corruption and venality in the administration of justice both in pre-revolutionary France and in Burke's England. Barlow was confident that it could be reformed by changing the principle of government. The courts should be easy of access to poor and rich alike, and the legal process should be simplified and divested of mystery. In England, for example, it perpetuated the ignorance of the people. It was "a fathomless abyss . . . studied not to be understood . . . not to give information, but to breed confusion." Justice in France before 1789 was a commodity. It profited the king who sold the judgeships; the judges who sold decisions; and the numerous lawyers who "covered the iniquity of the judges under the impenetrable veil of their own." Yet, said Barlow, Burke lamented the abolition of this antiquated system of jurisprudence. For the benefit of Englishmen who considered their laws and legal process models of perfection, Barlow showed with some detail that, as in France, their courts were "effectually shut against the great body of the people." The administration of justice was costly, intricate, entangled in masses of records and complicated by an army of law-practicing cormorants. Even in America, he continued, drawing on his experience as a lawyer, even in his own country, where the legal process had been stripped of useless forms, the heritage of the English common law served "to increase the expense and to mysticize the business, to a degree that is manifestly inconsistent with the dignity of a true republic."[45]

This concluded the first part of *Advice*. Of the second, only one chapter, entitled "Revenue and Expenditure," was completed and published. Its composition was apparently slow and deliberate. Discussions with reformers had undoubtedly marked its lines of thought, and much of its substance was drawn from the best authorities of the day. The chapter was considered so subversive that it had to be brought out in Paris. His English publisher feared to print it.

Barlow went at his subject with deep conviction. It stemmed in part from the early reforms of the French Revolution and in part from the overwhelming evidence furnished by such reputable writers as Timothy Cunningham,[46] Sir John Sinclair,[47] Jacques Necker[48] and Adam Smith.[49] Though the relation between national revenue and the cost of government was relevant to his general subject, he avoided treating it at length. It would have meant plowing ground already turned up by the second part of the *Rights of Man*.[50] For the same reason he abstained from presenting a welfare program. Barlow shared with Paine and other contemporaries the belief that the best government was that which governed least.

Governments in Europe, Barlow charged, practiced the policy Cardinal Richelieu had formulated in his *Political Testament*. It said plainly that the people had to be hoodwinked and treated like pack animals if they were to bear their burdens submissively. The policy was implicit in the system of indirect taxation. It was a means of disguising levies to render their payment imperceptible. It arose, first, from the necessity of concealing the purposes to which they were applied, and second, from the division of society into oppressors and oppressed. Therein lay the reason why the former, for whom Burke spoke, regarded the French Revolution with abhorrence. Using Sinclair as his authority, Barlow said that only about one-seventh of the revenue received by the English Exchequer derived from direct taxes. In France, according to Necker, it was a little less than a third. In both countries the remaining portion of the revenue was raised by imposts on consumption. Barlow concluded that the system of indirect taxes was morally wrong, vicious in practice and founded on the belief that men had to be governed by fraud. Every vestige of these taxes had to be abolished. The same should be done with lotteries, tontines and annuities.

He then assailed the arguments against direct taxes. Their collection would be difficult, said their opponents, for the poor could not pay them. They were in the habit of spending all they had, even on superfluities. Also the selfish would find ways of evading them. With regard to the poor, Barlow answered that their condition and improvidence were the products of their abject environment. The great majority of them would be retrieved in "a nation organized as human reason would dictate." In such an order "the greatest quantity of our physical wants" would be supplied, "with the corresponding improvement of our moral faculties." He replied to the second argument that under a government founded on violence and geared to the interests of a small minority, any rational estimate of private property would be improbable. It inevitably became an outer sign of merit and instilled a desire for external pomp.

Barlow listed a number of evils traceable to the passion for property. It excited emulation and rivalry; it warped man's moral nature and it was a cause of outrage and assault. The list was shorter than Godwin's.[51] Nor were the conclusions communist, as Godwin's were. Perhaps as a concession to Godwin and others of the day, he granted the possibility that "in a more improved state of society, the time will come, when a different system may be introduced; when it shall be found more congenial to the social nature of man to exclude the idea of separate property, and with that the numerous evils which seem to be entailed upon it."[52] A similar thought may be read into his saying: "establish government universally on the individual wishes and collective wisdom of the people, and it will give a spring to the moral faculties of every human creature, because every human creature must find an interest in its welfare."[53]

Nowhere else in Barlow's works do we find him admitting the contingency of collectivism. His closest approach to it was a social order that would provide sufficient material wants and stimulate moral improvement. But this vision grew out of confidence in individualism.

What was the source of his collectivist ideal? One literary historian has suggested that Barlow leaned on Morelly's *Code de la nature*.[54] Published anonymously in 1755, it caused little sensation in Paris, according to a contemporary observer.[55] It was attributed to many litérati, among them Rousseau and Diderot, despite his efforts to disclaim it. Its republication in a two-volume work of Diderot's philosophical writings[56] revived an interest in it. Barlow might have discovered it in this edition.

He might also have come upon the collectivist idea in more available writings, such as More's *Utopia* or in those that derived from Rousseau's philosophy. Novels by Rétif de la Bretonne, for example, proposed collective ownership as the solution of the social problems. And numerous social plans were circulating that did away with thine and mine. Among them were Jean Meslier's *Le Testament* [57] and Francois Boissel's *Catechisme du genre humain*. Published in 1789, while Barlow was in Paris, Boissel's book was given free publicity by the bishop of Clermont who denounced it in the National Assembly. [58]

In the quest for the source of Barlow's idea of collectivism we must also concede a possible English inspiration. For at his meetings with friends in London, with Godwin, for instance, the question often arose respecting private property and its bearing on human relations.

The works of Cunningham and Sinclair plunged Barlow into the question of the national debt. It was an issue in his own country and a cause of much debate in Europe. Its two great advantages, according to its advocates, were commercial and political. It put a mass of capital in the service of trade, they said, and it aided governments in waging war. In Barlow's opinion, its mischiefs far outweighed its benefits. It enabled rulers to enter upon the most expensive operations without consulting the nation's representatives; it resulted in higher taxes; it burdened future generations; it converted commerce into a weapon and ally in wartime; it rendered the mass of the nation wretched; finally, it was a means of prolonging the established system. Barlow expected France to set an example by extinguishing the national debt. But whether she did so or not, the problem could not contain the progress of liberty. [59]

The *Advice* not only passed sentence on the institutions and practices of European governments. It also implied a censure of the philosophical and ethical superstructure. The belief was current in the eighteenth century that the universe comprised a continuous scale of beings from the lowest to the Absolute. Man was the middle link. He was as inferior to those above him as he was superior to those below him. Here was a cause for his humility. His duty was to know his place in the social scale and not attempt to rise above it, and it was equally idle for him to hope for an improvement of the political and social edifice. Besides, so ran the creed, imperfections were inherent in government. [60] Evils existed, of course, but they were also productive of good, said Soam Jenyns, the English vulgarizer of the doctrine. [61] This amounted to sanctioning Bernard Mandeville's crude morality, "Private Vices, Public Benefits." [62]

Such a philosophy was alien to Barlow. Its complacency and cynicism were calculated to make man satisfied with the state of affairs; it served despotism and privilege; it pronounced man forever doomed to remain in his fixed state. In sum, it was a weapon of oppression. Clearly, both its premise and conclusion were irreconcilable with the thesis of the *Advice*.

Several concluding remarks are in order, regarding the effect of Barlow's book. The number distributed amounted to a fraction of the figure given for the *Rights of Man*. According to the publisher, the *Advice* sold a maximum of one thousand copies. However, its British audience seems to have been greater. Spies reported that it was read in political clubs outside of London. The Society for Constitutional Information of Manchester resolved on November 27, 1792, "That this society do congratulate the public on the appearance of such works as the Advice to the Privileged Orders and the Letter to the National Convention of France by Joel Barlow; and they are of the opinion that the cause of liberty will be essentially promoted by extending the knowledge of publications so masterly on subjects so important." [63]

The growing popularity of the *Advice* led to its suppression the same month. *The St. James Chronicle* took particular notice of the chapter on the administration of justice. It commented approvingly on the author's "minute and accurate comparison" of the British and American methods of jurisprudence. The same ends, it said, were reached in America with one-hundredth part of the trouble and expense. But *The Morning Chronicle* was hostile as was *The British Critic*. [64]

Jefferson had nothing but commendation for the *Advice*. [65] It was perhaps at his suggestion that an American edition was brought out in 1792. Freneau was enthusiastic. He cited it to support the argument that monarchical governments needed wars to continue oppressing the people. [66] The *New York Daily Advertiser* was full of praise.

The *Advice* became popular in America after the arrival of Gênet and was republished in 1794. It lifted the author's reputation on both sides of the Atlantic. It was his first extensive declaration of faith in the French Revolution, which he reaffirmed in *The Conspiracy of Kings* and *A Letter to the National Convention*.

Chapter VI
An Urge to Reform the World

1

The American Revolution had roughened the surface of British politics, which the French Revolution agitated. A closer inquiry into the established order, pressed upon the politically minded by the shower of polemics, showed them that it violated the doctrines they had learned from Locke. The fact that these doctrines bore a close resemblance to French revolutionary principles made them ominous in the eyes of conservatives. They might revive the social issues and bitter disputes of 1647-1649.

Looking back on the British agitation of the 1790s, after a lapse of more than a quarter century, Robert Southey ascribed it to dissenting literary men.[1] The judgment was superficial. Actually the agitation was neither the work of disaffected intellectuals nor an exotic, as others alleged. It had a history, dating from the 1760s, when a multitude of associations came into being that demanded parliamentary reform and greater country representation. But they went into slumber[2] until they were awakened by French events. They were made up of elements going all the way from upper-class liberals, or Whigs, to working-class democrats. Liberals were divided into moderates who united in the Friends of the People and liberal democrats who formed the Revolution Society. The first, consisting essentially of peers and parliamentarians, aimed "to tranquilize the agitated part of the public," as Thomas Erskine wrote in 1797, "to restore affection and respect for the legislature, so necessary to secure submission to its authority."[3] The second, the Revolution Society for Commemorating the Revolution of 1688 (to use its full title) was a target of censure because it sanctioned French ideas. As early as November 1789 it addressed the French National Assembly on its "glorious example" for other nations "to assert the unalienable rights of Mankind, and thereby to introduce a general reformation in the governments of Europe, and to make the world free and happy."[4]

The Revolution Society, however, never raised as much antagonism as did the Society for Constitutional Information and the London Corresponding Society. Both societies, based in London, kept a running correspondence with like bodies in Manchester, Sheffield, Birmingham, Norwich and smaller towns. The Society for Constitutional Information taught "that the great end of civil society is general happiness; that no form of government is good any further than it secures that object; that all civil and military authority is derived from the people; that equal active citizenship is the unalienable right of all men—minors, criminals and insane persons excepted; that the exercise of that right in appointing an adequate representative government is the wisest device of human policy and the only security of national freedom." [5]

The London Corresponding Society was labor's arm of political action. Three of its propagandists were Thomas Holcroft, John Thelwall and Thomas Spence who had assisted Hardy in its establishment. Spence was the author of pamphlets advocating common ownership. [6] His weekly penny periodical, *Pig's Meat*, a sarcastic variation on Burke's "swinish multitude," was devoted to the cause of liberty and equality. If the memory of one of the Corresponding Society's members can be relied on, the average number attending its several divisions in London, Westminster and Southwark was, for years, probably no less than eighteen or twenty thousand. The great mass of its membership was composed of shopkeepers, artisans, mechanics and laborers. [7] It appealed to citizens "to keep a watchful eye on the government"; and it held that equal representation was the remedy for "oppressive taxes, unjust laws, restrictions of liberty and wasting of the public money." Preliminary to equal representation was the abolition of "all partial privileges." It declared "its abhorrence of tumult and violence." It neither called for a republic, nor for levelling property. Still, members undoubtedly entertained these objectives. Primary in the reforms, said the Society, was an annually elected parliament, fairly chosen by all. [8]

Enemies accused the two London societies of conspiracy to revolutionize the country. But the charge fell in with the torrent of abuse. All that could be established was their spirited support of Paine's program and their sturdy defense of the French revolutionaries against émigrés and crowned heads. Yet, neither one of these actions caused the middle and upper classes to panic as did their frontal attack on the political edifice and their advocacy of labor's claims.

A word about the relation of the societies to the Polish and Irish questions. The presence of Polish refugees who had risen against the partition of their country evoked sympathy among English democrats. Subscriptions were opened and meetings scheduled that denounced the robber states. [9] The fraternal connection of English democrats and Irish patriots is too involved to be told here at length. It merely needs saying that democrats stood for the abolition of penal laws against Catholics and the extension of the franchise to them. United Irishmen joined English and Scottish reformers to demand the renovation of the political order. Symbolic of that unity was the friendship that grew up in Paris between Paine and Lord Edward Fitzgerald, head of the Irish movement for independence. [10]

The reform agitation, even more than the progress of industry, brought the existence of trade unions to the notice of the authorities. [11] Workers in all trades combined in defiance of official laissez-faire policy. Before the enactment of the well-known Combination Laws, there were already more than forty acts of Parliament to prevent workers from uniting. [12] To stem the labor and reform movements, "Church and King" clubs came into being; counterdemonstrations and riots were staged, with the complicity of local authorities; newspapers were kept in line by government subsidies; [13] and a substantial literature was turned out to refute the doctrines of liberty and equality. Simultaneously, reform publications were suppressed, their authors indicted and their vendors prosecuted. A system of terror was initiated with the King's Proclamation of May 21, 1792, against "seditious writings and their dispersion."

The pivot of the anti-reform agitation was the "Association for Preserving Liberty and Property against Republicans and Levellers," founded in November 1792 with official backing. Apart from organizing mob demonstrations and plotting assaults on reformers, publishers and book dealers,[14] it issued a series of penny tracts [15] in which it advanced the following presumptions: the will of the majority was an offense to private property; the principles of the *Rights of Man* would result in the insecurity of the individual; reform agitation brought an increase in the number of poor; a society could not exist without a class of poor; "the excellence of the English Constitution" derived "from the harmony subsisting between the several ranks of citizens"; it was shocking to see Englishmen attempt the imitation of the inferior, frivolous French. A set of verses read:

> *Come rouse up my lads*
> *And defend the great cause*
> *Of our Country and King,*
> *Our Religion and Laws;*
> *These, in spite of the maxims*
> *Of Priestley and Paine,*
> *Each true-hearted Briton*
> *Would die to maintain.*[16]

The volume of the Association's literature was exceeded by that of the reformers. It consisted of pocket pamphlets and penny periodicals, songs and political broadsides, such as "Citizen Guillotine, A New Shaving Machine" and "God save the Rights of Man." The "swinish multitude" was turned into a popular theme, with titles like "The Rights of Swine," "Husks for Swine," "Pig's Meat" and "Hog's Wash or a Salmagundy for Swine."

A keynote of British democratic thought, dating from the English Revolution, was the brotherhood of man, according to one of its historians. [17] But it was more articulated during the French Revolution. In their addresses to the French British reformers announced their solidarity with the revolutionary government struggling in behalf of the human race. [18] In the organ of the London Corresponding Society we read: "Man is a citizen of the world; his duty, therefore, is threefold: to his family, to his country, to the human race." His duty to country was to preserve and improve its rights and liberties; it was inseparable from his duty to the human race. As long as "slavery exists in any part of the world, freedom is not secure from danger. . . . Free nations ought then to unite with one heart and hand to extirpate despotism and bigotry." [19]

The spirit of brotherhood was echoed in America as in Europe. Freneau caught a glimpse of the future, "When erring man shall all his rights retrieve, / No despots rule him, and no priests deceive." [20] Burns cherished the hope:

That sense and worth, o'er a' the earth,
May bear the gree an' a' that.
For a' that, an' a that,
It's coming yet for a' that,
That man to man, the world o'er
Shall brothers be for a' that.

And his lesser known lines in "The Tree of Liberty": [21]

Wi' plenty o' sic trees, I trow,
    The world would live in peace, man;
The sword would help to mak a plough,
    The din o' war wad cease, man.
Like brethren in a common cause,
We'd on each other smile, man;
And equal rights and equal laws
    Wad gladden every isle, man.

And Paine said in Part Two of the *Rights of Man,* "My country is the world, and my religion is to do good." [22]

The dream of world peace was shared by littérateurs and philosophers from the seventeenth century to the eighteenth. We need but mention Sully's peace project and La Bruyère's savage satire against war. Peace and fraternity were causes common to eighteenth-century intellectuals, from the Abbé de Saint-Pierre to Rousseau and from Mably to Pallier de Saint-Germain. [23] After 1789 the ideas filtered down to the inarticulate masses, and even invaded the stage, as a comedy of 1791 showed. [24] Among the revolutionary champions of international peace, Anacharsis Cloots and the Abbé Henri Grégoire were well known. The first dwelt on the Republic of Humanity; [25] the second wrote a declaration of the rights of peoples, guaranteed by an organization of the human family, made up of free, independent nations. [26] A similar sentiment runs through Kant's *Perpetual Peace.* Man endowed with intellect and humanity would develop his full capacities, remove the obstacles to freedom and eventually organize the means of everlasting peace.

British Tories could not contemplate with equanimity the diffusion of subversive doctrines. The Royal Proclamation against seditious writings was endorsed at officially sponsored meetings. Clergy and local magistrates initiated loyal addresses; indecent writings against Paine were subsidized with secret service funds; his effigy was burned by terrorizing mobs and the government went into action against the propagators of his ideas. The heresy hunt was in full swing in the early months of 1793.

2

Barlow had meanwhile been in the thick of the British reform movement and had affiliated with the Society for Constitutional Information. At the meeting of March 30, 1792, at which he and Paine were present, a communication from the London Corresponding Society, signed by Hardy, was read, inviting concurrence on resolutions calling for universal suffrage and parliamentary reform. The members gave complete assurance of their "sincere desire to continue to correspond and to cooperate with them [L.C.S.] for the purpose of obtaining a fair representation of the people in parliament." [27]

A diverting interlude broke into Barlow's political activity. After the appearance of the *Advice,* he and Ruth traveled to the estate of the poet, William Hayley, in Sussex, to pay a visit that had been planned through the intermediacy of Hayley's friend, the Reverend John Warner, chaplain of the British embassy in Paris. Warner, like Barlow, was a lively observer of French events. He was agog over the coming election of the Legislative Assembly and cited "the excellent Robespierre" in saying that on its outcome depended the destiny of France and Europe. [28]

We shall pass over the flattering Alexandrines Hayley and Barlow exchanged before their meeting. The lines are dreadfully monotonous.[29] The Englishman's invitation was warm and irresistible. He sent detailed instructions on the route to Sussex and even offered to meet the American in London. Hayley waited impatiently. "I hope America will not rob us of the pleasure of seeing Mrs. Barlow," he wrote on August 28, 1791. Finally, early in February 1792, the Barlows were escorted by Warner to "the little Paradise of Eartham," as Gibbon portrayed it.

The host was noticeably energetic, despite a crippling disease. He led the life of a country gentleman, generously entertained men of talent and wrote essays, plays and poetry. But he is best remembered for his book *The Life and Posthumous Writings of William Cowper.* Southey said of him that "everything about that man was good except his poetry." [30] It belonged, according to a student of the literature, to the "most barren era" of English poetic writing. [31] A contemporary satirist pronounced the following verdict on Hayley, the poet:

The polish'd period, the smooth flowing line,
And faultless texture, all must own are thine;
For these thy rank thou shalt unenvied keep,
While all must praise, but while they praise they sleep;
No flames of genius thro' thy verses burn,
Langour and sweetness take their place by turn
Nor force or vigour there . . . [32]

(It was to Hayley's credit, however, that he discovered the talent of William Blake whom he housed and employed for months.)

Barlow's visit lasted but a few days. They were spent in talk of poetry, literature in general, the French Revolution and possibly the epic—for Hayley believed that it was still fruitful. His dream was a national epic poem. [33]

Barlow was apparently in the proper milieu, for he had been meditating a revised edition of *The Vision of Columbus*. Before leaving his gracious host, he left a copy with a request for his judgment. Hayley was obliging. Together with James Stanier Clarke, a young clergyman Barlow had met during the visit, he studiously went over the poem. His principal criticism was its length. It would have been more effective, he observed, had it been reduced to six books. But Barlow was of the opinion that it needed only a revision of the contents. [34]

Several days after Barlow's departure, Hayley put down these comments: "Our hermitage has been enlivened in the course of last week by a visit from our cheerful friend, Dr. Warner, and a very amiable American poet for whom he has the highest regard.

"They stayed only three nights; but we could not well expect to enjoy their society longer, as they are both preparing to take their leave of this island for some time. Our American brother of Parnassus returns to the new world; and his fellow-traveller, to rejoin the English Ambassador in France." [35]

Barlow and Hayley continued to correspond. The American promised to send him "the little mad poem" when it came off the press. He was referring to *The Conspiracy of Kings* he had sent to Johnson. In October, acknowledging the receipt of *A Letter to the National Convention of France*, Hayley expressed delight that his friend was still in England, "endeavouring to render Europe more rational and happy." It was the occasion to invite the Americans to revisit the Hermitage. But Barlow was wrapped up in the reform movement.

The "little mad poem" was brought out on March 20, 1792. Clarke wrote Barlow several days later: "We see your Conspiracy of Kings advertised. Should think it would make a great noise. I think I shall hear of you in the tower before long. If so take care to procure good apartments, for we will certainly come to see you very often." [36] It was an angry poem, in a fortissimo way. It declared against "the sceptred horde" with "crusted souls," pillared by mitred divines. And it scorned Burke, "degenerate slave!" In a mood of indignation, the poet asked:

And didst thou hope by thy infuriate quill
To rouse mankind the blood of realms to spill?
Then to restore, on death-devoted plains,
Their scourge to tyrants, and to man his chains?

Burke and kings had had their honors and glories of war. But they were nearing their exit from history. Men were uniting, and people were awakening to the call of France, where a new order was in the making.

Wide o'er the gazing world it tow'rs sublime,
A modell'd form for each surrounding clime.
To useful toils they bend their noblest aim,
Make patriot views and moral views the same.
Renounce the wish of war, bid conquest cease,
Invite all men to happiness and peace.

As in *Advice*, Barlow proudly pointed to America

. . . where the dawn began,
The full fruition of the hopes of man:
Where sage experience seals the sacred cause;
And that rare union, liberty and laws,
Speaks to the reas'ning race; to freedom rise,
Like them be equal, and like them be wise. [37]

Thus ended the "mad poem." Its passion was mixed with bile. Yet, it never had a place among the enduring pieces of literature. It was turgid and rhetorical; the verses lacked ease and natural rhythm. It was wrathful, but had no rage. Its epithets failed to pillory the opponent.

It was an arresting polemic for all that. It at once voiced the author's warmth for the French Revolution and echoed the crescendo-like sentiment in England. Beyond that, the poem uttered the hope of human brotherhood that Burns and Blake and Freneau sang in tones audible to the common man.

For a better understanding of Barlow's state of mind it may be useful to sketch the European setting in which the poem was composed. The attempted flight of Louis XVI, we said earlier, had set on foot a republican party. But it had little support in the National Assembly. This body, in fact, hastened to clear the king of guilt under the fiction that he had been kidnapped, and fostered a movement to the right. Petitioners for a republic were imprisoned and democratic sheets suppressed. Deputies were conspiring to compromise with reaction.

The arrest of the king roused the European monarchs and princes. The emperor of Austria, backed by the king of Prussia, proposed simultaneous action by the European rulers to save the French monarchy. But the emperor's zeal cooled, and the king of England preferred to remain neutral. The empress of Russia and the king of Sweden supported intervention. But Austria distrusted Prussia and Russia with regard to Poland. Thus the French royal cause became less urgent. The heads of Austria and Prussia simply issued the Declaration of Pillnitz, saying that the restoration of order in France was the concern of Europe. To attain that goal, they invited the cooperation of other monarchs.

The Declaration was interpreted by the French revolutionaries as an ultimatum and as a step toward war. To aggravate matters the emperor of Austria called on the monarchs to consider the formation of a coalition. At the same time aristocrats and clergy were instigating uprisings in France. French popular sentiment was aroused. In the Legislative Assembly the Girondins who had risen to power voted measures against the clergy and against the armed émigrés on the eastern frontier. The king vetoed the law against the first but assented to that against the second.

The Revolution was menaced, notwithstanding the powers' conflict of interests. Austria and Prussia were coming to terms in the early months of 1792. By coincidence Leopold of Austria died on March 1 and was succeeeded by Francis II, hastening intervention. [38]

Three separate parties in France looked to war to achieve their respective ends: the court party, the Girondins and the Fayettists. The first believed that war would restore the king's power; the second hoped to turn it into a war of peoples' liberation and the third, to become the ruling party. Robespierre almost alone stood out against war, but his arguments were swept away by a wave of bellicose hysteria. On April 20, 1792, France declared war on Austria.

Such, in brief, was the international climate in which *The Conspiracy of Kings* was written. Certain of the ultimate victory of the Revolution, Barlow confronted the coalition of kings with the coalition of peoples which, by delivering Europe from oppression, would inaugurate an era of liberty and fraternity. The poem, therefore, was at once a warning to despots and a greeting to the dawn of a new order. To that extent it supplemented the poem *Advice*.

The Conspiracy of Kings had a moderate sale. It was circulated by British political societies and was reprinted in Paris, London and in two American cities. [39] But the range of its impact cannot be determined.

4

The year 1792 was fruitful for Barlow. The two defenses of the Revolution appeared in the first quarter. Within less than four months, he edited with notes an English edition of Trumbull's *M'Fingal,* in the preface of which he called attention to the poet's object of ridiculing monarchy and exposing "the absurd arguments and shallow subterfuges" of its supporters. [40] Also in 1792 he translated Brissot's *New Travels in the United States of America.* [41] The book, he said, would exhibit to the English public the true character of America and the effects "of habitual liberty on man in society."

The business prospect also seemed brighter in 1792, if only for a relatively short period. In April Barlow received word from James Swan to meet him on the Continent, the purpose being to petition the Legislative Assembly to set up a tannery in the Haute-Loire. Swan asked for an advance of 100,000 livres or for a bonus on the product. [42]

A word about Swan. He was born in Scotland and taken to Massachusetts in his early years. Apprenticed to a mercantile house in Boston, he revealed quite early an acquisitive bent. He joined the Sons of Liberty, took part in the Boston Tea Party and served in the Revolution, ultimately rising to the rank of colonel. He married an heiress and speculated in trade and real estate. But the depression of 1786 reduced him to near bankruptcy. After helping to suppress Shays' uprising, he went to France and renewed acquaintance with French officers he had met in America. In Paris he published a book showing how an increase in trade between France and the United States would be mutually profitable. [43] He formed a business partnership in 1791 and through proper connections obtained good contracts with the Ministry of the Navy and got entrée into other government departments. [44]

Barlow and Swan had probably met in Paris in 1788 or 1789. They had friends in common, and they were both signers of the petition requesting the privilege of participating in observing the first Bastille Day. Swan seems to have trusted Barlow's ability as a negotiator.

After twenty-two hours of hellish seasickness, Barlow arrived in Ostend and thence proceeded to Coblenz. In "that seat of 'Forsaken Villains,' " as he termed it, he and Swan worked out a project for which they sought the advice of LaFayette. To reach the general's headquarters it took three days and three nights of rough travel. LaFayette sent Barlow to the Minister of the Interior in Paris. But the conferences dragged on for weeks and without results. The project was finally turned down. With respect to business, the journey was a failure. Looked at from the viewpoint of Barlow's experience it was inestimable. [45]

For Barlow had come to Paris in a critical time. Arriving on May 31, he found the city in a state of tension. The peoples' uprisings that the Girondins had vaingloriously predicted in response to their propaganda did not happen. Ill-prepared for combat, France suffered reverses. Matériel was lacking; officers had deserted; the troops were raw and confusion prevailed in the higher echelons of government. To aggravate matters, counterrevolutionairies instigated revolts in France.

Defeat unloosed fierce passions. Patriot and revolutionist became synonymous. A popular movement, like a tidal wave, swept the nation. Democratic clubs and fraternal societies sprang up; loud were the demands for the total abolition of feudal dues and a *jacquerie* rapidly spread in regions of the south. Inflation, want of necessities and precarious grain supplies brought on rioting. Calls were heard for price controls, even for curbs on private ownership.

The breach widened between Fayettists and Girondins. LaFayette planned a coup d'etat to put down the Parisian *sans culottes*. The Girondins feared them likewise, but they had to fall back on their strength, as in the mass movement of June 20, for that day the demonstrators invaded the Tuilleries and demanded the reinstatement of the Girondist ministers. The king listened with dignity but did not yield.

The Girondins were in a plight. The force they had reluctantly summoned to their aid was a standing threat. They could only wait for developments while attempting to contain the menacing populace. At heart they were not inimical to monarchy, despite their republican professions, for monarchy was a barrier against equality and its dangerous breed. But they were outmaneuvered. The popular movement erupted again and overthrew the monarchy.

That event occurred on August 10, when Barlow was already back in England. He had, however, witnessed the demonstration of June 20 building up to a climax. He assured Ruth that those who were forecasting the collapse of the Revolution had been misguided. The nation was bracing itself for resistance. The people, he wrote in surprisingly good French, were recognizing the need of unity and discipline. Men were amassing to enlist, confident that France could stand up against all Europe. [46] And after the demonstration: "You will hear frightful stories about the riots at the Tuilleries on the 20th. You must believe but little—there was no violence committed. This visit to the King by armed citizens was undoubtedly contrary to law, but the existence of a king is contrary to a law of a higher original. The constitution of nature is older than that made by the last assembly—the people feel this truth, they must express it in their own way, & they always will express it by like irregular movements till they shall have enough to settle the matter according to the laws of nature, which admit of no king." [47]

He was pledged to the Revolution. The events that had brought down the monarchy [48] did not amaze him. On September 20 the National Convention assembled and abolished monarchy in France. The rise of the first Republic coincided with a turn in the tide of the war. By the end of the month French troops were invading enemy territory.

Barlow was enthusiastic. To Jefferson he wrote that France "is now taking the proper ground on which to establish a glorious republic, nor will it be in the power of all the combined despots to prevent it . . . they seem now to be removing all the rubbish out of the way, in order to lay a proper foundation for a national government."[49]

The same enthusiasm imbued *A Letter to the National Convention* he published less than a fortnight after the establishment of the Republic. Addressing the French deputies, he wrote: "Your cause is that of human nature at large. You are the representatives of mankind; . . . I not only consider all mankind as forming but one great family, and therefore bound by a natural sympathy to regard each other's happiness as making part of their own; but I contemplate the French nation at this moment as standing in the place of the whole. You have stepped forward with a gigantic stride to an enterprise which involves the interest of every surrounding nation; and what you began as justice to yourselves, you are called upon to finish as a duty to the human race." [50]

This was his strongest avowal of international brotherhood. It was a product of the climate in which sprouted visions of human development that were exemplified by Condorcet's famous *Esquisse d'un tableau historique des progrès de l'esprit humain* and Cloots' *Bases constitutionelles de la république du genre humain*. It looked forward to terrestrial happiness after the eradication of monarchy. With thrones overturned, peace would reign, peoples would unite in a federation with one legislature made up of deputies from all the republics. In other words, republicanism was the key to the great triad of liberty, equality and fraternity.

A Letter to the National Convention evidenced trust in the republican ideal. The mind once set loose from royal shackles, said Barlow, "finds itself in a new world. . . . Human nature assumes a new and more elevated shape, and displays many moral features. . . . We are so much used, in government, to the most complicated systems, as being necessary to support these impositions, . . . that it is an unusual task to conceive of the simplicity to which the business of government may be reduced, and to which it must be reduced, if we would have it answer the purpose of promoting happiness."[51]

Implied here was a concern for the future of the French Republic. The framework of the government the National Assembly had erected was obsolete now that the monarchy was ended, observed Barlow. The constitution that had been voted was filled with contradictions due principally to the desire for retaining royalty. He was not derogating from the achievements of the Assembly. In fact, few in his day estimated better than he did the immense labor it had performed. [52] Nevertheless, the shortcomings of its constitution needed pointing out, if only to avoid them in the contemplated revision in government. So steeped had the French been in monarchical ideas, said Barlow, that the king's faithlessness had had little effect in dispelling the fiction that monarchy was necessary. Yet, the French limited monarchy, though of short duration, was an unforgettable lesson. It taught the people "that kings can do no good." [53]

He presented a bill of indictment against them. They were expensive to maintain; they corrupted legislators; they rewarded knavery and they helped prolong the legend that the people were unfit to govern. If the object of government was the good of the whole community, the whole "can best know the means of pursuing it." The people could frame a better constitution for themselves than "the most learned statesmen in the world." [54]

He applied the same reasoning to colonial peoples. Even with the best intentions to promote their good, the mother country was incapable of knowing their wants. Hence, he concluded: "The sure and only characteristic of a good law is, *that it be the perfect expression of the will of the nation.*" [55]

The above reflections were meant for the consideration of the French Convention. He put down three requisites for drafting a new constitution: It should be absolutely free of any vestige of royalty; its language should be simple, for it had to serve the legislature as a handbook and the citizens as a political grammar; and its governing law should be *"that all men are equal in their rights."* [56]

He recommended fourteen amendments to the old constitution, should it continue to be the fundamental law of the land. Only the most important can be noticed here: population in place of property as the basis of representation; the right of suffrage extended to every citizen of twenty or over; the legislators to be elected annually without property qualifications; salaries of officers restricted to a sum sufficient for their work; abolition of imprisonment for debt and of capital punishment, on the ground that society itself was "the cause of all crime." [57]

The last recommendation condemned the social order that presumed to punish when it itself was at fault. Crimes, he said, arose "out of the conflict between governors and governed;" and punishments were an indication "that the nation is in a state of civil war." Consequently, before deciding to punish the criminal, inquiry should be made into the condition of society rather than into the nature of his offense. [58]

The logic bore the marks of several origins. Beccaria's famous essay at once comes to mind. Another likely source was Marat's *Plan de législation criminelle* in which crimes were traced to private property and the conflict between rich and poor. The same causes of crime had also been advanced by Nicolas Pinel, [59] Brissot de Warville, [60] and William Playfair.[61] But there was an essential difference between Barlow's argument and theirs. His reasoning stopped, as Marat's and Brissot's had not, before its continuance would challenge the claims of private ownership.

The *Letter to the National Convention* was the high point of Barlow's political thinking at the end of 1792. The severe critic of prescriptive rights and outdated institutions dear to Burke, rose to the level of a political sage, advising the French deputies how to build a model of government that would be the cynosure of all Europe.

It was also distinguished for its good prose and firm purpose. It was at once an example of stylistic vigor and a stout affirmation of republicanism at a time when republicanism was considered synonymous with subversion. A literary historian has ranked it "among the state papers of the period." [62]

It won praise in England and France. The English novelist Charlotte Smith was so gratified by it that she predicted its good effect on the Convention, as well as on people generally. [63] Hayley addressed the author as "Dear Politician of the World" and went on to say that though he was not yet a republican, he was "particularly pleased with the sensible advice you give to the Convention respecting the important articles of a standing army, & future improvements of the new Constitution." [64] And John Warner wrote from Paris: "A thousand thanks to you my dear jewel of a Joel, for the 'feast of Reason and the flow of Soul' with which you have this day regaled me in your kind letter and that to the N[ational] C[onvention]. It will, I flatter myself, do great credit to the writer and great good to the glorious cause of which he is so able a support. . . . You must come here and be made a Conventionalist et Citizen, as I think you will, whether you come or not." [65]

Warner was notifying his American friend that his name was on a list with six Englishmen who were all candidates for French citizenship. The Convention expressed complete satisfaction with the criticism and recommendations of the piece addressed to it, gave it honorable mention in the minutes, ordered its translation and referred it to the constitutional committee. [66] The decree, granting Barlow French citizenship, was voted on February 17, 1793. Obliged to remain in France, Barlow entered heartily into the spirit of the Revolution.

Chapter VII
Propagating Revolution

The insurrection of August 10, 1792, that had brought down the monarchy had the foreseen diplomatic consequences. England, Russia, Spain, Holland and Venice broke off relations with France. By good fortune, France was saved from invasion by the artillery duel at Valmy on September 20, 1792. The Prussian army was forced to retreat. The revolutionary victory at Jemappes on November 6, opened Belgium to the French.

A contest for power ensued in the Convention between Girondins and Mountainists. Neither party had a defined program. Events, however, pulled them in separate directions: the Girondins to the bourgeoisie; the Mountainists to bourgeois remnants, the small middleman, artisan and laborer.

The trial of the king separated them more effectively. The Girondins were inclined to avoid putting him on trial. Had they succeeded, they would have found themselves in a dilemma. For if he were not guilty, Robespierre argued, then those who had dethroned him were, and the existence of the Convention was as illegal as the proclamation of the Republic. In the public mind, in the opinion of the sans culottes especially, he was culpable. He had summoned foreign powers to his aid; and he was responsible for the many casualties in the attack on the Tuilleries.[1]

The debate took a sharper turn when the king's secret correspondence with foreign princes was discovered. The defense took its stand on two points. The first contested the legal competence of the Convention to try the king; the second revived the old principle that the king's person was inviolable. The majority of the deputies was not convinced. The Girondins tried to prevent a final decision, first, by calling for the banishment of all Bourbons, then, by proposing a popular referendum on the king's guilt. Finally they contended that his execution would unite all Europe against the Revolution. The Girondins were reminded that they had been the advocates of war to a finish.

The balloting started in January 1793. A referendum was ruled out. Rejected too was the proposition that the king be banished to America. The death penalty was voted at last, and Louis was executed on January 21, 1793.

The effects reached far. The struggle between republicans and royalists at home became harsh and cruel. Monarchs formed a league to exterminate the Revolution and partition France, much as Poland was being partitioned. In France the war took on the aspect of a crusade. The Convention offered fraternity and help to all peoples desiring to gain their freedom. But the borderline between liberation and annexation became blurred as the war progressed.

1

The trial of the king was at times interrupted by addresses from foreign societies, [2] one of them from the Society for Constitutional Information, which was brought by Frost and Barlow. Instead of returning with Frost, Barlow decided to remain in France. Meanwhile he was calumnied in England. [3]

The whole situation distressed Ruth. To begin with, the Revolution in France was incomprehensible to her. At the time she was living in London under conditions she declared insufferable. She had been used to village life; talking with neighbors had been a daily routine and attendance at church, a social event. But in the British metropolis she was cooped up in a small place on a narrow street. To be sure, as the amiable wife of a man of letters, she enjoyed the hospitality and respect of his friends and basked in his glory. She knew a number of Joel's associates in the Society for Constitutional Information and formed a lasting friendship with Mary Wollstonecraft. But she disliked Joel's politics and talk about equality and fraternity. To crown it all, he had gone off to the hotbed of revolution with that radical agitator, John Frost.

She was lonely and longed for her homeland. Without children, she depended on her husband for companionship. Now that she was alone in London she felt slighted. "Would to Heaven you had not left me," she wrote him on New Year's Day 1793, "that is, unless it has given you satisfaction; if so, I have nothing to say. Here you cannot return at present; everything evil is said of you, and I am obliged to avoid company not to hear you abused. I hope you may be provided for in some eligible way in Paris, or what is to become of us? For myself it matters little. I can and shall go home in the spring. Our friends in Paris wrote that they expected me there; why should I go unless you are like to continue? . . . Our friends the P's have quite withdrawn their attentions . . . on account of your politics, I suppose, but am not sorry. . . ."

Eight days later she returned to the slander against him. Burke, for instance, called him "the prophet Joel" and charged him with the intent of altering the British Constitution. The impending war between England and France would aggravate difficulties, she feared. She could not enjoy staying in Paris. Nor could she safely travel to America. Then this reproach: "I fear, my love, you did wrong in going to Paris with Mr. F[rost]: his character here is so bad it has injured yours, hitherto spotless. I shall send you Mr. Fox's speech upon the Kings [*The Conspiracy of Kings*] at the opening of Parliament; it is excellent."

She felt humbled and lacerated. Her Joel was considered guilty by association and regarded as a fomenter of revolution. It was too much for a Connecticut-bred woman with middle class mores. She wrote on January 28: "My feelings have been much wounded, as you may suppose, to see my beloved, my best friend thus scandalized as he has been here, when I know so well the goodness, the rectitude of his heart and intentions." [4]

Ruth found herself in an atmosphere of war hysteria. Ever since the Convention's decree promising aid to peoples striving to gain their liberty, the British government was suspicious of French intentions and with the occupation of Belgium and the opening of the Scheldt estuary to shipping, was convinced that war was imminent. The Whigs supported the government, though Fox came out against war and ridiculed the measures designed to whip up hostile sentiment.[5] A request for 20,000 sailors was made on December 20. On December 31 the Alien Bill passed, increasing the government's repressive powers. After the execution of Louis XVI, it was only a matter of days before the final break between the two nations. On February 1, the Convention declared war against England.

The British government meanwhile proceeded against reformers. Memberships of societies fell off; reformers disowned the French cause. In December 1793 a convention of reform organizations was dispersed, and leaders were tried and convicted. Thomas Hardy's indictment for treason in 1794, however, ended in an acquittal, which a large crowd loudly applauded. Pitt finally succeeded in achieving one of his war aims, namely, breaking the back of the British reform movement. Reaction gained new strength. "It is astonishing," wrote Mary Wollstonecraft from France on June 14, 1795, "what strides aristocracy and fanaticism have made since I resided in this country." [6]

The day France declared war on England, Ruth imparted to her Joel the mounting anti-French opinion in her entourage, and her own sentiments. "I am distressed at the thought of a war between this country and France. The death of the unfortunate French king is the present pretext. Surely they could not have done so impolitic an action, setting aside the injustice of it, which I think unparalleled. Their friends condemn them equally as their enemies. The National Convention have most certainly greatly disgraced themselves and their country by showing such passion and violence in their debates and being directed solely by their passions. . . . They have showed themselves too cruel and bloodthirsty for the legislators of any country, particularly of a free one.—Their friends are ashamed of them." [7]

Her husband had a more considered understanding of the event. What concerned him was that the king's execution might be used to distort the cause of liberty in America as well as in Europe. Taking all circumstances into account, he concluded that, irrespective of the bloody deed, faith in the French republic was inseparable from the defense of freedom. The triumph of the European coalition would also be a defeat for America. Seen from this standpoint, the death of the king had to be evaluated in terms of its benefit to the French republic. If it advanced the struggle against the allies, it was good for the public interest.

Despite all her disapproval of the Revolution, Ruth preferred being with her husband in France to returning home. But she was ill at ease in the French capital. She confided to a friend in New York that "had your letter reached me in London, it would have staggered my resolution about coming to Paris, which you rightly judged must be disagreeable to one who possesses the least sensibility. My feelings are daily wounded beyond description, and I can never be happy here." [8]

2

Barlow stood high with the Girondins. As intellectuals, they valued his literary work in behalf of the Revolution. Beyond that, his American origin and connections might prove useful to the plans they were devising for the Louisiana territory. Meanwhile he was called upon to accompany a commission to Savoy, headed by the Abbé Henri Grégoire.

For centuries the road to Italy lay through Nice and Savoy. One estimate has it that no less than eighteen different peoples, at one time or another, invaded, ravaged and settled in the area. After the outbreak of the Revolution, French émigrés steadily crossed the border, until Nice became a second Coblenz. Party strife became acute. Francophiles and Francophobes eyed one another like foes, awaiting the command to attack. The issue was resolved at the end of September 1792 when French troops marched in and sent émigrés fleeing to different points of the peninsula. Popular clubs supported the occupation. The communes sent delegates to Chambéry where, on October 21, 1792, a vast majority voted for union with France. They confiscated the properties of the Church and émigrés, abolished serfdom and privileges, chose a provisional government and sent four deputies to the Convention with a petition for incorporation. [9]

The report Grégoire submitted to the Convention set the stage for annexation. His principal point was that if people, living in an enclave within the limits nature had fixed for the French republic, wished to unite with it the request could not be turned down. On November 27 the Convention decreed that Savoy was an integral part of the French Republic. [10]

The priest with whom Barlow went to Savoy was the Constitutional

Bishop of Loire-et-Cher, having served the Revolution from the start. He was instrumental in founding L'Institut de France, the Conservatoire des Arts-et-Metiers, the Bureau des Longitudes and the botanical gardens. The oppressed looked to him as their champion. He advocated the rights of Negroes and other minorities, and refuted the claims of the whites to superiority. The faults attributed to Negroes, he argued, were not peculiar to them. Any people, subjected as they had been, would show the same failings. Given the chance of their masters, they would be their equals in all ways. [11] He also presented arguments supporting the thesis that the Jews were entitled to the rights and duties of Frenchmen. The charges that money was their idol, that they were rootless and without a country should in effect be brought against the governments that had forbidden them to own real property and to practice a trade, that is, to have a footing in the land they inhabited. [12]

Joel explained to Ruth why he was going with the Commissioners of the National Convention to Savoy. They were on their way to organize its internal government and teach the inhabitants how "to act in forming themselves and in choosing their deputies to the National Convention. They intend a certain friend of yours shall be chosen. Of this you must not be sure, but he will at least see much of the south of France, the city of Lyons, the Alps, etc." [13]

With respect to the Savoyards he wrote: "Here is a people, vigorous and hardy, just born to liberty. They have long struggled under the worst and most complicated species of tyranny without being broken down in their spirits or debased in their morals. Their character bears a strong resemblance to the mountains which gave them birth. . . . Their patriotism and morals appear to me the purest of any people I ever knew." [14]

Barlow, it was apparent, was a candidate for deputy. Just how much compaigning he did is not known. In the public mind he was identified as a Girondin at a time when the Girondist-Mountainist contest in the Department was gaining in acrimony. Meetings of the popular societies were stormy. Girondins were labeled aristocrats by the Mountainists; and the Mountainists, anarchists by the Girondins. [15] The election resulted in Barlow's defeat.

His defeat at the polls occurred late in February 1793. By then he was a French citizen and had two more pieces of writing to his credit. The recommendation to honor him with French citizenship rested on these grounds: He had served the American cause, disseminated its principles in Europe, aided the organization of democratic societies in England, published works in defense of the Revolution and preached liberty in Savoy. [16]

The last item had reference to a *Letter Addressed to the People of Piedmont, on the Advantages of the French Revolution, and the Necessity of Adopting its Principles in Italy.* [17] It was a programmatic pamphlet meant for all Italians, written in Chambéry in December 1792. With intense emotion calculated to compel action, he called on the Piedmontese to cast off monarchy. The time was propitious. France now stood ready to assist people struggling for their freedom, especially her neighbors. She was not only the most powerful nation in Europe; she was a match for all the combined powers. Having brought liberty to the door of the Piedmontese, she invited them "in the name of all that can bind you to the interests of human nature in general to accept the blessing at her hands."

The world was in debt to France, he asserted. She taught peoples "how public happiness is to be acquired and preserved. She has addressed herself to the great principles of reason which are common to all men; she has cleared away the mass of prejudice, of false doctrine, of superstition in the science of morals. . . . She has laid down and clearly defined the rights and duties of man and citizens, explained the great doctrine of equality, the true design of government, the nature of the trust to be reposed in the public officers, as servants of the people, by whom they were paid. She has taught you a great practical truth . . . that you are the sovereigns in your own country; that you have not, that you cannot have a master, unless you choose to give up your reason, and renounce the character of men. She has conquered liberty for all men, and laid the foundation for universal public felicity." [18]

Under these circumstances Piedmont could not resist a revolution. The government of Turin had to be overturned, and power restored to the people to whom it naturally belonged. [19]

The political and religious masters, he went on, were deceiving the people on the meaning of the French Revolution. The people were kept ignorant that they might not see how the proceeds of their labor were appropriated by the privileged orders. This abominable system of pillage had to be replaced by one "which should secure to every man the fruits of his own labours, protect the innocent, punish the guilty, and instruct every member of society in his duties and his rights." This was what the French had done. To vilify the Revolution the court and clergy of Piedmont invented falsehoods, portrayed the French as a nation of plunderers, assassins, atheists and violators of property rights. Actually, he answered, all in France were free to worship in their own way. And they had "a most sacred regard to individual property."[20] A revolution in Piedmont would spread wavelike over the entire peninsula. Liberty victorious in one of its states would inevitably triumph in the rest. He grew prophetic and anticipated a free Italy, united in one great republic.[21]

The forty-eight page *Letter* revealed Barlow an adept propagandist. Its language was vigorous and warm, yet controlled by reasoning. A test of its persuasive power was denied by an efficient suppression in Turin.

It was an exuberant profession of faith in the principles of the Revolution. The *Letter* reminds us of Barlow's chaplaincy. Like his camp sermons, it aimed at instilling the belief that the fruits of revolution would be freedom and security. Nothing in the same key appeared again from Barlow's pen, save the fifth chapter of the *Advice*. This, however, had been written the previous year.

His estimate of the Revolution changed with its character. He disliked the Mountainist policies and he deplored the execution of the Girondins. Yet he stayed firm in the conviction that the Revolution had put guide posts to an improved order. He did not falter in the belief that the French and American republics were bound in a common effort to liberate mankind.

3

His upbringing had indelibly stamped Barlow an American. Though drawn into the revolutionary ferment abroad, he never forgot his origin. Proud of his country's pioneering in democracy, he found every occasion to talk to Europeans of America's advances. In his enthusiasm for the French, he gazed back at their revolutionary model of the western hemisphere. At times a yearning for the homeland came over him, which even high-pitched feeling for French deeds could not master.

A few weeks after writing the *Letter to the People of Piedmont* a poignant feeling for home took hold of him. It was soothed by a dish of Indian meal mush served him in a Chambéry inn. His nostalgia was set afire and his memory darted from "Alps audacious" to "dear New England."

"The sweets of hasty Pudding," like a folk song, came back to him. He sat down to write what turned out to be his best known poem. "The Hasty Pudding," since its publication in 1796, [22] has been a favorite of many readers.

The Yankee's homespun palate eclipsed the "death of kings," and "Gallic flags." He chose a "softer theme" for his mock heroic:

> *A virgin theme, unconscious of the muse,*
> *But fruitful, rich, well suited to inspire*
> *The purest frenzy of poetic fire.*
> *Oh! could the smooth, the emblematic song*
> *Flow like the genial juices o'er my tongue,*
> *Could those mild morsels in my numbers chime,*
> *And as they roll in substance, roll in rime,*
> *No more thy unpoetic name*
> *Should shun the muse or prejudice thy fame*
> *But rising grateful to the accustomed ear,*
> *All bards should catch it, and all realms revere!*

He traced the humble lineage of the noble mush. It was the American Indian's sacred legacy to the world. But it was hard to come by.

> *Dear Hasty Pudding, what unpromised joy*

Expands my heart, to meet thee in Savoy!
Doomed o'er the world through devious paths to roam,
Each clime my country, and each house my home,
My soul is soothed, my cares have found an end;
I greet my long-lost, unforgotten friend.

For thee through Paris, that corrupted town,
How long in vain I wandered up and down,
Where shameless Bacchus, with his drenching hoard,
Cold from his cave usurps the morning board.

London is lost in smoke and steeped in tea;
No Yankee there can lisp the name of thee;
The uncouth word, a libel on the town,
Would call a proclamation from the crown.

Not so in distant Savoy where:

With mutual glee, we meet and laugh once more.
The same! I know thee by that yellow face,
That strong complexion of true Indian race,
Which time can never change, nor soil impair,

• • • • • • • • •

Where grows the maize, where thou art sure to reign.

The rest of the three cantos describes "The Hasty Pudding" from planting to harvesting and finally to the luscious mush. Youthful memories of plowing and husking bring us back to the poet's farmboy days in Connecticut. Inebriated with joy, he hails the "mound of corn" the "sifted meal," even the "Blest cow," "Were I to leave my God, I'd worship thee."

His playfulness and wit roam over rules of eating the Hasty Pudding, the "choice in spoons," the "wide-mouthed bowl," and table manners. "Fear not to slaver; 'tis no sin."

The Connecticut Yankee was irrepressible. Though tucked away in Southeastern France, amidst snow-capped Alps, writing appeals to Italians and politicizing in a foreign tongue, his Yankee blood continued to course through his veins. His attachment to his native land remained unshaken.

4

In December 1792 the French republican government named Edmond Gênet minister plenipotentiary to the United States. He was a young diplomat of aristocratic origin, who had served the Bourbons in several European capitals. Two motives lurked behind his appointment: To resolve the question of the King's guilt by deporting the royal family to the United States under Gênet's escort and, of particular relevance to the general plan of the Girondins, to embroil neutrals in the war against the coalition. The envoy's instructions were calculated to implement this policy. He was to strengthen the harmonious relations of the two countries, negotiate a new treaty, pledge the American government, if not to make common cause with France, at least to provision her to the amount of the American debt, secretly incite the inhabitants of America's interior to separate Louisiana from Spain and finally to stir up the Canadians to revolt against Great Britain.[23] In other words, the new French minister was directed to plot against Spain and Great Britain on the soil of a neutral power.

Gênet arrived in the United States after France had declared war on England, Holland and Spain. His instructions were therefore supplemented to include outfitting privateers, authorizing French consuls to judge prizes taken to American ports and organizing military expeditions into Louisiana. How much Brissot's unfailing interest in land speculation in America furthered such aggression is still unknown. The available evidence shows that he sponsored several plans designed to make Louisiana a French possession.

Gênet's mission to America need not long occupy us. Before his official reception in Philadelphia, he behaved like a Roman consul in a conquered territory. He was impulsive and shockingly tactless. He failed to appreciate the value of America's neutrality to France, "a manly neutrality," as Jefferson termed it, one that would not lean to reaction. Jefferson defended the right of France to purchase American goods despite English protests. His reasoning was that America's entry into the war, while not seriously affecting the military outcome on the continent, would be detrimental both to America and France. American commerce would, under the circumstances, be subjected to prey by the British navy, and France would be in want of American supplies.[24]

Friends of the French Republic were disconcerted by Gênet's conduct. Washington had no sooner learned of his landing at Charleston than he issued a proclamation of neutrality. The envoy thus had to choose between abstaining from conspiracy against foreign states and a conflict with the American authorities. He chose the latter course and appealed to the people against their executive. The United States government was obliged to ask for his recall. The case Jefferson presented against him [25] did not need special pleading. For before the request reached Paris, the Girondins had been expelled from the Convention. The policy of respecting the rights of neutrals replaced that of exporting revolution. Robespierre's report of November 17, 1793, vigorously censured his country's aggressive stand with regard to America, promised French observance of the subsisting treaty and declared it to be the resolve of France to strengthen the friendly relations of the two nations. [26]

Meanwhile Barlow was expecting to sail home. This time his return related to a long held plan of making France heir to Spain's empire in the West.

The grand objective antedated the French Revolution. After the loss of Canada, French statesmen looked longingly on the Spanish territories of the West, of which Louisiana appeared to be the most desirable. It had a suitable climate and incalculable resources; its products could reach the sea via navigable rivers and it bordered on a young vigorous nation whose westward expansion and eventual mastery of the continent had to be contained. An apprehension of its ultimate might was shared by political minds in France and even aired in 1777 in what turned out to be an important journal. [27] A decade later the French minister to the United States submitted to his government a memoir, the purpose of which was to induce it to take possession of Louisiana. [28]

The outbreak of the French Revolution cast the memoir into obscurity. Its aim, however, continued to motivate French policy makers and was the cause of at least eight plans that were drafted from 1792 to 1793, under Girondist inspiration. All of them had two points in common: the small manpower and little expense needed to conquer the area and the diversionary effect of the undertaking on Spain's anti-French policy in Europe.

Let us take a quick look at the plans. [29] One, by Paine's friend, Dr. James O'Fallon, called for an expedition commanded by General George Rogers Clark. [30] A second, from an anonymous source, gave Gênet extensive power to prepare the conquest and recommended General James Wilkinson of Kentucky as its leader. A third was submitted by Stephen Sayre, an American-born French citizen and a bankrupt, and by General Beaupoils, a French officer who had served in Poland and a friend of the Barlows and Blackdens. Sayers and Beupoils proposed the spread of revolution into all Latin America after the occupation of Louisiana had been accomplished. A fourth plan by Pierre Lyonnet, who had lived in New Orleans and claimed to have an intimate knowledge of the territory, reasoned that French interest would be better served if the area, following its conquest, were united with the American republic, provided France was guaranteed her economic rights.

The fifth plan, credited to Gilbert Imlay, had some support at the Ministry of Foreign Affairs. [31] He was an American businessman abroad and the lover of Miss Wollstonecraft. After serving in the American Revolution, he went West, bought land in Kentucky, speculated in real estate, accumulated debts and somehow managed to escape the sheriff. He went to London where he published two works, *A Topographical Description of the Western Territory of North America*, which established his authority on America's West, and *The Emigrants*, a novel that echoed sentiments he had probably heard in English radical circles. In France he was courted by Girondins, especially by Brissot who discovered in him the brains needed for an expedition to Louisiana. Perhaps at Brissot's suggestion, Imlay submitted a report to the committee of Public Safety, in which he argued the advantages of occupying Louisiana. [32] It was the key to Spain's American empire; its conquest would compel her to increase her forces in Latin America, upset her finances, oblige her to abandon the European coalition and make peace with France. Futhermore, since the expedition would probably be undertaken by American citizens, the United States would eventually be drawn into the war, which was a Girondist objective. The report also stressed the economic benefits of the territory—Its vast food supply needed by France and its great potential in producing tobacco, sugar, coffee and cotton. Also, New Orleans in French hands would be both the great entrepôt of the West and the Antilles and an excellent haven for French privateers.

Imlay's plan failed to win official endorsement despite Brissot's earnest support. [33] Possibly the Ministry had greater faith in a scheme of its own adopted in March 1793, about the time Barlow returned from Savoy. The scheme, the sixth in our catalogue, called for the appointment of a committee that would go to the United States, and there, under the direction of the French envoy, that is Gênet, concentrate on three objectives: To explore the means of conquering New Orleans and Louisiana, to stir up the Spanish colonies, and to send to French colonies such commodities as wheat and salt provisions that were two-thirds cheaper than those imported from the United States.

The personnel of the committee requires some attention. Its four members were Barlow, Sayre, Beaupoils and Lyonnet. What were Barlow's credentials for the enterprise? The author of the project said that he was an American and a French citizen, "a genuine friend of liberty, a philosopher with a high moral character, who merits every kind of confidence. He has well served both the American and French Revolutions. He might be made general director under Gênet and entrusted with the handling of the funds." [34]

The committee's instructions were detailed and precise. Its mission had to be a dark secret. Before departing, its four members would consult Louis Otto, chief secretary of the Foreign Ministry, who was said to have extensive knowledge of what was available in the United States for the success of the expedition. No time should be lost in settling on a plan. It would be well for the four persons to sail on different vessels. If they left within a month they would arrive in July, and would not have too much time to complete the affair this year, unless Gênet did it in advance. To expedite matters he should be authorized to start an uprising in the Spanish colonies, and for this purpose to employ a portion of the American debt to France. The uprising, once begun, would be carried to a successful finish by the Venezuelan, General Francisco de Miranda, who would be released from the French army and sent to Latin

America.

Noteworthy is the absence of Imlay's name from the committee. Faith in him declined possibly as a result of his underhand dealings. Mary Wollstonecraft was at one time disturbed by what she termed "this crooked business" he was involved in. [35] His biographer suggests that he might have been engaged in trading with France on British capital. [36]

The sixth plan called forth a counterplan. It dampened French hopes of succeeding to the Spanish-American Empire and concentrated on Louisiana alone. It recommended the dismissal of Sayre and Barlow from the committee of four. The draft of unknown authorship saw little or no worth for the object in view either in Barlow's character or in his revolutionary past. All that mattered was the serviceableness of the men, and by this test he found Sayre and Barlow useless: "Both were incapable of risking their skins, which is essential in an expedition of this type. Having been away from America for many years, their knowledge of its interior can be but superficial." Their removal from the committee could be explained on the ground that the government feared to compromise the neutrality of the United States. [37]

Whether or not Barlow was to be on the committee turned out to be of little moment. For the counter-scheme, the same as the other plans, went by the board after the ousting of the Girondins from the convention on June 2, 1793. Their leaders were impeached October 3, tried the fifteenth and executed the thirty-first. Their aim of making Louisiana a French possession was subsequently realized by Bonaparte.

The dream of the Girondins survived their leaders. It appealed to adventurers and fortune hunters. To friends of the Revolution it imaged the feasibiltiy of supplying France with necessities. And it animated Barlow and his Connecticut-born friend, Mark Leavenworth, to present their own project to the Committee of Public Safety.

Their "Plan for Taking Louisiana, " as it was entitled, is dated 3 *frimaire year II* in the revolutionary calendar, or November 23, 1793. [38] It was probably drawn up by Barlow, and it shrewdly underscored the interest of France rather than that of the planners.

Sections of the Plan bore a strong similarity to the drafts we have already considered. It stressed, for instance, the fertility of the land, its favorable location, the industry and peacefulness of the inhabitants, who looked forward to their deliverance from Spanish rule. Then followed a typical Barlowan theme:

"To restore the liberty of these people by giving them the political standing of a French colony would be not only an act of humanity. It would also be immensely advantageous to them, and at the same time be a great example to the neighbors in Mexico and Florida, with the result that Spanish despotism would before long be cast out of all of South America."

Such an outcome belonged to the future. The more immediate and foreseeable benefits were the shipment of timber to the French islands and of low-priced provisions to France, provided the Mississippi was kept open to navigation. France could also be the furnisher of naval stores to other countries, for Lousiana had more than was needed by all the European navies. The same was true of tobacco that could be grown more abundantly and cheaply than in Virginia. French exports would have a new market on the condition that they had free entry at New Orleans. Finally, French soldiers could be settled in Louisiana once the European war ended.

Delay in executing the plan would be detrimental to the enterprise. Decisive action alone could achieve victory over Spanish despotism. Who would bear the cost of the expedition? According to the planners, the end would be achieved without the financial aid of France. The expense of recruiting and equipping the necessary force of 2,000 men would be borne by a company they would establish. They promised to take possession of Louisiana in the name of the French Republic and then await further orders.

The plan is quite vague as to the kind of company that would pay and direct the operations. Perhaps Barlow and Leavenworth took as their model the British East India Company. But the British found a greater reservoir of wealth. The Americans, however, could count only on the development of the territory. Meanwhile, after taking possession, they would confiscate the properties of the Spanish government and its officials and distribute them among the soldiers and entrepreneurs, that is, the company's stockholders. That would be the first payment on the investment. A government would be organized according to the principles of the French Constitution and commercial regulations would be the same as in other French colonies. Neither France nor the colonial government would interfere with the free navigation of the Mississippi and of other rivers emptying into the Gulf of Mexico. A clause was introduced to protect the company against unforeseen developments: "If, contrary to all anticipation, France yielded Louisiana to Spain at the peace settlement the French government would refund the entrepreneurs and their associates the cost of the enterprise."

It turned out to be but a paper project. Preoccupied with war and internal troubles, the French Republic could scarcely become involved in Louisiana affairs. To be sure its need for food and armaments was acute. But it managed to get them despite the British blockade.

The plan made it evident that while Barlow was propagating the principles of the French Revolution, he was on the lookout for a way to economic success which he believed, in common with others, could be achieved in the virgin land west of the Mississippi. Fortunately he found less risky opportunities in Europe.

Chapter VIII
Conservatism versus Reform

1

The extension of the coalition against France was detrimental to French commerce. Georges Lefèbvre pointed out that from about May to December 1793 it suffered from gradual paralysis, but slowly regained vitality during the next four months. From April and May 1794 to the beginning of 1795 it went on after a fashion.[1] The principal causes of the sluggishness were the blockade of French ports, the falling value of the paper money (*assignats*), the flight of capital, the embargo on exports and the exclusion of products made in Great Britain. Among the internal effects were merchants' hostility to the revolutionary government, business failures and a dearth of vital commodities. Economic curbs were concessions to popular demands for tight control. War needs forced the Committee of Public Safety to permit the importation of necessities.

The Food Commission (*Commission des subsistances*), set up in October 1792, was an essential arm of the Revolutionary government. It had the burden of requisitioning at home and purchasing abroad wheat, meat, naval stores, potash, saltpeter, leather and other essential products. In January 1794 it was empowered to place orders with neutrals.

Trade between France and the United States recovered. Several merchants and special agents were dispatched to America. In exchange for imports from the United States the agents were permitted to export luxury articles, even bullion. The fact that many American products reached their destination via Copenhagen and Hamburg suggests the deviousness and secrecy of the traffic.

The minutes of the Food Commission disclose its dealings with many Americans in Paris. Swan's name appears most frequently. His connections in London, Amsterdam, Lisbon and Hamburg, in Spanish ports and in the United States gave him a broad field of operations and means of evading British surveillance. Other Americans included Benjamin Jarvis, Mark Leavenworth, G. W. Murray, Benjamin Hichborn and Joel Barlow. Swan was the biggest importer of foodstuffs, powder, leather and shoes. Jarvis supplied tinware; Murray, cotton; and Barlow, potash and pearlash. [2]

The functions of the Food Commission were taken over in 1794 by the Commission of Commerce and Provisions, under which the system of purchasing was reorganized. Trade with neutrals was placed in the hands of four business firms, one of them James Swan and Company. By the end of August 1795, it reported having sent to France 105 shiploads of provisions. The figure rose to 113 by the end of the year. [3]

Barlow's business affairs are often difficult to track down. Early in December 1793, bargaining went on between him and the Food Commission over the price of potash, pearlash and other unspecified commodities. Shortly thereafter a contract was made that brought him a substantial gain. [4] Pieces of evidence show that from the end of the Scioto venture to his relations with the Food Commission, he was constantly in search of quick returns. In April 1792 he had his eye on goods in England that might be traded lucratively. A month later, in Paris, he accepted Blackden's offer of partnership in some unexplained enterprise. Then, toward the middle of 1793, he entered into a shipping brokerage with Colonel Hichborn of Massachusetts, Mark Leavenworth and Daniel Parker. The four chartered vessels, several of British origin, were to transport contraband to France. The risk was high; but the profits were even higher. In 1794 he was in business with Imlay and Elias Backman, a Swedish merchant, to ship goods to French ports from Scandinavia. His affairs prospered, so that by 1796 his investments in France amounted to $120,000.

He was business oriented. Even during his mission to Algiers, he studied the prices of wheat and barley in the English market, bought into a shipping firm, speculated in wines and salt and acquired part ownership of merchant vessels. By 1800 he was a rich man, living in one of the best houses in Paris. [5]

Experience molded Barlow into a star negotiator. One of his functions in the partnerships with Americans was to treat with responsible persons in Paris, of whom he knew many. He spoke French; he was a French citizen and he was respected for his services to the Revolution. So appreciated was his adroitness with officials that Swan wrote to General Knox at the end of 1793, commending him to succeed Gouverneur Morris as U.S. Minister to France. [6] This was a far cry from the innocent Barlow of the Scioto days.

2

Approximately four months after Swan wrote the recommendation to Knox, Barlow was on his way to Hamburg. The reason for his going can only be inferred. Possibly it was his business involvement with Imlay and Backman. Possibly, too, it was to escape the severity of the Terror.

The Barlows felt insecure under the Montagnard regime, [7] especially after September 17, 1793, when the Law of suspects was voted. Friends of the Girondins could expect detention and interrogation. The Terror became more intense in 1794. Jacques Roux, the *Enragé* priest, committed suicide on January 12 to avoid appearing before the Revolutionary Tribunal. The Hébertists were executed on March 23, and the Dantonists on April 5.

An event occurred toward the end of 1793 that touched the Barlows closely and warned them of approaching danger. At eleven A.M. on December 28, they were surprised by the arrival, at their residence on rue Jacob, of Tom Paine under police escort. (His biographer has documented the story of the way he maneuvered to be led to his friend and countryman to entrust him with the first part of *The Age of Reason*. [8])

Three weeks after Paine's arrest, a petition drafted by Barlow and signed by eighteen Americans, appealed for the liberation of "one of the most earnest and faithful apostles of liberty." [9] The petitioners significantly kept clear of Gouverneur Morris. Paine languished in prison until November 1794, when James Monroe, the new minister to France, claimed him as an American citizen and asked for his release.

Hamburg was the independent North German emporium where foreign merchants were making fortunes. It had the best natural harbor on the German North Sea coast, was the exit of the Elbe and the contact point of traders from the German plain, England, France and Holland. Of the 2,000 ships that annually visited the port, only 160 were owned by residents. It was unique among German cities. It was large, prosperous, full of economic, political and intellectual activity; and it was reported to have over forty millionaires. It had the first Masonic lodge, named Unity and Tolerance, composed of democrats, artisans, shopkeepers and white collar workers. In neighboring Altona a Jacobin club had existed during the Mountain's ascendancy. But these organizations had dwindled by the time the Barlows arrived. [10] During the Revolutionary War, many neutral ships, most of them American, could be seen anchored in the harbor. Nearly all were carriers of provisions and war matériel to France, though they were officially destined for England's allies.

Hamburg was vital to France. It was not only a distributing center of "neutral" goods; it was also a lookout point for what went on in the German states. It was, however, in an extremely difficult position. On the one hand it was pressed by Prussia and Austria to stop trafficking with the enemy. On the other, in the interest of its merchants, it endeavored to be on good terms with France. It speaks well for the diplomacy of the city's magistrates that they were able to maintain neutrality despite threats from the opposing sides. This course was advantageous to the North German towns which served as outlets for goods France needed. France could not pay in cash. Only in Hamburg were its bills of exchange acceptable. A French consul estimated in September 1795 that the annual balance of French trade with the Hanseatic cities was 48,000,000 livres. Hamburg in particular benefitted [11] and consequently reciprocated accordingly. It refused to join the coalition, permitted the observance of Bastille Day and put restraints on the approximately 12,000 émigrés and their nearly 1,300 prostitutes.[12]

It was a densely settled city of 130,000 people. Here business was the absorbing subject of conversation. Barlow was a business agent, which meant that he received commissions on incoming and outgoing goods he neither saw nor owned. This did not hinder him from buying and selling cargoes on his own.

The Barlows lived close by in Altona, which was part of Denmark. The town was more residential and quieter than Hamburg, and more congenial to Babbitry. Social life was without sparkle. Thoughts were occupied with market quotations or with the gossip of the traders' exchange. Living in Altona must have been a drowsy existence for Barlow.

He missed the sparkle of Parisian gatherings where ideas were exchanged. The Terror, to be sure, had sent a number of his friends to their graves and silenced others. Lost were Roland, Vergniaud, Condorcet, "men of rare talent" and "profound learning," as he had estimated them; and Brissot, an "active genius"with a capacious mind, "a sober, uniform, and indefatigable defender of the rights of mankind," who had gone to his death singing the "Marseillaise." [13] Missing, too, was the Protestant minister and deputy, Rabaut Saint-Etienne, who had written an illuminating account of the Revolution during its first two years. [14] Fortunately others remained whose company he craved.

Two English friends, Mary Wollstonecraft and Helen Maria Williams, funneled news from France. Mary, writing from Le Havre, relayed facts on the Leavenworths and Blackdens, and mentioned in passing the impediments to shipments Imlay was plagued with. She even introduced a homey reference to her recently born Fanny, whose head size was too big for the caps Ruth had made. To bring Joel up to date on her literary work she reported progress on her book on the French Revolution. Helen, in Paris, alternated between anger and sorrow over the execution of the Dantonists. She was lonely and of a mind to visit the Barlows in Hamburg. Should they sail to America she would like to follow them, "to form a ménage with you." [15]

Of the small number of Barlow's friends in Hamburg, Christoph Daniel Ebeling was the most intellectual. He was a teacher of Greek and history in the local gymnasium and in later years the head of its library. His magnum opus was a geography and history of the United States in seven tomes on which he had spent twenty years. He had a collector's passion for all kinds of prints of America, including maps. To that end he corresponded with Ezra Stiles, Reverend Jeremy Bellknap, the historian, Reverend John Eliot, Corresponding Secretary of the Massachusetts Historical Society, Professor Joseph McKean of Harvard and Joel Barlow. [16]

Barlow and Ebeling probably saw one another frequently. It is safe to assume that the German's hobby turned the talk to the United States, during which the American was plied with questions on the geography, history and people of New England. Perhaps they also entered upon European politics and events in France. For Ebeling, the same as Barlow, defended her revolutionary principles and rejoiced in her victories.

Barlow did what he could to promote the professor's research. To his former teacher, Ezra Stiles, he wrote on May 27, 1794, enclosing a letter of Ebeling and describing his project.

"Every such attempt to instruct the European world in whatever concerns America deserves our warmest encouragement, as it serves to induce the oppressed of all nations to come to us; a migration which at once augments our prosperity and their felicity. And I know no man who possesses more ability and inclination to serve the cause of humanity in this way, than he whom I have the honor to recommend to your correspondence." [17]

Stiles, in answer to Ebeling, wrote eighty-six quarto pages, which contained a history of Connecticut.

Let us take a longer look at Barlow's letter to Stiles. For it genuinely mirrored the man. His inquiring mind discovered the beauties of the German writers. And he ventured the opinion that they were "more excellent than those of any other modern nation." The overstatement is pardonable if we recall that this was the age of Wieland, Lessing, Goethe and Schiller. Barlow's emotions might have leaped at his meeting the seventy-year-old German poet, Friedrich Klopstock. The Germans, wrote Barlow to Stiles, "think [him] as much superior to Milton, as we think Milton superior to him." He "makes odes, with as much fire as [William] Collins." [18] It may be noted that most of Klopstock's odes were like Christian psalms. Madame de Staël named him "the David of the New Testament." His chef d'oeuvre, the Messiado, an epic poem, has sometimes been likened to *Paradise Lost*. But as Madame de Staël remarked, Milton drew a gigantic figure of the rebellious Satan. Klopstock was content to abide in the pure Christianity of the New Testament. [19]

3

Save for Paine, Barlow was the most lettered of the Americans in Paris. Nearly all of them seem to have been activated by the acquisitive instinct. Barlow was. Yet, to place him in their category would eclipse the side of him that set him apart. This may explain why he liked to escape the company of business hawks. The Swans, the Hichborns, the Leavenworths did not care a tinker's damn whether the French republic survived. They would worship their golden calf under any régime. Not so in his case. Barlow forever stood by the democratic and republican principles, the warp and woof of his credo. His was a world of liberated peoples, living peacefully together and utilizing their resources for the public good.

The argument has been advanced that free enterprise buttressed by the rights of man was the dominant idea of Barlow's thinking.[20] This point would make him but another Yankee trader, without concern for human welfare. Such a construction of his thought is possible only if free enterprise as a concept is disengaged from its historical context. For in its pristine meaning, it was a rebellion against the claims of privilege, monopoly and despotism. Men like Barlow, Paine and Jefferson, to name but three, considered it inherent in a republican-democratic order, and a way of man's improvement. But history drained it of its noble promise, leaving only a dry, brittle shell to misguide unhistorically minded commentators.

Barlow spent much of his leisure on study. His interests were encyclopedic in the eighteenth-century manner. He filled notebooks[21] with data and comments on ancient history, religion and the origin of fables, on epic poetry, philosophy and science, on inventions and the history of printing. He remarked that the allegedly authoritative historians of antiquity were wanting in scrutiny. They were embellishers of fable and allegory. Herodotus had set the pattern by equipping them with a historical form. Greek historians in general, said Barlow, had "sought rather to be brilliant than exact." Thucydides was an exception, but he left only a small portion of his history of Greece. Reading Roman history fortified in Barlow a hatred of military conquerors who brought "unbounded and endless calamities" to countries and barbarism to society. The razing of Carthage was shocking, unnecessary and unexampled in cruelty, and he chanced the opinion that it was the beginning of Rome's decline and fall.

He was versed in natural science and philosophy. Descartes, Copernicus, Galileo, Newton, among others, aroused in him unending curiosity. He enjoyed reading the philosophical writers of the century and their precursors. And he had the ambition of becoming a historian, with the object of tracing democratic ideas to their roots and showing their effect on the formation of national institutions. He planned a history of the United States of which the American Revolution would be an important part. But mounting hostility to French Revolutionary principles in Great Britain and at home convinced him to write first a history of the French Revolution. Since the work was intended for Great Britain and America, we must preface it with a review of opinion on the Revolution in the two countries.

4

By 1795 the British reform movement had bent before the government's vigorous assault. Only the London Corresponding Society and a number of similar organizations in the provinces held together several years longer. [22] In the relatively short span from 1795 to 1800, nine repressive acts were voted with the design of severely restricting the freedom of speech, press and assembly.

The legislation bespoke a sense of alarm in the British ruling class. For the country passed through a series of cyclical crises, in 1793, in 1797 and 1797-1800. The dates show a close correspondence between the crises and the oppressive acts. The British workers paid heavily with rising prices, falling wages and unemployment.

Industrial investment slowed down in the same decade. Those with reserve funds either bought government bonds or, because of the high price of corn, invested them in the building of merchant ships or put them into agriculture. The number of enclosures rose from 246 in the previous decade to 469, totalling an approximate 274,000 acres. The war period was the golden age of the Brtitish landlords. They lived lavishly and paid off debts. [23]

This may account in part for the climate of reaction. Secret government funds went into subsidizing newspapers and periodicals with the object of ridiculing the French, their Revolution and its British sympathizers. Contributors portayed the immense superiority of the British in resourcefulness, virtue and courage, and decked out with the logic of Burke the wisdom of Britain's political system. The verbal war against reform was waged with prose and verse and with torrents of scorn and abuse pumped from a reservoir of invective. Both lords and commoners entered the lists to preserve the order of estates and defend the natural laws of trade.

One of their effective publications was *The Anti-Jacobin: or Weekly Examiner*. [24] Its readers, it was estimated, rose to around 17,500, and according to a more zealous calculation, to 50,000. Its underlying theme was that the happiness of all peoples hinged on Britain's unabating struggle against France. Britons who opposed the war and who were partial to French principles were traitors and Jacobins. And a Jacobin was a visionary and an incendiary. He inflamed the poor against the rich; he aimed at levelling the orders and gradations of society; and his object was desolation and anarchy. Thanks to Providence, Great Britain was safe from the Jacobin scourge.

A feature of *The Anti-Jacobin* was its clever verse. The purpose was always the same:

To Trace the deep infection that pervades

The crowded town, and taints the rural shades. [25]

It cast a sacred light on domestic institutions and raised to sainthood Burke:

. . . Whose prescident scan
Pierc'd through foul Anarch's gigantic plan. [26]

The cause of reaction had many crusaders. One vindicated the British constitution and the Establishment against the Voltaires, d'Alemberts, Condorcets and Rousseaus, whose progeny were "the vulgar and illiterate blasphemy of Thomas Paine," "the contemptible nonsense of Willian Godwin" and the idolatry of Volney. Facing them was "that uncontrolled genius," Edmund Burke, who had seen through their wickedness and rung the alarm. [27] Another, a former friend of Paine, told his countrymen that the condition of the English peasant or mechanic was "prosperity itself when compared to that of a Frenchman." He declared that "Rational freedom had nothing to do with the French cause" for the French were fighting to establish the worst kind of despotism. [28] A third, after inquiring into comparative government, came up with the conclusion that the British monarchical system was preferable to a democracy. [29] A fourth, John Bowles, a Burkeite, discovered the seeds of subversion in Locke's *Treatises on Civil Government*. Embedded there were the doctrines of consent and the natural equality of rights (both of which had been wrought into a system by a set of philosophers) that unsettled the minds of men with regard to their obligations and social status. The way was opened to the French Revolution with its train of evils and its metaphysical constitution making. [30]

At the heart of the controversy was the problem of poverty. It was impossible to solve it by leveling ranks and property, said partisans of the existing order. The process would do violence to man's nature. There was no guarantee that giving land to the poor would prompt them to cultivate it, for the causes of poverty, the argument continued, were in the poor themselves. They indulged their tastes, spent too much time in barrooms and fell into such vices as drunkenness and gambling. Consequently, it was wrong to teach them, as agitators were doing, that their misery proceeded from oppression by the rich. The wages of the workers were sufficient not only to support them but also to lay by sums that would in time lead to opulence. The employers were the workers' best friends and patrons, for they made it possible for them to rise to independence. Besides, the workers never had the anxieties of the employers who took all the risks. In fact, if the poor balanced the good against the evil of their situation, few of them would exchange it for that of the employers. [31]

Of special interest was the argument of Arthur Young. No society, he said, can nor ever did exist without the distinctions of rich and poor. For that reason equality was a phantom, good enough for romantics. As long as the world endured, the rich would be the purchasers of the labor of the poor. To be compelled to labor for life was no greater evil than sickness or death. The antidote to French doctrines was teaching the poor that a revolution in England would be to their loss. It was "the undoubted and genuine interest of all lower classes to keep things as they are, because every change must be for the worse." And on further reflection, "if Christianity be not a fable, their eternal welfare is at stake." [32]

The last point had become a commonplace in the anti-reform argument. Religion, ran the reasoning, was necessary to the stability of the state. France would have been better off if the writings of the philosophers had not been published or had been kept from circulation. Hannah More acknowledged a greater apprehension of French principles than of French bayonets. The armed forces, she trusted, could guard the nation against the latter. But its protection against the former demanded the vigilance of every one who valued "religion and the good order of society in this world, and an eternity of happiness in the next." [33]

The threat of everlasting hell, backed by legislation and prosecution, brought the desired effect. By 1798 the voices of protest and reform had been reduced to but a few. One was *The Brazen Trumpet*, a weekly, which said fearlessly:

"Every endeavour to make the industrious poor man acquainted with the cause of the poverty, and other evils he has to contend with, is called *seditious* by those who would fatten their acres with the sweat of their labourer's brow. . . . Whatever property every man holds but by the avowed or tacit consent of the majority of the people is not legitimate property, any more than that which may be seized and held by the soldiers of a camp or army, whose titles are to be looked for in the mouths of their cannon." [34]

With the same forthrightness, it told the rulers of Great Britain that they were deceiving themselves in thinking that the people would rush on the French invaders with the eagerness of former years. "What will they defend?" it asked, "the liberty announced by Pitt and Grenville which the people do not have?" [35] To have asked the questions was to invite the eventual suppression of the periodical and the prosecution of the publisher.

However charged with danger, the question was asked nevertheless and answered by a professor of the classics, Gilbert Wakefield, [36] who had left the Established Church to become a Unitarian. He was gentle and amiable, but, thrown into a polemic, his mildness turned into vehemence. The change of temper was observable in his reply to Dr. Watson, Bishop of Llandaff, an unbending standby of the British Constitution and the author of an address to the people, in which he narrated in recitative the virtues of the governing ministers and the excellence of the political and religious systems. Wakefield replied by listing the ministers' misdeeds: Their crushing taxes, their unexampled prodigality, their burdening England with an overwhelming debt, their utter disregard for human life, their deluding the people with sham plots and false alarms and their deportation of fellow citizens. He rejected the grounds of the social order. Only those distinctions should prevail that arose from merit and public service. This applied equally to the church hierarchy which he defined as "the despicable trumpery of priestcraft and superstition." Finally, like *The Brazen Trumpet*, he came head-on to the war issue. The war was hopeless, expensive and beneficial to "a few, greedy, obstinate, tyrannical, and sanguinary men in office." Was a system like Britain's worth fighting for if the French invaded the country? His answer was a direct negative:

"Let those, who have an interest in these fooleries and aims; let those, who have brought us to this most alarming crisis, step forward on the day of danger and fight the battles of their Baal and their Mammon; . . . We, *sons of peace,* see, or think we see a gleam of glory through the mist . . . a general fermentation is working for the purpose of general refinement through the universe." He would await the event in defiance of penalites.[37]

Wakefield's reply cost him two years' imprisonment, which probably hastened his death at the age of 45.

Thus were silenced the British champions of principles made popular by the French Revolution. A reactionary flood tide set in. But the principles and what was stigmatized as Jacobinism survived the war years in shops and taverns and behind closed doors, only to reemerge in new forms.[38]

5

Barlow was well acquainted with the struggle between conservatism and reform in Great Britain. Information was reaching him of a similar struggle going on in his native land. There the opposing sides were not quite as unequal as in England. The Federalists, with a design to curtail democratic practices, had on their side the executive branch of the government, the clergy and a large press. These powerful molders of opinion undoubtedly gave them the upper hand. Still the republican democrats eventually triumphed.

American opinion of the French Revolution developed in two stages. The first, from 1789 to 1794, was one of general acclaim. The second, from 1795 to 1800, was torn by dissension between Francophiles and Anglophiles. For the present let us consider briefly the earlier stage when the French Revolution was regarded as the twin of the American. The Revolution in France was therefore hailed as the herald of a golden age and likened to an exterminating angel sent by the Creator to hasten the coming of the millenium.

From north to south it was greeted in prose and verse. News from France crowded out other foreign reports, and pamphlets supporting the Revolution were advertised. Among the titles were Paine's *Rights of Man*, Barlow's *Advice to the Privileged Orders*, Rabaut Saint-Etienne's *History of the French Revolution*, Robespierre's speeches, and publications of British reformers. The following dates were observed: February 6, (the signing of the treaty of alliance between the United States and France), July 4, July 14 and August 10. Francophile democrats had support among small farmers, artisans and mechanics, western settlers, merchants operating with their own capital, scientists, school teachers and painters, in sum, among diversified segments of America. They were united by opposition to Hamilton's monetary plans, to the funding system especially, and they looked to establishing a social order that secured individual economic independence.

Any attempt to survey pro-French revolutionary sentiment in the United States must take into account the role of the popular organizations, better known as the democratic republican societies. They were indigenous, traditionally descendant from the Sons of Liberty and ideologically indebted to foreign and home-grown thinkers, that is, first to Locke, Montesquieu and Rousseau, and then to Jefferson, Paine and Barlow. Their programs lacked uniformity. Each set of demands represented the needs of the locality where the society functioned. Yet they had these aims in common: To preserve the rights of man; to watch over public servants; to maintain the democratic process of government; to check the political designs of the wealthy; and to prevent the severance of Franco-American relations.

The credo of the societies had its origin in the thought of the seventeenth and eighteenth centuries and included such tenets as the Lockean doctrine of consent and Paine's teaching that governments had to go on changing in order to be the genuine expression of the people's will. It called for popular instruction, and it held that democracy would be jeopardized in America if counterrevolution triumphed in Europe.

The defense of the French Revolution was a motivating tenet of the societies. According to their historian, every popular society, from north to south had in its constitution a clause supporting France and the Revolution, for "in the event of the overthrow of the French Republic, the United States, then without an ally, may be forced to yield to European confederacy." [39]

An article of faith shared by the societies was the saving of the Franco-American alliance from infraction. Consequently they leveled their criticism at the Jay Treaty. From north to south it was rejected with disdain and regarded as a sinister design to enslave the nation. Jefferson was called on to assume the nation's leadership in order to cleanse it of the accumulating rot.

The number of American societies was only a fraction of the thousands of clubs in France. Only forty-two maintained themselves from 1793 to 1798. But their lush growth was from 1793 to 1794, that is, during the heyday of the French and English clubs.

The American societies, like the British, became objects of calumny. The accusation by President Washington that they had instigated the "Whisky Rebellion" did them great injury. The fact was that they had neither direct nor indirect links with it, as a student of the record has shown. [40]

The societies disintegrated during the next five years. The causes lay in a number of blighting events, among them the slave insurrection in the French West Indies, which gave plausibility to the Federalist charge that the societies were formenters of civil war. Also, a qualitative change had come about in the French revolutionary war that chilled the members' zeal. From a war of liberation it became into a war of annexation.

Democratic republicanism continued to be militant. It gained coherence and vitality under the leadership of the Republican Party. This developed during the second stage of American opinion of the French Revolution.

Chapter IX
French Revolution Historiography

1

The histories of the French Revolution written in the 1790s corresponded to the drawn-out debate between conservatism and reform. Most of them were diabolically critical of the Revolution, in particular of the period after August 10th. Works by French émigrés excelled in that respect and were taken as authoritative by British and American maligners. Assessed in terms of modern research, they are distortions. They serve only to depict the emotions that agitated the anti-revolutionary cause.

Of the hostile British accounts, only those by Helen Maria Williams and William Playfair merit notice here. In the first series of her *Letters from France*, [1] Miss Williams rejoiced at the march of events. Her golden age of the Revolution ran from July 14, 1790, to August 10, 1792. Then came the macabre years, years of conspiracy, assassination and struggle for mastery between Girondins and Mountainists. To this period she devoted another set of *Letters*, [2] in which her heroes were the Girondins, and her villains, the Mountainists. France breathed again after their execution.

Missing in her story were the ideas that impelled people to action. The hidden, volcanolike forces escaped her. Her panorama sufficiently deformed the Terror to gratify its foes. Consequently, her second series of *Letters* was publicized in Great Britain and the United States, along with works by such irreconcilable critics as Mallet du Pan and the Abbé Barruel. [3]

Yet Miss Williams was a model of restraint compared to William Playfair, Barlow's associate in the Scioto business. He was unabating in his antipathy to the Revolution. A pamphlet he turned out in 1794 maintained that the war against France was necessary to protect the British constitution, religion and property as well as to preclude the misfortunes that would follow a French victory. Hindsight and foresight, he argued, ought to teach the rich to be generous in supporting the war, for they profited most by the existing order. Otherwise they might expect the fate that had befallen the French nobility and the citizens of Lyons. Jacobinism in England would lay the axe to the roots of institutions and replace them by a permanent Guillotine. [4]

The pamphlet prefigured *The History of Jacobinism*, the thesis of which was epitomized in the lengthy title. [5] Its single asset was an analysis of the causes of the Revolution. But when Playfair entered upon the narrative he ceased being an analyst. The great reforms of the National Assembly were metamorphosed into a record of crime, murder, iniquity and anarchy. The confiscation of Church property and the abolition of feudal rights were a signal for the destruction of what remained of rank and order. The fault for the mischief lay partly with the powers, for they had been dilatory in recognizing the danger.

The rest of *The History* was a mutilated story, filled with invective, misrepresentation and spurious moralizing. The Girondins were the same as the Mountainists, "equally culpable and equally immersed in guilt." The dethroned king was an example of human moderation next to the republican rulers. Playfair's longest pause in his furious assault was an inquiry into the reasons for the French success, which he attributed to the ingenuity of the revolutionary government, especially to its law of maximum and its encouragement of science.

Of the English works favorably disposed to the Revolution, only two are worthy of notice. One was by Mary Wollstonecraft and the other by Sampson Perry. The first,[6] embracing only the first six months, is didactic and historical. Its motif is man's steady progress of which the Revolution was a consequence. The French, however, had moved too rapidly, Miss Wollstonecraft believed. They were impatient to achieve their ends. The National Assembly had failed to prepare the nation to understand and safeguard liberty. Its first task should have been the drafting of a constitution that would have served both as a standard and as a bond of national unity. But constitution-making had a subordinate place on the agenda. After the October days, the despotism of the multitude was set up over the people's representatives. Peaceful orderly action succumbed to Parisian violence.

Miss Wollstonecraft, like Godwin, was partial to gradual change. Yet she was not altogether opposed to revolution, since the morality of the ruling classes had sunk so much that no remedy was possible save through violence. That at least rooted out the poisonous forms that blighted society, and cleared away impediments to progress. Generally, however, she stood for moderation. The nobles should have been given enough power to balance that of the people's representatives. This is not to imply that she failed to appreciate the momentous popular movements like the storming of the Bastille or the dramatic unity of citizens to resist the country's invaders.

How she would have treated the subsequent course of the Revolution, had she completed the narrative, can only be surmised. If the title is an indication, she might have estimated at length the revolutionary principles and their effect on peoples. But her premature death deprived us of her further reflections.

What she was prevented from doing was achieved by the better informed Sampson Perry. He was a surgeon who had been fined and imprisoned in 1791 for having libeled the British government. The following year he fled to France where he was arrested in 1793, together with other British subjects, and held in prison for fourteen months. Returning to England in 1795, he was put in custody until 1801. His history of the Revolution was a product of this long confinement. [7]

His observations of men and events were remarkably balanced. The overthrow of royal power was due to the king's ignorance, manifested by his actions. The strong position of the Jacobin Club was both necessary and unavoidable. It was at once the intermediary between the government and the people and the sentinel of the Revolution. The September massacres, however regrettable, were the result of convergent circumstances. The people had been thrown into a fit of fury by the invasion of France, which sparked the belief that the imprisoned aristocrats had helped to plot it. To slanderers of Robespierre, Perry replied that his fall had the effect of inciting royalists to hoist their standard.

Perry's interpretation of the Revolution was meant to counteract British Francophobia. Instead of writing history in the conditional mood, as Mary Wollstonecraft had done, he clung to the evidence. Viewing the Revolution philosophically, he discerned what was imperceptible to others, namely, the prospect of freedom and its effect on peoples.

Whether Mary Wollstonecraft's and Sampson Perry's books cooled anti-French passion in Great Britain cannot be answered. The first had a second edition in 1798 [8] and another in Dublin in 1799, believed to have been pirated. After the critics had had their say, her book was forgotten. The second work went into oblivion after the first printing, perhaps because it appeared during a towering wave of reaction.

2

Histories comparable to the above, whether friendly or hostile, were lacking in the United States, as far as we know. Instead of full-length narratives, Americans were served only sermons and polemics. A case in point was a sermon by the Reverend David Osgood, pastor of Bedford, Massachusetts. [9] In keeping with the conduct of the New England clergy, [10] he had stepped out of his role as a Christian minister to tar the French Revolution. It was, in his words, "a despotism the most ferocious, cruel and bloody recorded in history." The Massachusetts politician, James Sullivan, replied that the sermon was an exhibition of glossy rhetoric to conceal a dearth of facts. Comparing the American and

French Revolutions, Sullivan found them similar in methods and objectives. The excesses laid to the French also happened in America, though to a lesser degree. The difference arose from separate sets of circumstances. The French committed imprudent acts, to be sure, but in the overall record of their Revolution they were minor. Gênet's conduct in the United States was inexcusable. But to call him "a foreign incendiary" was to invite a like condemnation of Franklin and Dean. For they, too, had attempted to win the aid of the country they had been sent to. Sullivan finally charged the pastor with the sin of omission. He had calmly passed over the enormity of reaction that had resulted in the death of millions of Frenchmen.[11]

The Osgood-Sullivan polemic was a symptom of the turbulent climate of opinion. "Lying tongues!" "Anarchists!" Federalists shouted at Republicans. "Aristocrats!" "Hirelings of England!" came back the reply. Odious epithets replaced evidence and argument. To damn a critic of Jay's Treaty with England, for instance, it was sufficient to label him a "Jacobin," a nasty word in the Federalist dictionary. The use of it in party warfare was deftly described by a republican-democratic sheet:

"In America every man who is principled in his attachments to the Equal Rights of the People, to the incontestable privileges of the Federal House of Representatives, is a Jacobin. . . . If we have waged a wanton and expensive war with the Indians on our frontiers, it is Jacobinism to speak of it. If we say, the institution of the Federal Bank was intended to corrupt the morals and destroy the frugal habits of the people—that is Jacobinism. If it is insinuated, that the *virtue* and *piety* of the leading Federalists is much the same with other people—that too is Jacobinism. . . . It is to be a Jacobin to oppose a war with France; to object to an intimate Union with England; and to wish the whole world to be as free, as happy, and to have as Good Constitutions of Government as the Citizens of New England." [12]

Barlow was disturbed by the violence of the Anglophiles. He confided to his New York publisher on May 23, 1795, that he was distressed by the "slavish spirit of aristocracy" in America. However, he foresaw its retreat "as soon as the French Revolution shall be understood, and especially when a like change in government shall take place in England, which is an event as irresistible as the march of Time." [13]

His thoughts turned to his Connecticut friends. Nearly all of his Yale class were either well-posted Federalists or devotees of Federalist policy. Not one of the Hartford wits shared his democratic belief. Lemuel Hopkins satirized the republican societies and opponents of the Jay Treaty; [14] Humphreys was a confirmed Federalist; Theodore Dwight, brother of Timothy, edited the *Connecticut Courant*, organ of the Federalist Party; and Richard Alsop was a foe of every new idea. [15]

Painful to him was the political role of Noah Webster. He was conservative in the Connecticut tradition and was a loyal Federalist. He had already written a carping critique of the *Advice to the Privileged Orders,* which Barlow thought better intentioned than reasoned. With the spirit of a crusading knight, Webster went forward to slay the French revolutionary infidel. His weapon was an angry pamphlet. [16]

Save for the concession that the Revolution in its initial state was "necessary" and "just," the pamphlet was a philippic. The auspicious beginning of the Revolution was succeeded by the despotism of the infernal Jacobins. Their taking the helm of power brought forth the Terror. Their conquests would cause not only the overturn of all governments, but also a general desolation like that of the sixth and seventh centuries, and the destruction of works of art. In France proper they had replaced Christianity with *"deism," "atheism"* and *"materialism."* The effects, Webster predicted, would be sorrowful. The nation would be set adrift on the sea of doubt and tossed between the hope of immortality and "the modern legislative assurance of everlasting sleep." In an effort to demolish old beliefs and superstitions, the Jacobins, he charged, had set up their own errors, pronounced by them as *reason* and *philosophy.* It was his firm opinion that the revolutionary legislation would bring forth these demoralizing tendencies: people released from the restraints of law and religion; allurement to licentiousness by the authorization of divorce; and a test whether atheism and materialism could make men happier than belief in God. His closing remarks were in the nature of a warning to Americans to beware of societies like the Jacobins.

Barlow rated the work of little or no value. To his publisher he wrote that Webster knew nothing about the Revolution. "He took his text, I suppose, from an English Ministerial paper, where a decree was made for the Convention that 'Death is an Eternal Sleep.' " Barlow regarded the pamphlet as an illustration of the way Europeans had been "perpetually imposed upon with respect to the affairs of France." Nor was it strange, he added, "that the people of America should share in this imposition as long as you find grave historians who will sit down in their closets in New York, and give them the French Revolution from the mouths of their enemies." [17]

Webster's account of the Revolution was just what leading Federalists had been looking for. "It is precisely the thing which I have long wished to be published," wrote Oliver Wolcott in acknowledging the receipt of a complimentary copy, "and will eminently serve to fix public opinion on national principles, and to tranquilize those passions which have threatened the peace of this country."[18]

To our knowledge, no one then in America, save President Ezra Stiles of Yale, was equipped to write a refutation. He was learned and one of the best informed Americans on the Revolution. But declining health and preoccupation with other matters prevented him from entering the controversy.

A word is appropriate about Stiles' views on the French Revolution.

He wrote to Barlow on March 20, 1793, to congratulate him on "the celebrity which your poetical and political writings have justly merited and acquired to you." He went on to praise the National Convention, "one of the most important and illustrious Assemblies that ever sat on this terraqueous globe: an Assembly charged with the highest Betrustments and coming up from the people with the express power and authority for accomplishing three great works, *The Formation of a Constitution*, the taking into their hands the *public Administration and National Government* in the interim and sitting as a *Judiciary Tribunal* on the life of the king." [19]

He stood up for the Terror and the Jacobins and, in this state of mind, wrote a defense of tyrannicide. His biographer is of the opinion that "it was the finest piece of writing he had done." It affirmed the right of the people to judge their rulers. Relieved of the royal yoke, they could well set government on such simple principles "as would be intelligible to the plainest rustic." [20] He applauded French military successes, for they would hasten the advent of "the mild and just Government of Liberty and Laws and the Rights of Man." [21] Stiles' death in April 1795 silenced one of the best defenders of the French Revolution in the United States.

Webster was surpassed in venom by the British immigrant, William Cobbett, known to Americans as Peter Porcupine. He loathed the Irish and scorned Americans. He was brassy, scurrilous and wrong-headed. Jeremy Bentham once epitomized him as an "odious mixture of egoism, malignity, insincerity and mendacity." [22] Democrats, in his opinion, were the same as Jacobins, as the title of his tirade against them informs us. [23] He berated them for arousing enmity to the existing government by the sanguinary spirit they had injected in the republican societies. He defined them as groups of needy, discontented, indolent men, foreigners for the most part, primarily motivated by the object of inciting the people to imitate the French. Without a shred of evidence to rest on, he ascribed the Whiskey Insurrection to the "democratic fuel, paid for with French gold." [24] Then followed the moth-eaten cliché that democrats were atheists or deists.

Cobbett's *History* had everything but originality. The torrent of abuse and the famine of facts showed that he had merely joined the anti-French chorus. It must have lifted his British pride to hear Federalists deplore America's separation from the British Empire. By her independence, he said, America had exchanged a settled government for mobocratic, lawless freedoms. The American Revolution was, therefore, a great blunder.

Republican democrats fell upon the weaknesses of the Federalist case. Remarked the *Independent Chronicle*:

"The enemies of the American and French Revolutions have artfully attempted to confound the means with the ends: and to impose on the public understanding by representing those measures which the necessities of a revolutionary system demanded as the indispensable consequences of a free republic." Paper money, for example, an unavoidable feature of the Revolution, was made out to be a kind of permanent currency produced by revolution. Similarly, continued the *Chronicle*, the antagonists of both Revolutions dwelt on the sufferings they had caused, without crediting them with any benefits. They applied the same method in judging Robespierre, said the *Chronicle*. They forever talked of his tyranny, but they forgot to say that the American government had been indebted to him for the recall of Gênet.

To condemn revolution in general, answered the republican sheet, was unrealistic. A revolution was, of course, a tempest with ruinous results. But it also purified the atmosphere. Asked the *Chronicle*, "shall we condemn the French, then, because the rich soil of the Revolution has produced weeds as well as flowers? Shall we go in mourning, in imitation of certain concealed Royalists, for the death of Louis XVI, because there might have been some irregularity on his trial? And yet, never was there an individual who had so fair a trial." [25]

The errors of the Revolution, said its vindicators, stemmed more from the execution of its laws than from their intention. Yet they were necessary, brought about by the march of events. The Revolution, wrote another commentator, had probably been premature. But this was no reason for attributing to it the crimes and cruelties of revolutionaries. Like Sampson Perry, he traced their source to the combined powers. French cruelties were acts of vengeance or means of defense against ruthless foes. [26]

The furious debate emitted sparks which ignited minds. Actually a better understanding of the significance of the French Revolution percolated among Americans. Their great number, however, it is safe to say, were taught by a hostile press and by an equally hostile clergy to fear and hate it both. The consequence was a misshapen and terrifying tale in which hideous men had the star roles.

Barlow planned a documented account of the Revolution to correct the story. He had already conveyed the purpose to Oliver Wolcott in a letter from Hamburg on November 6, 1794. The Revolution was "an event of such an extraordinary nature," he explained, "as scarcely to stand a chance of being treated impartially by its friends or enemies. Though I cannot call myself an indifferent spectator, I might, perhaps, be able to trace the causes of things with more coolness than some others who have attempted it or will attempt it." [27]

3

In preparation for the history, Barlow assembled a small library, containing historical works, writings and memoirs by participants in the

Revolution and files of periodicals. A great many of the prints were anti-Robespierreist, exemplified by such titles as *Portrait de Robespierre, Les crimes de Joseph Le Bon,* Babeuf's *Système de dépopulation* and Fréron's *L'Orateur du peuple.* This violently anti-Jacobin paper was offset by the liberal *Journal des hommes libres.* [28]

His object was to write a balanced or nearly balanced story of the most controversial subject of the time. Its nature is best shown in his introductory notes and outline of twelve chapters. [29] They were probably written in September 1797, upon returning from the mission to Algiers. How a revolution is brought about was a question that long occupied him. He held with eighteenth-century writers that it was difficult in a far spreading monarchy. A revolution was achieved either by a general insurrection, "which is almost impossible," or it was set in motion by a meeting of the national representation, which the king might prevent. Barlow was thinking of France and America. In France the Estates General was summoned. In America the general insurrection of 1775 was preceded by the meeting of the first Continental Congress. With respect to France, he continued, the Revolution, even at the outset, was the outcome of an extraordinary coincidence of events that no one could have foreseen. Nor could any one know beforehand the direction it would take, although men of Condorcet's stamp had forecast that once the Estates General convened, things would not stop short of a republic.

Another question that troubled Barlow was the kind of government that was best adapted to the changed situation. Here, we are confronted with a problem that caused much discussion in his day. In keeping with the Greek tradition, *philosophes* and political theorists believed that a republic was better suited to a small state, and monarchy in its absolute form, to a large one. A limited monarchy, said Barlow, either went to pieces or degenerated into despotism. Above this generalization, however, loomed the striking case of the English monarchy. Why hadn't it turned despotic or fallen apart? The answer, said Barlow, lay in the nation's insularity. Its best defense was a navy, and that could neither be marched into the country nor quartered on the people. Had England's means of defense been a standing army, its constitution would have been destroyed long ago.

His speculation on limited monarchy was but an intervening feature in his reflections on the preliminaries of the Revolution. Pertinent to the matter was the Estates General, a perplexing subject for one raised in the American tradition. French kings had sometimes had recourse to that body, Barlow discovered, but it was "unknown to the monarchical constitution." The history of the Estates General seems to have intrigued him. His research turned up the exciting fact that its meeting at Pontoise in 1561 had set a revolutionary precedent by proposing the liquidation of the state's debt with the properties of the Church.

The above considerations were meant to be prefatory to his introduction. Here he intended to draw in heavy lines the political character of Europe, with its feudal structure, and the "progress of Society," subsequent to the age of Charles V. The purpose was to pick up the story where William Robertson had left off in his lengthy introduction to *The History of the Reign of the Emperor Charles the Fifth*. Robertson had traced man's advance from the end of the Roman Empire to the beginning of the sixteenth century, that is, through nearly eleven centuries. The period Barlow expected to cover spread over fewer than three. Under the "progress of society" he hoped to embrace European expansion, the opening of trade routes and the founding of settlements in the West.

The rest of the narrative would center on France before May 1789. Here he aimed at showing how the Revolution grew out of a meeting of long developing circumstances, such as the monarchical constitution, the role of the Church, the general progress of knowledge and the expensive wars. Accessory to these four causative factors were four others: new views on political economy, that is, the principles of the Physiocrats and Adam Smith; the impact of the American Revolution; the deterioration of French finances; and finally, to cite him, the "various causes which conspire to dissolve the charm and destroy the idolatry for the court—royalty—the clergy—religion—nobility—and all privileges."

It may be observed that, while Barlow shared with eighteenth-century *philosophes* a belief in the inevitability of progress, he did not, like them, appeal to natural laws as the cause of human destiny. With Robertson and Gibbon as examples, he would hew closely to empirical inquiry, that is, interpret the historical process in terms of experience and evidence. It can be noted, therefore, that his projected work on the Revolution promised to be comparatively free of the passion and moral judgments of previous accounts.

It was not Barlow's intention to turn the introduction into a history of modern Europe. He merely intended to include what was "indispensably necessary to the right understanding of the French Revolution," and to establish that it was the outgrowth both of progressive and deteriorative tendencies. Primary among the latter were the privileges of the feudal orders. He defined a revolution as "a bankruptcy of privileges" and not "a national bankruptcy" as contemporaries were saying. For it was not the nation that had had a direct part in accumulating debts, but "a set of illegal guardians, who have plundered the heritage and loaded the estate with incumbrances not contracted for its benefits."

Barlow was prospecting for the roots of the Revolution. The longer he studied its currents and eddies the more he came to believe that its full history resembled in brief the history of man. "All his predominant passions," he said, "are there developed and acted out without disguise." Consequently "each day of the revolution becomes an age; and he that has seen it has lived a thousand years." But no one could pretend to have seen it all.

He divided the critics and historians of the Revolution into three principal classes. In the first were those who were wholly wrapped up in certain parts of the Revolution. They were usually active participants who justified every favorable event by their own actions and sought the reasons for everything disastrous in the deeds of their opponents. The second consisted of those who had neither been in France nor been acquainted with the persons and characters of the leaders. The example of Noah Webster might have passed through his mind. The third was made up of individuals who had lost or gained by the Revolution, and who saw everything "through the mist of their personal anxieties."

Was Barlow better equipped to judge the Revolution? He answered that he had something of the fitness and inadequacy of the above commentators. But he also had what they lacked. We shall let him speak for himself. "Being a decided friend to the great principles and general movements of the revolution, I have felt a strong interest in its success; but it was the interest of Philanthropy arising from a belief that it would enlighten the world and promote the happiness of mankind." He had still another qualification: "I have been generally near the center of action, perhaps sometimes too near, tho' I never have been an actor; but, being a foreigner, my acquaintance with the leaders, their connexions and motives has not been so particular as I could wish; but it would be difficult even for a native to have an acquaintance more particular and at the same time more general than mine has been; especially with several successive setts [sic] of the early leaders who began the business and directed the first and most characteristic movements."

Barlow's notes, it should be recalled, dated from 1797, when the Revolution was retrograding. Nevertheless, his faith in its principles remained sturdy. "I will not pretend to say," he confessed in one of his notes, "that the . . . revolution . . . will succeed in that direct and complete manner as could be wished; or whether this and other nations will be immediately benefitted by it. But could I know that it would not succeed, I should nevertheless retain the opinion that the object of amelioration is still attainable, and that revolutions in favor of representative democracy ought to be encouraged. It would still be my opinion that the fault was not in the inherent nature of the operation, but in the manner of conducting it. The mistakes that may have been committed ought to be clearly pointed out, the causes of the failure detailed in a most candid and critical examination; so that other nations, or a future generation here need not be unnecessarily deterred from a like attempt, whenever they shall feel themselves able to avoid the errors and seize the advantages held up to view in this example." In the absence of such confidence despair would darken the horizon.

This was as far as Barlow planned to go in the introduction. The story of the Revolution, outlined in twelve chapters, ran from the Assembly of Notables to the Treaty of Campo Formio, that is, from about

1787 to 1797. The first chapter focused on changes in public opinion wrought by the discussions at the meetings of the Notables, on the mode of electing the Estates General and the drafting of *cahiers*. Seven of the twelve chapters, namely, two to eight, comprised the body of the narrative, from the meeting of the Estates General to the overthrow of the Mountain. The four remaining ones dwelt on the French military triumphs and the several attempts to set up an enduring political system. One senses a mood of disenchantment in Barlow's repeated observation, "Small progress yet made in republican principles." With regard to the military campaigns, he emphasized what contemporary writers ignored, that is, the growing resistance and rising national sentiment of the conquered peoples.

Let us turn back to the earlier chapter notes. He duly stressed the king's intrigue and the Parisian popular movement that upset his plotting. The taking of the Bastille, in Barlow's view, was far bigger than a local event. It hastened the liquidation of feudalism, stimulated a reform movement and so intensified popular mistrust that the King and Assembly were compelled to move from Versailles to Paris.

Barlow was one of the first in his day to look upon the Revolution as a European upheaval. He reserved space for a consideration of Burke's book and its bearing on reaction. But he missed considering why the King's flight gave a conservative instead of a democratic turn to events. Nor can one find reference to the party strife in the Convention. He reflected the general opinion that Robespierre had been a murderer. Yet the outline is not free from the impression that he was motivated by selflessness.

Barlow's failure to write the book was a loss to the historiography of the French Revolution, for he had marked out lines of thought that reached into still unexplored areas. On the basis of his brief headings, it is plausible to say that his narrative would have surpassed in inquiry, perspective and interpretation most contemporaneous accounts on the subject.

He was abstracted by other interests. He was involved in business speculation; he was planning a new version of *The Vision of Columbus*; and he spent much effort to prevent the outbreak of hostilities between France and the United States. These preoccupations left the preliminary sketch of the history in the background, and there it remained.

Chapter X
Mission to Algiers

On January 13, 1796, Barlow wrote from Marseilles to his wife in Paris, asking her to buy Mme Roland's posthumous writings and a history of August 10, both of which he considered essential for his history of the Revolution.[1] Obviously the project was in his mind, even while he was on his way to negotiate treaties between the United States and the North African States.

1

America's relations with the Barbary powers dated from post-revolutionary years. Starting in 1785, their corsairs took American prizes and held the crews for ransom. Apart from its inhumanity, the piracy was very costly to American commerce. According to a report by Jefferson in 1791, about one-sixth of the country's exported wheat and flour had the best markets in the Mediterranean ports. From eighty to one hundred ships, manned by about twelve hundred seamen, were annually required to carry the cargoes. Consequently, the American government dispatched agents to the three North African states to establish amicable relations with them, especially with Algiers, the strongest and most aggressive.[2]

The government knew little either about Barbary affairs or about the Barbary rulers. Primary in its instructions to its envoys was that a peaceful settlement was preliminary to any agreement on the ransom of captives. Jefferson ruled out the purchase of peace with naval stores, for that would simply furnish the states the means of continuing their piracy.[3] In the course of ten years almost as many agents were appointed to treat with them. A few failed; a few others died before reaching their destination. By 1793 the burden of the negotiations fell on David Humphreys, minister to Portugal, who soon discovered that the way to an agreement was strewn with many obstacles.

The American government first toyed with the idea of using naval force. That course would have been hazardous without the cooperation of Great Britain, France and the Netherlands. But these nations, especially Great Britain, secretly sanctioned the piracy. The only other method was diplomacy.

Humphreys was given full charge of the mission to Algiers, with instructions that were more flexible than those hitherto given. [4] To make the assignment less difficult he was promised the appointment of a consul for the Barbary coast. Much of his information on what would be acceptable to the Dey of Algiers came to him from a sea dog, Captain Richard O'Brien, a Maine Yankee who had served as a privateer in the American Revolution. This seasoned sailor of many voyages, imprisoned in Algiers since 1785, was permitted by the Dey to serve as go-between in the negotiations.

Humphreys welcomed O'Brien's advice. Studying the Dey's conditions of peace, the captain calculated that the entire cost would be close to 2,500,000 Mexican dollars. The duration would be one hundred years. These terms should be rejected, he said, and then followed by a series of bids that would bring the total sum above 600,000 Mexican dollars for a peace lasting 60 years. Knowing the Dey as he did, he recommended the following course of action:

"If the Dey Gets in his usual Blustering Convulsions of Passion, and orders the Ambassador to be gone from his presence and depart, Obey these orders Instantaniously [sic], but remember that, from the fluctuateing [sic] and variable character of the Dey, the Ambassador should leave some person of Confidence empowered to Conclude with the Dey on the Terms you offered or proposed." [5]

Assuming that peace could be had during a century for 2,500,000 dollars, reasoned O'Brien, the price would still be cheap. For during that time, American Mediterranean commerce would profit immensely. But who would guarantee the peace for so long a period? The Algerines would say that the treaty had been signed by a dead Dey. Besides, he added, peace with Algiers might not be respected by Tripoli and Tunis. Also, enemies of the United States would bribe the Dey to tear up the treaty.

Toward the end of 1794 the Dey submitted his terms for a century-long peace. The price was more than two and a quarter million dollars, plus an annual tribute of naval stores. He pledged an advantageous treaty with Tunis and every commercial privilege equal to that of the most favored nation. He furthermore promised to comply with any reasonable request made by the American representative. The counterproposal fell far short of his demands.

Here we must interrupt the narrative to introduce another American captive, through whom the Dey communicated his terms. He was James Leander Cathcart, Irish by birth and American by adoption. Captured by the British during the American Revolution, he found a way to escape. But in 1785 he was made prisoner by the Algerines. During the long captivity his shrewdness served him well. He not only acquired wealth; he also rose to become the Dey's Chief Christian secretary. [6]

Cathcart described two tempestuous scenes when he was the target of the Dey's passionate explosions. Offended by the American proposals Cathcart had brought back, the robed corsair flew into a rage and thundered, "go out of my sight immediately, thou dog without a soul, and never presume to bring such trifling terms into me again under pain of my displeasure." Later, while waiting impatiently for the American payment to arrive, he roared and sprayed his secretary with profanity. [7]

In response to the Dey's figure, the American envoy Joseph Donaldson, offered only $543,000 for peace and ransom. The Algerine replied with contempt and ordered him to leave the country, if he had nothing further to submit. Pressed by his advisers, the American increased the sum by more than $40,000. A provisional agreement was reached at last on September 5, 1795, by which the United Stated pledged to pay $642,000 for peace and ransom and an annual tribute of $21,600 in naval stores.[8]

Humphreys had meanwhile gone to Paris to win French aid. Here he consulted with James Monroe, the new American minister, respected in France both for his integrity and his advocacy of amicable Franco-American relations. The United States could not have had a better representative in France at this time if the intention was to preserve the long-standing friendship of the two nations.

The evidence gives the impression that Humphreys had only a lukewarm interest in associating France with America's negotiations in Algiers. Consistent with Federalist policy, he preferred to have English rather than French help. But there was good ground for suspecting the English of double-dealing.

Monroe solicited French intervention as he had been asked to do. But he was embarrassed, he informed the Secretary of State, for the reason that the Jay Treaty had meanwhile been submitted to the senate for ratification. For French aid to have full effect, he wrote to the Secretary, "our agent should be clothed with a French passport, and if possible be a French citizen and even appear to be an agent of France. . . . By this mode it would seem as if France interfered as our friend, and chiefly from motives of humanity, in regard to our prisoners, whereby we should avoid inculcating any idea of wealth on our part." [9]

Two Americans abroad fitted Monroe's standards, namely, Paine and Barlow. The first was disqualified on two scores: He was recuperating from an imprisonment of more than ten months; and the shrill controversy his *Age of Reason* had raised in the United States would only further inflame party strife if he were selected. The second, Barlow, was still in Germany. For the time being, Benjamin Hichborn was asked to serve, but he declined. [10]

It is fairly possible that Barlow was urged to hasten his return to Paris, for the American position in Algiers was insecure. Someone, other than Donaldson, was needed there who could contain the irascible Dey, and Barlow was the best possible choice. He was experienced, sociable and could adjust to difficult conditions. By contrast Donaldson was ill-tempered, undiplomatic and stubborn. Moreover, he was sickly, gouty and uncouth in appearance. If we are to judge by the detailed instructions left with him, his superiors probably doubted his resourcefulness in treating with the capricious ruler of Algiers. Monroe and Humphreys must have concluded that since they could not replace him they could at least provide him with a colleague.

The two American ministers called for Barlow's speedy departure by the most direct route. But the uncertain climate brought about by the Jay Treaty caused several weeks to elapse before the French Foreign Office issued the important credentials. Then more weeks were consumed by the problem of getting the money for purchasing the customary presents for the Dey.

In the interim, news arrived that a provisional treaty had been signed. The question arose whether that put an end to Barlow's mission. And if it had no further purpose, what should be done with the presents? Cogent reasons, however, necessitated his going, reasons Monroe explained to the Secretary of State in the communiqué of October 4, 1795: "If any errors had been committed at Algiers, and which it was possible to rectify, we knew he would be able to do it; and we were also persuaded that, in other respects, a trip to that coast, whereby he would be enabled to gain an insight into the policy of those powers, could not otherwise than be of great advantage to the United States." Barlow was ready to act as consul for Algiers. And Monroe added "that no person can be found willing to accept the trust, in whom it can be so happily vested."

2

Apart from the primary purpose of the mission, Barlow had two other duties. He had promised Bishop Grégoire he would send information on captive slaves in North Africa. Also, in the interest of intelligence, he would gather information on political, military, economic and religious conditions in the Barbary countries. It can be said at the outset that he discharged both obligations. The facts he conveyed to the bishop told a depressing story. About eight hundred European captives were rotting and dying in prisons. They were helpless victims without the prospect of redemption by their respective governments. Fifty of the slaves were French. The rest were Spanish, Portuguese and Italians. [11]

Among Barlow's manuscripts [12] are two complete notebooks of observations on the North African coast. Here are recorded data on coinage, the religious habits of Mohammedans, their annual feasts, big events, great men and principal rulers in Arabian history; he recorded information on the languages of Algiers and Tunis. The Algerian language was a jargon, with corrupt Spanish as a base; the Tunisian language was essentially Frankish though based on Italian. In Algiers

Barlow discovered few writers and not a single printing press. The notebooks contain information on manners, ways of living and the low status of women, figures on the number of Jews and Christians, brief accounts of the privileged role of the Turkish soldiers and many notations on the geography of the region. Algeria and Tunis together, he said, formed "one of the richest little portions of the earth that has ever been known, if we regard the fertility of the soil, or the variety and value of its productions."

In a report to the Secretary of State after his first fortnight in Algiers, Barlow gave a compact survey of the vassal status of the Regencies and the Dey. The country was held in subjection to Turkey by a handful of strangers, essentially Turkish adventurers who despised and plundered the natives. The Dey and the high military officers who formed the Divan acted in concert to commit piracy. He was subject to no other check, said Barlow, "than what arises from the Necessity he is under of distributing foreign presents, and sometimes his own Money, among the principal Officers, to secure himself from Assassination and Mutinies." [13]

Missing in Barlow's notes is any reference to the European-Barbary relations. For relevant to their understanding is the point, recently developed by an American scholar, [14] that the European powers were for centuries pursuing a predatory policy with regard to the North African States, pillaging their coasts, ravaging their cities and enslaving their people. It can be added that one of the major maritime powers in the Mediterranean and one of the most plunderous was the Order of Malta, a military arm of the Catholic Church, propagating the faith by means of piracy and trade in Moslem slaves.

3

Barlow left Paris toward the end of December 1795, bearing the costly presents for the Dey that Monroe had helped him select. He was also armed with considerable knowledge of Algiers, soon supplemented with what he learned from a group of Algerines he met in Marseilles. Humphreys had instructed him to go to Alicante, the southeastern Spanish seaport, and there to wait for the arrival of the specie Donaldson had pledged to the Dey in the provisional treaty. Captain O'Brien had sailed to England to get it, but he was told by the bankers, the Baring Bros., that the United States bonds they held could not be converted into cash without lowering their value. O'Brien returned to Lisbon empty-handed.

Meanwhile the American position in Algiers was growing increasingly precarious. The Dey, who had been promised the money by November 1795, was becoming impatient. Barlow described him as "a man of a most ungovernable temper, passionate, changeable and unjust, to such a degree that there is no calculating his policy from one moment to another." [15] Thoroughly unacquainted with the American treaty ratification procedure or with the baffling problem of obtaining the required sum, the Dey wrote to Humphreys on January 4, 1796, expressing his irritation at the incompletion of the arrangements and doubting the authenticity of Donaldson's credentials. He asked not only for their confirmation but also for the reason of the delay in the payment. More than six weeks elapsed before Humphreys replied. He verified the credentials, explained the slowness of ratifying treaties in the United States and gave notice that it might take considerable time before the money would arrive, since it was unobtainable in the country he had counted on. He notified the Dey that in view of Donaldson's illness all the power of the agency had been delegated to Joel Barlow. [16]

The answer only provoked the Dey. O'Brien wrote from London to the Secretary of State that he was "very apprehensive of fatal consequences"—the Dey would tear up the treaty. To soften him Cathcart suggested that Donaldson give him a present. But the agent, a rigid adherent to instructions, said he had no authority to do so. Summoned by the Dey for questioning, Cathcart tried to clarify matters. The Dey disbelieved everything and charged that the American representatives in Algiers were trifling with him. He warned Donaldson that unless the affair was settled within one month after the arrival of the packet he would annul everything that had been done, treat Americans as a set of impostors, send all their captives back to hard labor, order him out of the country and refuse all further negotiation. Cathcart pleaded for more time and begged high officials to intervene. This had an effect. The Dey's anger subsided like a hurricane that has lost its force. He told Cathcart that if Humphreys had sent but one-half or even one-third of the required sum, he would have been persuaded of America's sincerity to fulfill its engagement. But five months had gone by without having received the least assurance that the treaty would be observed. [17]

Barlow waited in Alicante for the signal to speed to Algiers. Instead he learned that things were going from bad to worse. "Our affair is daily becoming more critical and the outcome less certain," he wrote to Ruth on February 22, 1796. "This entire difficulty would have been averted if they had taken my advice last September and transferred the credit from London to places within easier reach." [18] Again to Ruth, five days later, he reported that the state of the business was much worse than it had been before its start.

He decided to sail to Algiers, irrespective of orders. The interest of the United States, he wrote to Humphreys, necessitated the conclusion of the business "at almost any rate. I shall not hesitate to make use of all the means in my power to keep the treaty in suspense till we are furnished with the funds to fulfill it." A note of reproach was sounded in Barlow's communiqué. It seemed to him that Humphreys had been dilatory, even negligent, in persuading Portugal "to act in concert with us, or at least not to counteract us again in this troublesome business." [19] And two months later he confided to Ruth: "The most conspicuous talent that I can discover in him is that of keeping a secret, keeping it from those whose knowledge of it is absolutely necessary to his own success. . . . All would have been finished before now and sixty thousand dollars saved to the United States if we had had a good Banker's clerk at a certain place for a minister." [20]

Arriving in Algiers on March 5, Barlow found the Dey intractable. Loudly he threatened to send him and Donaldson out of the country, to end at once the negotiations and to declare war on the United States. Nearly three weeks of uncertainty followed, during which the Dey waited for the arrival of the money.

Barlow went sightseeing. Algiers, he described to Ruth, rests on the slope of a mountain dominating the port. About one hundred thousand people lived in small houses close together on narrow, dark alleys that ran and bent in all directions. A newcomer, without losing himself in this labyrinth, would need a guide, preferably a Turk, to avoid being insulted or crushed by the mass of Moors. The houses had no window panes and were without furniture or utensils. The only distinguished buildings were the numerous mosques and churches.

He wrote at some length of the degradation of Mohammedan women. They could not appear in public or be seen by any man except the husband. These were sacrosanct rules and their violators were severely punished.

The saving features of the city were the climate, the scenic beauty and the fruit. Otherwise it was a "sad abode and pirates' nest," a "sewer of all vices that the imagination can bring forth or monsters practice." [21]

The uneasy period grew more disquieting. Still without the money, the Dey informed the American agents on April 2 that they would be turned out within eight days. After that, war would be declared and prizes taken after thirty days. [22] A dark curtain fell on Barlow's hopes. If the treaty failed, the one hundred captives would continue in their misery and the ransom cost would undoubtedly rise sharply. If the Dey declared war, more American captives would have to be redeemed at the same high price. It was a predicament that afforded no escape.

Three days later he felt reassured. He had established friendly relations with a Jewish broker in Algiers, Micaiah Cohen Baccri, who, to cite Barlow, had "more influence with the Dey than all the regency put together." The Americans and the broker watched for an auspicious moment. The hauling of Danish prizes into port seemed to put the Dey in a good humor. This was the time Baccri chose to engage him in conversation on cruisers and prizes and to surprise him with an offer by the Americans. The United States would build a fast ship of twenty-four guns and present it to his daughter provided he waited six months longer for the money. The Dey answered that he would see the agents on the matter. He bargained, demanded a cruiser of thirty-six guns and in return promised to let everything remain as it was for three months. The Americans readily assented.

It was a tour de force of which Barlow had reason to be proud. He had gained a respite of three months and saved the treaty from being scrapped. Pleased with the maneuver, he wrote to Humphreys:

"We consider the business as now settled on this footing, and it is the best ground that we could possibly place it upon. You still have it in your power to say peace or no peace; you have an alternative. In the other case war was inevitable, and there would have been no hope of peace during the reign of this Dey."

The entire arrangement, he calculated, would cost the United States over fifty thousand dollars, counting the cruiser and the broker's fee. This was of course an unforeseen expense for which he expected to be blamed, but one had to be on the spot, he said, to have a complete understanding of the circumstances. Besides, the price of peace was cheap, if everything were taken into account.

He reverted to the funds. He believed their transfer to Algiers could be facilitated through Leghorn, and he notified Humphreys that Donaldson was sailing there "to await your orders on this head." Knowing the failings of his superior, Barlow added: "There is no time to be lost. You will please to instruct him as soon as possible and let our measures from this time forward be effectual." [23] It seemed as if Barlow and not Humphreys was in charge of the Algerian business.

The temporary settlement with the Dey lifted the spirits of the American captives. They were elated by Barlow's presence. His warm personality softened hard-faced officers and won their favor. Cathcart reported to Humphreys a day after the arrangement: "He is a Gentleman I much esteem and who I make no doubt will in a great measure contribute to the happy completion of our affairs in this Infernal Regency." And again to Humphreys on April 15:

"The agreeable contrast between Mr. Barlow and Mr. Donaldson makes us pass our time with as much pleasure as people in our disagreeable situation is susceptible of. Mr. Donaldson took the greatest pains to make himself disagreeable to every person. Mr. Barlow is respected by every one that has the honour of his acquaintance." [24]

A plague broke out in May. Informed that Humphreys had sent Donaldson a credit in Leghorn and obtained another in Lisbon, Barlow borrowed on them from the house of Baccri a sum sufficient to free the slaves. The same brokers, he reported to the Secretary of State, had likewise "become answerable to the Dey and Regency for the remainder of the money we owe here for the price of the peace. Without this the Dey would not agree to the Redemption." On the face of it the ransom money seemed excessive. But there was the consolation, Barlow went on to say, "That it is not expended on worthless and disorderly persons, as is the case with some other nations who are driven, like us, to this humiliation to the Barbary States." He hoped that the liberated, suffering men would receive consideration and encouragement in their own country. A number were helpless; others were disabled or nearly so. He drew a pitiful picture: "Several of them are probably rendered incapable of gaining their living. One is in a state of total blindness; another is reduced nearly to the same condition; two or three carry the marks of unmerciful treatment, in ruptures produced by hard labour." [25]

The liberation of the captives was a diplomatic feat. It took tried patience, resolute courage and steady caution, so much so that the Danish consul was heard saying: "The American agent is not a man, but an angel. God has sent [him] here to save the interests of his country." Barlow gave his wife some idea of the moving scenes as the freed men were leaving the pestilent city. They showered him with blessings; tears rolling down their cheeks bespoke their gratitude. Were it not for him, they said, they would all have perished in slavery. [26] They were stating a fact, though they did not know the full story. Nor did they know that he had succeeded without a penny from his own government and without orders from Lisbon. Still more, he had stayed at his post at the risk of his own life.

It was a measure of the man. In the event that he fell a victim of the plague, he sent Ruth what he thought might be his final words. They were at once a last testament and a confession of his duty to humanity. What were Barlow's reasons for remaining in the city during the pestilence? Many prisoners, he said, "have wives at home as well as I; from whom they have been much longer separated and under more affecting circumstances, having been held in a merciless and disappointing slavery. If their wives love them as mine does me, . . . ask these lately disconsolate and now joyful families whether I have done too much." [27]

Captured in these lines were the histories of men who had come to a dead end, and could only look to a lingering death that would rob hard labor and disease of their ravages. To have seen them at close range was a perturbing, unforgettable grief. It lifted Barlow out of himself, blacked out his own happiness and everything he had striven for. He was determined to get the captives out of their Gehenna even at the cost of his own life. Fortunately he came out of the ordeal unscathed, probably due to his robust health and his "pretty extensive and dear-bought knowledge of mankind," as he wrote to Ruth.

Lacking the means of sending the liberated Americans home by a direct route, Barlow ordered their passage to Leghorn, but they were landed instead in Marseilles. The problem of getting them to their final destination raised several difficulties. The most embarrassing was the case of Samuel Gravis of Boston, captain of the schooner Eliza. He was unscrupulous in a buccaneer's way. In total disregard of Barlow's orders, he loaded his vessel in Sicily with a cargo bound for England and behaved like a freebooter. One passenger, a Jew from Algiers, was not only robbed of his belongings; he was also brutalized and put ashore only with the clothes he wore. This act of piracy nearly ruffled relations between Algeria and the United States. [28]

Another complication arose after the ransomed Americans had been put in quarantine in Marseilles. The ship, owned by the firm of Baccri, sailed away under the American flag only to be captured by the British on the ground that it had been taken as a prize by the Algerines. Its estimated value of forty thousand dollars was billed to Barlow and listed as an American debt. [29] A Swedish vessel finally had to be chartered to bring the Americans home.

4

The humanitarian aspect of Barlow's mission was brought to a successful conclusion. But the treaty engagements still had to be fulfilled. He received two pieces of good news from Humphreys—that the long awaited money was on its way and that the State Department appreciated his diplomatic talent and wanted him to continue at his post until all objectives were accomplished. [30] During this stay, he learned the native tongue, cultivated the friendship of influential dignitaries, became a favorite of other consuls to the point where they referred to him as "the father of all consuls" and kept his eyes open for a good investment. He had, also, taken on the functions of America's consular service.

All this time he was playing a clever game with the Dey. The ruler, he had discovered, succumbed to ingratiating ways. The result was that the Dey developed a sentimental attachment for him and protected him against enemies. Nevertheless, Barlow was circumspect.

The game took a new turn when Barlow announced that the vessel Sophia with $200,000 on board, which Captain O'Brien was taking to Algiers, had been captured by Tripolitan corsairs. To the Dey this was a gross insult. The Sophia was sailing under his special passport, which, in Humphrey's words to the State Department, "was looked upon as being absolutely sacred with all the Barbary Powers." [31] Filled with resentment, the Dey ordered the release of the vessel and its property. Barlow thought the time propitious to say that if the other Barbary States continued to violate his passport, the United States would find it impossible to send him presents and naval stores. The Tripolitans obeyed his order and the Sophia sailed into the port of Algiers on October 1.

Thereafter, the Dey and Barlow were on the best of terms. When Barlow announced that the money had arrived, the Algerine pirate gushed apologies for his harsh treatment of the American, for the worry and suffering he had caused him. He had felt down deep in his heart, he said, that Barlow was telling the truth. He pledged friendship for the United States as long as he lived, even though the British were tirelessly contriving to undo it. He then asked Barlow if he had any favors to request.

It was the moment Barlow had been waiting for. He related how America's relations with Tunis and Tripoli had been steadily deteriorating. The first power demanded a high price for peace, but after seizing an American vessel it refused to talk any terms at all. Barlow then turned to the Bey of Tripoli, who had captured two American ships, one of them in defiance of the Dey's passport. The money it had carried for the Dey had been detained for a long time. The Bey's intent of affront was further evinced by his keeping in service Peter Lyle, an English captain who had refused to take notice of the highest Barbary sovereign. Barlow rose to the peak of blandishment. He spoke of the Dey as the "father of justice" who alone could force the heads of Tunis and Tripoli to act reasonably and thereby "save the honor of Barbary."

Having showered the tyrant of Algiers with fulsome flattery, he asked for two favors. He desired two letters, one to go to the Bey of Tunis ordering him immediately to make peace with America at his original price of 50,000 piastres for the ship and crew he had been holding; the other, to the Bey of Tripoli, containing these terms: to receive 40,000 piastres for peace and prisoners, to beg pardon for the insult to the Dey and to send the head of the captain for having disavowed his power and name. The American was asking for too little, answered the Dey. He would not only write the letters; he would also lend Barlow the 90,000 piastres for the two treaties. Barlow had but to get ready a vessel under O'Brien's command. The Dey had not the slightest doubt that the proposed terms would be accepted. He was particularly severe with the Bey of Tripoli. Unless he sent back by the same vessel a signed treaty and the chained captain that he, the Dey, might have the pleasure of decapitating him, he would send 60,000 men to behead the Bey. To cap it all, he told Barlow that the American government could repay the loan when it pleased. [32]

Barlow hoped that the entire business would be settled within the next month. But affairs did not run as smoothly as he had expected. Tripoli assented to the terms brought by O'Brien. The Bey of Tunis, however, was defiant. The sum offered, he said to O'Brien, was but a third of what he had looked for. Barlow promptly informed the Dey of the Bey's obstinacy, and played on the pirate's sentiments as on a keyboard. He stressed the Dey's *amour-propre*, his sense of honor and his friendship. This had its effect. The Dey promised to have the Bey's head and sent an army into Tunis. "You may be assured," Barlow reported to Humphreys on January 12, 1797, "that the present war which the Dey of Algiers has undertaken against Tunis is wholly on account of our Treaty. He will succeed, and our peace with Tunis as well as with Tripoli will be established on the most solid foundations." [33]

Foreign representatives in Algiers were astonished by a friendship that could impel the Dey to invade Tunis. But they knew their American colleague. "Today," he wrote to Ruth on November 20, 1796, "he would give me his beard, hair by hair, were I to ask for it." [34]

Barlow's negotiations for settlements would have run a smoother course had it not been for impediments raised by English, Spanish and French agents. The underlying reason was their hostility to American competition in the Mediterranean. The French of course had still another cause, namely, the Jay Treaty. Their consul, Jean Bon St. André, a former Robespierrist, enjoyed telling Barlow that the treaty with England was likely to bring about a war between America and France. He challenged the important principle of the flag covering the cargo, on which were founded the treaties with the Barbary powers. Barlow and other consuls took the matter to the Dey and finally persuaded him to shut the port against prizes brought in by French privateers. [35]

Barlow's responsibilities seemed to grow with the lengthening of his stay in Algiers. Yet he received little encouragement from his superior. Humphreys was neglectful. The Secretary of State, who did not write for eight months, finally acknowledged: "In a country where principles are unknown, or what is equal, have not the smallest influence, it has been fortunate for the United States that their interests were at so critical a period in the hands of a citizen who had intelligence to discern and confidence to seize the fittest moments to secure them." [36]

Much as Barlow yearned to return to France, he waited obstinately until Tripoli and Tunis signed the respective treaties. The Bey of Tripoli accepted the terms presented to him on November 4. The arrangement with the Bey of Tunis took longer to conclude and required the use of force.

In the interval Barlow amused himself; he was invited to a hunting party and spent three days pursuing wild boars. When urgent problems did not possess him, his mind turned to business. He became part owner of two vessels, bought and sold cargoes and realized substantial profits. Finally, when he was confident that the treaty with Tunis would be accomplished, he boarded one of his own vessels on July 17, 1797, and departed with the good will of his consular colleagues and with presents from the Dey to himself and Ruth.

In quarantine in Marseilles, he used the enforced leisure to convey to the State Department his advice on policy with respect to the Barbary States. He was apprehensive of Tripoli's growing power fearing that it might defy the Dey of Algiers and renounce the treaty with the United States. He warned against a possible combination of states to exclude Americans from the Mediterranean. And finally, he strongly recommended the appointment of talented Americans as consuls general in the Barbary States, at salaries nearly equal to those of plenipotentiaries in Europe. [37] To Ruth he wrote that to give himself a ferocious look in Barbary style, he had grown a long, dark mustache. But he came back clean shaven in September 1797.

There is an epilogue to the story of Barlow's mission. After he departed the amicable relations between Algiers and the United States continued for some time. The vessel the Dey had been promised was built at Portsmouth at a higher cost than had been estimated, particularly the masts Donaldson had agreed to include in the tribute, but not nearly as high as the naval stores. The original agreement had called for a frigate of thirty-six guns, nine-pounders on the main deck. But while the vessel was under construction, the Dey changed his mind and desired twelve-pounders, which the vessel was incapable of carrying. It was at last completed according to the architect's original design. Named the "Crescent," it was launched in July 1797. An expert seaman believed it was as "complete a piece of workmanship as he ever saw." [38]

A token of the Dey's good will to the United States was expressed by his desire to have Americans build him two cruisers at his expense. The request was granted at the recommendation of the President.

A word more about Cathcart and O'Brien. Cathcart served as American consul in Tripoli and other points in the Mediterranean. O'Brien, probably on Barlow's recommendation, was named Consul General of the Barbary States. He sailed to his post aboard the "Crescent."

Chapter XI

The Conquests of Science

1

Returning to Paris in 1797, Barlow expected to give full time to his literary interests. He had been reading extensively despite business and diplomatic interruptions. In his large library were well represented the writings of the *philosophes*, the economists and natural scientists. Here were Lucretius and Francis Bacon and the folio volumes of Pierre Bayle, Diderot's *Encyclopédie* and the *Encyclopédie méthodique,* published by Charles Joseph Panckoucke. Here, too, were histories by ancients and moderns, books on mythology and metaphysics and critiques of religion. The eighteenth century bulked large with the works of Voltaire, Rousseau, Helvetius and Holbach.

Of particular interest to Barlow was Constantin Volney's *Ruins, or Meditation on the Revolutions of Empires* which he and Jefferson had translated. A probable reason was that it contained in essence their own views on religion and historical progress. Published in 1791, it summed up the main points of the French Enlightenment on religion, politics and philosophy of history. Its line of reasoning was as follows: Religious notions which pretended to any other origin than sensation and experience were erroneous; man was the artisan of his own destiny; he was governed by natural laws inherent in his nature, but ignorance and the love of accumulation caused him to violate them; man armed against man; society was made up "of masters and slaves," which permitted ambitious heads of state to establish despotism; the better to forge its chains they allied with the clergy; thus arose misanthropic systems of religion, superstition, fanaticism and barbarous wars; however, despotism was doomed for progress could not be stemmed; the great majority of the useful members of society would finally triumph over the do-nothing minority and establish an order founded on the principles of liberty and equality.

A comparison of Volney's *Ruins* with Holbach's *System of Nature* discloses similarities which disposed a literary historian to conclude that

Volney "was Holbach's disciple."[1] Both rested their argument on the pain-pleasure theory and the sensational psychology; both rejected supernaturalism and asserted that reason and experience were the best criteria of human conduct. It was not surprising that Volney's book was denounced as "the textbook of infidelity."

Two other books, attrtibuted to Holbach, left their mark on Volney, on *Christianity Unmasked* and *Antiquity Unveiled*. They were published as the posthumous works of Nicolas Boulanger.[2] Barlow, too, was so impressed by them that he recommended their translation to his New York publisher.[3]

The above titles exemplified the current of materialist philosophy that had been gathering force since the first half of the eighteenth century. Despite the organized censorship and the vigilance of Jesuits and Jansenists, materialist teachings, diffused clandestinely and openly, were eroding the fundamental dogmas of the Church, spreading unbelief and rendering insecure the strongest prop of the French establishment. The number of materialist *philosophes* was legion. Here, we need only name Julien Offray de La Mettrie, César-Chesneau Du Marsais, Jean-Baptiste de Mirabaud, Nicholas Fréret, Jean Levesque de Burigny and the Holbach set, who in their respective ways wore down the basic tenets of revealed faith and undermined the authority of the Bible. Biblical criticism rose to a fine art.

The *Encyclopédie*, edited by Diderot and d'Alembert, was of supreme value in the antireligious movement. Begun in 1751, it was twice suppressed only to reappear secretly. It had 150 contributors and more than 4,000 subscribers. And it had its gods, too, Francis Bacon, Locke, Huygens and Newton. *The Encyclopédie* was important, to quote a student of the epoch, "not because it was necessarily read by a large public, but because it was the epitome of the age. It synthesized the scientific knowledge of the period. . . . It formulated a number of new hypotheses to account for facts, suggested new techniques, and above all, because of this basic activity, it was an instrument of war against all the prejudices of the Ancien Regime."[4] The common denominator of its principal contributors was Anti-Christianity.[5]

2

Barlow was well acquainted with Diderot's monumental work, but we do not know the topics that preoccupied him. His philosophical propensity might have drawn his attention to such articles as "theism", "atheists" and "atheism," the last two by the liberal Abbé Yvon, whom d'Alembert referred to as "a foe of superstition." The article, "atheists", was meant as a refutation of Bayle's argument that atheists could act virtuously and defend society as well as theists, if not better, because they were not restrained by religion. Yvon's method turned out to be a double-edged blade, for he cited at length Bayle's reasoning which in several instances was more cogent than the answers. In his second article Yvon summarized the principal themes of Spinoza's *Ethics* and justified theism, not for reasons of faith, but on political grounds, otherwise society could not exist. The same justification was to be found in the article, "Theism," so that belief in God was vindicated on practical grounds. The argument was little calculated to win the full sanction of the pious.

To Barlow, with his many intellectual interests, the *Encyclopédie* was virgin terrain. Nowhere else, save in this collaborative enterprise, could he find assembled so many seminal ideas from antiquity to his own day.

He also went through the massive work of Charles François Dupuis, *Origine de tous les cultes ou Religion universelle*, published in 1795. Here the author endeavored to prove with a store of erudition what Volney had already done in popular form. To get a reading audience, an abridged edition was put out three years later. It was an armory of fact and argument to foes of organized religion; and it defended "Republican virtue" against resurgent clericalism during the Thermidorian period. To that extent it was a political as well as a philosophical work.

Dupuis set forth a pantheistic view of the universe. God, he said, was in nature and its motive force, manifesting Himself to man "through the veil of the matter which he animates and which forms the immensity of the Deity." It included within itself everything, was the work of Nature and itself was Nature.[6] Such an understanding of the Supreme Being ruled out Revelation and priesthood. He went so far as to doubt the historical existence of Christ.

Dupuis likened organized religion to an epidemic. He ventured to say that "A philosophic history of the various kinds of worship and religious ceremonies and of the reign of the priests in the different societies, would offer the most frightful picture to man of his misfortunes and of his delirium."[7] Not the Deity ordered the introduction of worship, he asserted, but man himself, either through fear or desire.[8] Mediators arose who found a lucrative trade in interpreting the secrets of the Deity and in promising help with their incantations. Men were never more pious than when they were poor and unhappy. "Want far more than gratitude erected temples to the Gods," Dupuis declared. "What a contradiction to admit a God, who sees and knows everything, and who notwithstanding wants to be notified and enlightened by Man about his necessities!"[9]

There remained the age-old argument that religion was indispensable to hold the people in subjection. His answer was that it was more important to instruct than to deceive them.[10]

The originality of Dupuis was in his method. He retained the idea of a divinity, but he supported it with the reasoning of the materialists. Though he sanctioned their theory of knowledge, he did not fall in with their conclusions. In the estimation of Gilbert Chinard, he was a precursor in the study of the history of religion and comparative mythology.[11]

His theism resembled deism in several respects. It dispensed with organized religion and mysteries; and it recognized the Supreme Being in the order of the universe and in nature. The same as deism it opened a path to incredulity.

Barlow might have noticed in Dupuis lines of thought he had come upon in Pierre Bayle. Gibbon described him as "A calm and lofty spectator of the religious tempest," and quoted him as saying: "I am most truly a Protestant; for I protest indifferently against all systems and all sects."[12] A nineteenth century admirer likened Bayle's name to a "Tocsin of deathless power."[13] And a modern historian referred to his *Dictionnaire historique et critique* as "a vast reservoir of corrosive erudition."[14] As much can be said of his *Oeuvres diverses*.

Bayle set high criteria for the writing of history. "It requires a great judgment," he said. "a noble, clear and considered style, a good conscience, a perfect probity, many excellent materials, and the art of placing them in good order; and above all things the power of resisting the instinct of a religious zeal which prompts one to cry down what he thinks to be false, and to adorn and embellish what he thinks to be true." A historian, he continued, "can never stand too much upon his guard; and it is almost impossible for him to be altogether free from prejudices."[15]

Bayle traced the origin of divination and its practice from paganism to Christianity. The union of political and religious authority under the Roman Empire grew closer with the rising power of the Church. He then brought into focus the incompatibility between Christian practice and Christ's teachings. No nations were more warlike than those professing Christianity, he held, and none more intolerant of other faiths. The early Christians were persecuted not for their principles but for their cherished ill will to paganism.[16]

Experience showed, he went on, that the same springs of action—personal interest, selfishness or desire for reputation—impelled Christians as well as idolaters and atheists. As much dissolute or virtuous living existed among believers as among nonbelievers. It was false, he declared, that atheists were given to far greater vices than Christians. Of course, since a society of atheists never existed it was impossible to know its type of ethics. But a comparison of pagans and atheists of antiquity proved the greater cruelty of the first. He pointed out that religion did not restrain men from committing crimes. A society of atheists could well function, provided it punished criminals and honored or dishonored certain practices. In such a society would be found persons of good faith, ready to succor the poor, to oppose injustice, to be loyal to friends and to renounce profligacy. The desire for public approval would motivate them to perform the noblest deeds. For the ideas of honesty and glory were formed independently of religion.[17]

3

For many of his philosophical ideas Barlow was in debt to the religious criticism of the age. It dissipated whatever residue remained of his early Congregationalism; it left its stamp on his new version of *The Vision of Columbus* and it fixed his attention on things secular and scientific.

He reached the threshold of materialism, but did not cross it. He saw no contradiction between the moral code in the Gospels and the idea of progress. The code in fact was discoverable by the use of reason. The divine in man would manifest itself through his unshackled mind.

Still, Barlow's system had no place for the supernatural. He once put down a series of questions which stemmed from the persuasion that man had been imposed upon by a mode of terror much as children were by their nurses' ghost stories. "If men in all ages and countries had understood astronomy and physics as well as they do now generally in Europe would the ideas of God and religion have ever come into their minds? Have not these ideas been greater sources of human calamity than all other moral causes? . . . If we admit that these ideas are wholly chimerical, having arisen altogether from ignorance of natural causes, is it not the duty of every person who sees their evil tendency to use his influence to banish them as much as possible from society? Is it not possible wholly to destroy their influence and reduce them to the rank of other ancient fables to be found only in the history of human errors?"[18]

He stressed the deification of natural phenomena. Unexplained, they were "feared and adored as beings whom we could not control but might hope to soften by prayers as we might a passionate master who had us in his power." Thereby was laid a foundation of worship that served revealed religion.[19]

Bayle had raised the question whether polytheism was not worse than atheism. This was a pure hypothesis, according to Barlow. It was more relevant to ask whether monotheism was not worse than polytheism. The question should first be considered with regard to religious wars, and second, with regard to their influence on the morals of individuals and society. On the first point he agreed with Bayle that polytheists had never fought wars over religion. And he was at one with Helvetius that wars between sects were unknown among pagans. They were humane and tolerant. Evidence on the second point was more difficult to assemble. But Barlow believed that monotheists "would gain nothing by this comparison."[20]

On the question of matter and motion Barlow sided with the materialists. To say that matter needed some immaterial being to keep it moving was inconsistent with its nature. He was of the opinion that "Perhaps no particle of it ever was or ever will be at rest for a moment."

Following the scientific knowledge of the day, he concluded that all particles of matter were endowed with attraction and repulsion, so that they were incapable of rest. "These two qualities of matter," he continued, "and the circumstance of every particle being surrounded with a vacuum (which is the cause of elasticity) are perhaps sufficient to account for all the phenomena of matter." Eminently suited to his thesis was Francis Bacon's identification of Proteus and matter. Proteus, said Barlow, paraphrasing Bacon, knew all the secrets, but refused to tell them until he was constrained and forced into a thousand different forms. At last he was compelled to yield and confess all. [21]

To the Cartesian argument that matter being inert could have no motion but what was given it by something that was self-moving, Barlow replied "that neither the existence of matter, nor any form, quality, accident or production that can belong to it, is any proof of the existence of a God." Equally faulty was Descarte's dictum that "nature abhors a vacuum." If there were no vacuum, said Barlow, "matter indeed would be at rest, it would require something more than his immaterial God to give it motion. Motion in any case would be impossible."

He denied Bayle's assumption that productions adapted to a particular end must have been the design "of a preexistent intelligent mechanic." The assumption, he answered, suggests a chain of assumptions. "We may as well suppose that such a preexistent intelligent agent and the powers of his mind must have been previously *designed* and exactly calculated to produce the works he has produced, and this by some other preexistent intelligent being. And so on, ad infinitum." As for proving a negative, he said, it would not be difficult to demonstrate that there could not have been any intelligence employed in the production of Nature. The earth was not the workmanship of a Great Artificer, but the result of a long formation in a changing universe in motion.

As he saw it, the doctrine of rewards and punishments was entirely inconsequential. It could not serve any reasonable purpose with respect to what had been done in this life. "Damning a soul," he said, "may be an act of vengeance, an expression of useless and wanton rage, worthy the character that most religions give of their God." But the punishment could not be advantageous either to the victim or to any other being. The same was true of the doctrine of rewards. They were conferred as an encouragement to virtuous actions. But the policy of reserving them for a future life could never occur to a rational being. It defeated the moral purpose to which rewards could be applied. [22]

These views on matter and immortality led Barlow to conclude, as had many *philosophes*, that religion was an instrument of terror to hold the multitude in subjection. It was therefore detrimental to morals and to the intellectual powers of the mind. It weakened the foundation of society instead of strengthening it. Man's intelligence and morals were dependent on society, and this dependence was in proportion to its progress, which in turn bore a fairly just proportion to the advance of the arts and sciences. He thus placed men's morals and intellect on a sociological basis. A being totally out of society would be "necessarily destitute of any moral quality, as well as of intelligence." [23]

Like his French contemporary Henri de Saint-Simon, Barlow held that man's reasoning developed with the arts and sciences in his unrelenting effort to subdue nature. [24] The society anticipated by Barlow was many steps removed from the blueprint of Saint-Simon. Yet each looked to the progress of science and industry for its attainment.

4

"Toot, whenever in your travels you find any minerals that are rare or valuable, and you can get them for nothing or for little, bring them along. I wish to collect as many as I can conveniently, not for my own use, but for the advancement of science in America." [25] So Barlow wrote to Robert Fulton on August 18, 1802. "Toot" was Fulton's pet name in the Barlow household where he had been living.

Their acquaintance dated from 1797, shortly after Barlow's return from Algiers. Fulton, the younger of the two by about eleven years, had come to Paris to interest French authorities in his system of small canals. He met Joel and Ruth in the hotel where they were all staying, and thus began that affectionate attachment and devoted friendship which continued to the end of their lives. When the Barlows bought their luxurious home in Paris, they invited Fulton to stay with them as long as he remained in the city. "He resided in our family as a brother seven years," Ruth wrote after his death, "and during this period he learnt the French language and something of the Italian and German, studied the high mathematics, the sciences, physicks, chymistry and perspective." While he lived with the Barlows he invented several machines, set up the first panorama that had ever been seen in the French capital, drew plans for a submarine and proved it by experiment on the Seine. [26] He was on the way of becoming "the Archimedes of America," as Freneau described him. [27]

He was born in Little Britain, Pennsylvania, near Lancaster, where he stayed during the Revolution, drawing caricatures of British prisoners, making sketches of guns and calculating their force. As a young boy he displayed an artistic talent. At seventeen he was in Philadelphia painting miniatures, landscapes and signs for shops. He was successful enough to buy land for members of his family and to pay his voyage to London to study with Benjamin West, the celebrated American painter. West recognized the young man's genius, befriended him and invited him to live with his family. [28]

But the gifted pupil was sidetracked by a compelling interest in technology. Two reasons may be suggested for the shifted attention. To begin with, the British climate of invention was congenial to his bent toward the practical application of the principles of physics. Then, his discussions in England with Robert Owen and John Dalton, among others, on the "Connection between Universal Happiness and Practical Mechanics" [29] might well have instilled in him the belief that he could advance both his own interests and the welfare of mankind by devoting himself to the mechanical arts.

Fulton and Barlow were intellectual brothers. [30] They were not only in agreement on fundamental questions of politics; they admirably promoted one another's mental powers. The artist-scientist, apart from introducing his friend to an appreciation of art, West's work in particular, [31] initiated him into the recesses of science in its relation to technology. The poet-essayist, on his side, enlightened his companion on the history of the French Revolution and the far-reaching consequences of its principles. Together they studied science and political economy. Barlow lent Fulton money, helped him with his experiments and advised him in his dealings with the French government. "It is not too much to say," wrote a student of his naval projects, "that, without the help and encouragement of Joel Barlow, Fulton might be no more today than a name in some catalogue of obscure XVIIIth century artists." [32]

It is safe to assume that discussion with Fulton on the function of art fortified Barlow's view of it as a sociological matter. Studying the role of fine arts in history since antiquity, he came to the mortifying conclusion that they "have almost uniformly employed their services & lent their aid in favor of Despotism either in church or state, or both." That is because "they seem in their practice to be almost necessarily venal." The artist, without independent fortune, "must devote his labors" to those who can best reward him. In other words, he must look to patronage, which is but a form of condescension that inevitably "creates an obligation, probably an enthusiastic ardor on the part of the artist, to employ his talents on such subjects as are most agreeable to the interest and taste of his patron." Barlow believed that the fine arts could be directed, not to the glorification of princes, individuals or corporate bodies, but to the elevation of liberty and republicanism.

The trend of his thought and his unshaken faith in America left him with the conviction that she would become "the Muse of the Arts, perhaps the greatest & most durable that has ever been." Her citizens were well disposed to imbibe correct principles and to develop "good taste in whatever is ornamental to society." It was vital therefore to encourage the flowering of art to the end of serving the aims of republicanism. And he recommended the following subject for a prize essay: "What are the practicable means of rendering the cultivation of the fine arts in America the most beneficial to political liberty?" [33]

Around 1800 Fulton and Barlow began a joint work, "The Canal: a

Poem on the Application of Physical Science to Political Economy." Four books were planned, but only about half of the first was written. [34] It was "a scientific poem," as Barlow termed it in a letter to Fulton, "of which you were to write the geological and I the historical-mythological notes,—of which you were to furnish the philosophy and I the poetry, you the ideas and I the versification,—all of which we could only do together." [35] This turned out to be infeasible, for Fulton was at work to demonstrate the practicality of steam navigation.

Perhaps it was fortunate that "The Canal" was left unfinished. Tiresome hexameters, forced rhymes, shadowy myths, these were its undistinguished features. Its merit was faith in progress. The two authors were confident that nature and science would furnish:

The means of public happiness, the weal
That States may realize, the world may feel;
Blest, could we fix them in our native land,
Thrice blest, to see them o'er the earth expand.

Napoleon was the glittering star in France when Fulton submitted his plan of internal canals. It was rejected, although Fulton defended it as the unfailing means of national prosperity. A network of waterways would produce enough revenue to cover the cost of government, provide facilities for irrigation, run mills, increase the yield of agriculture and industry, raise land values and widen the domestic market. [36]

Fulton's plan was not original. Quite similar projects had been worked out in England and in France. For instance, James Brindley and Thomas Bentley, in England, had shown the advantages of connecting by water the sources of power and the factories depending on them. [37] In France, Joseph Marie Lequinio had antedated Fulton's arguments in support of internal water communications. [38]

Fulton's submarine, too, had a precursor in that of David Bushnell, an American. Bushnell's craft, however, had two principal defects. It was small, and it failed to submerge fully. It was more in the nature of a floating mine. Fulton's originality was in designing a boat that could submerge and surface at will and propel itself underwater. The Nautilus, as he called his submarine, was launched at Rouen in July 1800 and tested at Le Havre. All that was needed to prove its value to the French was an authorization to blow up British naval ships off the French coast. Thanks to Barlow's visits to the Minister of the Navy, authorization was finally granted. The submarine was towed out to sea, but British warships, having been forewarned, sailed off to a safe distance.

Fulton entertained exceedingly high hopes for his Nautilus. He had persuaded himself that it could be instrumental in achieving international peace, free trade and the freedom of the seas. Unless these ends were attained, republican nations, including his own, would be driven, in self-defense, to divert their resources to naval armament. "Seeing this," he recalled later, "I turned my whole attention to find out means of destroying such engines of oppression, by some method which would put it out of the power of any nation to maintain such a system, and would compel every government to adopt the simple principles of education, industry and a free circulation of its produce." [39]

His prescription for inaugurating a free and peaceful world order was as utopian as were others in his day. His immediate concern was the termination of the war between England and France and the security of his country from naval tyranny.

Fulton tried to sell his submarine project to the French government. The story of his negotiations, first with the Directory and later with Napoleon, has been told several times. [40] His proposal to found a company for constructing submarines was turned down. A clause in the contract he drew up stipulated that his invention "shall not be used by the Government of France against the American States."

His memorandum to the French naval ministry promised that his submarine would revolutionize international relations and change the course of history. It was a deadly challenge to England's mastery of the seas and to her predominant role in world affairs. After annihilating her navy, a fleet of submarines could blockade her major ports, sever the links of her empire, stop her export trade and bring her industries to a standstill. Without British aid the Continental powers would be compelled to sue for peace. Also the entire political and social structure of Britain would be changed. Ireland would break away; a republic would replace the monarchy; the aristocracy would be shorn of its privileges; the nation's productive capacity would be employed not for turning out naval armaments, but for manufacturing socially useful goods. In short, Great Britain would be revolutionized. The British ruling class could avoid violence by stepping down from its place of power. [41]

The revolutionary effects of his submarine were further elaborated in a projected letter to Pitt. [42] It was apparently a first draft, in Barlow's hand, which suggests that the two friends worked it out in common. The opening paragraph is a triumphal hymn to the glories of science and merits citation.

"Science in its progress towards the improvement of society has now begun the destruction of military navies; and a new field is opened to the contemplation of every government whose policy is in any measure combined with those enormous establishments. The time cannot be distant when maritime depredations will be found impracticable, and when the citizens of all countries will enjoy a perfect liberty of commerce. Which event, by offering to every man the prospect of security, will render his industry more active & more productive. In this manner the comforts of life will be multiplied; nations will begin to discern the true principles of their mutual intercourse, and learn that their real interests are founded on the equality of rights. We may then hope to see the day when the human mind shall have free scope for the developement [sic] of useful truths; and when those discoveries which tend to the general benefit of mankind shall not be perpetually obstructed by the mistaken policy of those who pretend to govern them."

Impelled by this sublime end, Fulton notified the Prime Minister that he had at his command the means of liberating peoples from England's oppressive might. This could be done with as little violence as possible, provided he persuaded the mighty of his nation to surrender their privileges, divest themselves of their authority and cooperate with the people to establish a free order. Only at such a cost would they avoid becoming miserable exiles.

The letter went on to say that large navies were the cause of an incredible waste of human values. The point of departure was the economic principle that the wealth of a nation consisted of the produce of labor. But navies were destructive of this wealth. An estimate had it, according to the letter, that for Europe as a whole, 680,000 men were required to build and maintain navies. The annual loss was 80 pounds per man, or 54,400,000 pounds a year. England's loss was 12,800,000 pounds. In other words, navies were a "monstrous misapplication of labor."

The letter inquired into Great Britain's price of empire. This raised the question whether Britain's colonies were her best customers. The example of America disproved it. America's trade with Great Britain was bigger after the Revolution than before it. Yet, to hold America in a colonial status Britain spent 139,000,000 pounds and the labor of at least 150,000 men for eight years, amounting to 36,000,000 pounds, or a total of 175,000,000 pounds, which could have prevented poverty, drastically reduced taxes and extended education in its many branches. The same sum could have been used to construct a city of 175,000 houses. With these comparative figures before him, Fulton asked, "is this what you call civil society? Is this that order & decorum for which you have again set Europe in armor & continued it for these eight years past?"

Still dwelling on the American example, the letter argued the cause of free trade and the independence of colonies. The fact that Great Britain derived greater profit from an independent than from a colonial America was solid evidence that trade restrictions and colonies hindered economic growth. They moreover caused rivalry and war. Consequently, the abolition of trade controls and the liberation of colonies were preliminary to sound economic development. Great Britain's market would be enlarged, her production stimulated, her population increased and technological innovation accelerated. Her heroes were the great inventors. She owed her prosperity to them, not to her dissipated aristocrats and corrupt legislators.

The same advantages would inevitably fall to other countries. For the principle of the Nautilus, Pitt was reminded, was "the true principle of equality among nations." It placed them all in equal safety and put an end to maritime wars. Their extinction would bring about the independence of Spanish and Portuguese America, the opening of its vast riches and the further progress of mankind in all its aspects.

The conception was impressive in its solemn grandeur. The great change would begin in Great Britain, provided she scrapped the navy and her ruling class renounced its privileges. In other words, Fulton and his friend Barlow called for revolution by consent. High labor productivity and increasing national wealth would easily enable the country to extinguish its debt. Another consequence would be the Church's sacrifice of its land and tithes. Provision would be made for those who had lost their posts in the Church, army and navy. The republicanized nation would enter upon a program of vast internal improvements, such as putting wastelands into cultivation and constructing a network of internal canals.

We have no evidence that a final draft of the letter reached its destination. The British intelligence informed the government of the submarine experiments, and Fulton was invited to confer with British authorities. His negotiations with the admiralty resulted in a contract granting Fulton a monthly salary plus a sum to cover his expenditures. Thus at a very small cost the inventor was kept from offering his services to France. But that was no longer necessary after the battle of Trafalgar. Thereafter, the British lost interest in the submarine project. The contract was terminated but not without satisfactory renuneration to Fulton. [43]

While the two friends were drawing the outlines of their preferred social order, events forced Barlow to turn his literary and diplomatic talents to the preservation of peace between France and the United States.

Chapter XII
The Cold War between the United States and France

On April 16, 1794, President Washington nominated John Jay envoy extraordinary to England. May 27th James Monroe was named minister to France. The two appointments, only six weeks apart, were more related than appeared to the average observer. Jay, a Federalist and an admirer of Great Britain's institutions, had the task of smoothing negotiations with her ministry, while Monroe, a disciple of Jefferson and sympathetic with French principles, was counted on to remove any suspicion in France that an American accommodation with her indefatigable foe was contemplated. Jay's instructions went as far as to enable him to conclude a treaty, a fact of which Monroe was kept in ignorance. An examination of the documents confirms what the historian of Monroe's mission wrote: "There appears to have been a deliberate purpose to blindfold France in regard to the Jay mission and to employ Monroe . . . as a means to this end." [1] In keeping with the subterfuge, the terms of the final treaty were withheld from him. At first he could not explain it, except that they were probably injurious to the nation to which he had been accredited. [2]

He went about strengthening the fraying ties between his country and France. Addressing the French Convention, he spoke of the mutual interests of the two republics and of the benefits they would enjoy from their closer friendship. [3] The cordial remarks were consistent with earlier American pronouncements. Nevertheless, he was charged at home with diplomatic error, with having committed his government to the support of France, departing from the American policy of strict neutrality. Behind the charges was the fear that he might hamper Jay's negotiations in London.

Yet Monroe succeeded in getting the French government to modify its policy with respect to American merchants. One decree gave them full rights as citizens of a friendly power. Another revoked the authorization of May 9, 1793, which permitted French warships and privateers to seize and bring into French ports neutral vessels carrying enemy goods. The two decrees in effect revived the treaty of alliance of 1778. [4]

1

Franco-American relations began to chill when news leaked out that Jay had signed a treaty in England. But the terms were not disclosed until later. It occurred to Monroe that the Federalist administration lacked confidence in him. He felt disconcerted, too, for the French suspected that his government had sent him to create a mirage of cordiality behind which it treated with their bitterest enemy. He met with cool reserve, even though, on instructions from home, he assured France that nothing in the treaty could arouse her opposition. If that were so, the French asked, why were its clauses kept from the public?

The publication of the treaty revealed the American government's pro-British leaning. In return for some American concessions, Great Britain promised to vacate the Western posts, which should have been done long ago had she kept her obligations. The treaty was silent on two touchy points: compensation for slaves carried off by British troops during the Revolution and the impressment of American seamen. And there was the humiliating article, number twelve, which prohibited America to export to any country sugar, coffee, cocoa and cotton. If the advantages and disadvantages of the treaty with regard to the United States were placed in balance, the second would far outweigh the first. After reading its terms, Freneau asked, "Was ever a nation treated with such indignity?" [5]

Defenders of the treaty claimed that, irrespective of its objectionable features, it gained an interlude of peace for the young nation. [6] Monroe's response was that war with England was not a real issue. In fact, in the light of French military successes, the time was propitious for America to insist on its own terms, provided it could convince the British government that it was prepared to take a firm stand. As he wrote to Jefferson, "of all possible calamities with which they [the English] are threatened, a war with us is that which they most dread," principally because of its effect on their commerce "by which alone they are enabled to support a war." [7]

The treaty was fairly unpopular in the United States. Criticism poured in from every part of the nation; protests and demonstrations inflamed crowds with statistical evidence of the sacrifices the treaty would entail, and people deplored the degradation to which the nation had been subjected. Monroe held that the agreement with England violated the neutrality towards France. Others accused the British minister in the United States of having been a prime instigator of this about-face in foreign policy. Still others predicted that the restored friendship with England would have unfortunate effects on republicanism. Flags were hung at half-staff. Boston, Philadelphia and other cities and towns voted resolutions censuring the administration. Jay was burned in effigy and Hamilton was stoned at a public meeting in New York. Even Washington was not spared the bitterness. [8]

Seen in the general frame of reference, after a long time-lapse, the treaty seems to have been the starting point of a long-studied plan to establish the power of the landed and commercial aristocracy. The attainment of this end depended on the success of a two-point program: the disorganization of the popular movement that had been activated by the democratic-republican societies and a reversal of America's foreign policy. In practice it meant dissolving the Franco-American alliance and repairing the broken bonds of Anglo-Saxon unity.

The course of the two objectives was strewn with obstructions, of which the popular movement proved to be the impassable one. Then too, the strategy of the Federalists failed. They had hoped to impose the treaty on an unsuspecting public behind a veil of secrecy. But rumors traveled. Monroe learned at the end of 1794 that a treaty had already been signed. The same report, reaching the French government in January 1795, had the effect of a bolt of thunder, according to Monroe. He foresaw trouble if the treaty were adopted. [9] To get the necessary two-thirds in the senate, Washington summoned it into special session and used his great authority. Federalist chiefs held wavering party members in line with the threat of England's declaration of war.

Had it not been for Monroe, the relations between France and the United States might have been strained sooner than they were. He marshalled all possible arguments to dispute the French contention that the agreement had annulled the nearly twenty-year-old Franco-American alliance; and his prudent advice stayed the French Directory from quick retaliation. An act of war, he said, would make the United States an ally of Great Britain and give supreme power to the American aristocracy. [10]

His position had been weakened. Despite his adroit diplomacy, he was unable to prevent the French government from decreeing on July 2, 1796, that France would treat neutral vessels in the same way they allowed themselves to be treated by England. In other words the concessions he had won were canceled. The Directory further showed its discontent by instructing its minister to the United States to suspend his diplomatic functions. But it was not to be interpreted as a mark of hostility between the two countries.

Monroe was recalled. But the Directory refused to receive his successor, Charles Pinckney, pending the reparation of wrongs. By contrast, it showed the warmest regard for the departing minister. By the time he came home, relations between the two countries had worsened. On hearing of his recall, seventy Americans in Paris expressed their "lively concern" and testified to his "unceasing vigilance for the honor and interest of our common country." [11]

His return set off a polemic that aggravated existing dissension. Republicans gloried in what he had achieved, but Federalists accused him of having created tensions between France and America. He was blamed for having exceeded his instructions and for lacking discretion. His answer was a book with a long title, in which he listed fourteen counts against the administration. [12] Washington's observations consisted of marginal comments in the copy he had read. A study of them shows that Monroe's main allegations were either ignored or met inadequately.[13]

The best Federalist replies were by Uriah Tracy, senator from Connecticut, [14] and Robert Goodloe Harper, of South Carolina, a convert from republicanism to Federalism. [15] A paper war broke out. Monroe was termed a Jacobin, [16] even charged with bribery. In retort his assailants were named "the Anglo-monarchic faction."

2

The epithets tended to becloud the drift of the nation's foreign and domestic policies. Observant Americans could see that the two were linked. An understanding with Great Britain would weaken the treaty with France, and perhaps even sever relations entirely. This was the objective of the Federalist Party, headed by such men as Hamilton, George Cabot and Fisher Ames. Given the occasion, it might have plunged the young republic into the European conflict on the side of Great Britain, torn up the American Bill of Rights, impaired the forms and practices of democracy and reinforced the aristocracy.

England was the polestar of the leading Federalists. "If England will perservere," wrote George Cabot to Oliver Wolcott, "she will save Europe, and save us." [17] America's "single hope of security," said Fisher Ames, was in the triumph of the British navy. [18] Looking back on events since 1789, he lamented the overthrow of the old French régime. Its hierarchy gave stability to society, and its aristocracy was respected. Europe and the United States would have been better off had there never been a French Revolution, which introduced mob rule.[19] The United States, to be sure, lacked the social gradations of Europe, yet it had an aristocracy of wealth, to which, he confessed, the mass of the Federalists belonged. This wealthy class necessarily had the responsibility of exercising state power. [20] In reality, Federalist reasoning led straight to the teachings of Edmund Burke.

To turn the tide of opinion in favor of these principles, the Federalists called all their forces into service. We have already observed with what vigor their press assailed the French Revolution. Republicans, to cite Freneau, were "stigmatized as disorganizers—aliens by birth—enemies to America in principle—Gênet's mob—institutors of democratic clubs, where darkness and drink make them shameless." [21]

A case was prepared against the Franco-American alliance. America's alleged indebtedness to France was without substance, ran the brief, for America had already proved its military capacity. Actually, France's prime motivation had been to humble her great rival, to reestablish her influence on the American continent and to dispossess the United States of a large part of her territory. In other words, she had plotted to use the American Revolution for her aggrandizement. [22]

Simultaneously the pulpit in the New England and middle states was turned into a political dais. Pastors likened the French Revolution to a plague God had visited upon a sinful world. As in France, so in America, Jacobinism and atheism were an "infamous combination," to cite the Reverend Joseph Lathrop of Massachusetts. Even the liberal William Ellery Channing declared that "the French Revolution had diseased the imagination and unsettled the understanding of man everywhere." [23]

The clerical offensive broadened into an attack against nonconformists, including critics of the Establishment, deists and sceptics, all of whom were equated with atheists, disciples of Satan and anarchists who thrived under a mobocracy. As a dissident pastor phrased it, the clergy became "the tools of the Federalists." [24]

The most controversial nonconformist writing of the day was Paine's *Age of Reason*. No sooner was it imported from France, where it had first been published, than it became a best-seller. During Paine's lifetime, it received more than thirty retorts, [25] not counting sermons and press editorials. The best planned refutation was *Evidence of Divine Revelation with Some Strictures upon Deistical Writers* that had been authorized by the Mendon Association of Congregational Pastors, a large and politically powerful club. [26]

One effect of Paine's book was the founding of the Deistical Society of the State of New York. It proclaimed the existence of one supreme Deity, credited man with sufficient faculties for self-improvement and the acquisition of happiness with the aid of education and science, considered the religion of nature "the only universal religion," and accounted civil and religious liberty essential to man's true interests. Finally, it declared "science and truth, virtue and happiness" to be the great ends to which the human faculties should be directed. [27]

The anti-French propaganda was fueled by the timely publication of two works. In 1797 in Edinburgh, Scotland, Professor John Robison's melodramatic book was published with an emotion provoking title. [28] Three London editions quickly sold out. It was republished in New York, and in Europe it was published in French, German and Dutch. In the same year began to appear a still longer work by the fanatical Jesuit, the Abbé Augustin Barruel, [29] which was turned into German and English and had two American printings. Its thesis was, in important respects, similar to Robison's, namely, that the abhorrent events and policies of the French Revolution were the result of an anti-Christian conspiracy in which the Encyclopedists, Freemasons and Illuminati had played a momentous part. A modified form of the thesis was later taken up by Joseph de Maistre and Louis de Bonald, and still later by Hippolyte Taine in his polemical history of the origins of contemporary France.

Neither Robison nor Barruel was the first to credit the Freemasons with the plot of overthrowing altars and thrones. The imputation had already stemmed from priests who, without exception, had traced it to the *philosophes*. According to the prelates, there was an unbroken connection between d'Alembert, Diderot and Voltaire, on the one hand, and the Freemasons and the other revolutionary leaders, on the other. [30]

The case against the Illuminati was pure fantasy, but Federalists transformed it into a terrifying indictment. The Illuminati, it was bruited about, were the instigators of the Revolution in France and the slave uprisings in Santo Domingo. Their secret agents were spreading impiety and the seeds of insurrection in the United States, with the connivance of the chief American Jabobin, Thomas Jefferson.

Robison's book was soon exposed in England as a fraud, and *The Analytical Review* could say confidently that the author "sees atheism in clouds, and hears it in the wind. The very words, *brotherly love* and *benevolence*, are enough for our professor. They are 'treason, stratagems and crimes.' " [31]

The exposé at first escaped notice in America. For on May 9, 1798, the well regarded Reverend Jedidiah Morse of Charlestown, Massachussets, declared in a sermon that the Order of the Illuminati, which had its roots in Freemasonry, had as its object the overthrow of American institutions through its emmissaries, the affiliated Jacobins. Atheism and licentiousness were their means. The pastor spoke with the conviction of one who had made a momentous discovery.

The alarm, sounded by Morse, stirred up New England divines and caused some hysteria. Timothy Dwight called for a "defensive war" against France, and the Federalist press intensified its assault against democratic-republicans. [32] Party struggles were further embittered. [33]

The emotionalism imparted by pastors and journalists boomeranged. Robison's book was soon discredited in America as it had been in Great Britain. Professor Ebeling's letter to the Reverend Bentley, which the latter allowed to be publicized, pointed out the insignificance of the Illuminati, and further evidence confirmed the emptiness of Robison's accusations. Also, American Freemasons resented their alleged alliance with conspirators against the social order. [34] Morse and other divines fell back on Barruel's work. But their new line of defense was just as untenable. [35] They were disgraced and hushed.

The clergy had undoubtedly overreached itself. Still it gave valuable service to the Federalist party. Republicans admitted that the Godly ministers did more "to stop the progress of republican light than any other class of men." [36] Government employees had to speak euphemistically with reference to things political. A prominent republican sheet wrote editorially:

> Already it is quite unfashionable among the dependents of the present administration to speak of liberty as a blessing. The expression must be qualified by some epithet which conveys a doubt of the position. It is not then liberty in the abstract; in the dialect of *pretended* federalism, it is 'rational' liberty, 'constitutional' liberty, or 'real' liberty. As if any liberty could exist in this country which did not merit the respective appellations. [37]

3

For five years and longer, after the ratification of the Jay Treaty, party rivalry took on a strident tone. Illustrative of the conflicting viewpoints were the declarations of two representative enemy sheets. Said the Federalist *Connecticut Courant* of December 12, 1796: "To pray for French success is to pray for the misery of Europe; and the corruption, *moral and political*, of your own country. These proceed exactly in the ratio of that success; and are as naturally the effects of it, as ravings are of the bite of a mad dog." On the other side was the republican *Independent Chronicle* which, on December 8, 1796, reprinted from the *New York Diary* an answer to Noah Webster's declaration in *The Minerva* that the cause of France was no longer the cause of liberty. "No longer the cause of liberty!" the *Chronicle* exclaimed. "Why? Because to term it so, would be injurious to the British party. Because, it would add weight to the opinions of the men who oppose that party, and who have ever been the friends of the French Revolution. Because, we have lately formed a new connection; and our affection for France, our old and tried friend, is incompatible with devotion to Britain, whose pride the philanthropist believes and hopes, she is yet destined to humble. Hence it becomes proper to asperse her. Hence 'the cause of France is the cause of ambition.' "

The dates of the two citations indicate that by the end of 1796 Franco-American relations had worsened. President Adams, while taking a firm and even belligerent stand against France, was disposed to start new negotiations. It is not clear whether this was due to a desire for a peaceful settlement that would also put to rest domestic strife, or whether it was in keeping with Hamilton's proposed way to disarm critics of the administration. Lurking in Hamilton's plan was the consideration that another attempt to treat with France would probably end in failure and demonstrate the unreasonableness of the Directory rather than the unwillingness of the American government. [38] Two of the negotiators he recommended were Pinckney and Cabot, both ardent Francophobes.

Be that as it may, Adams sent a commission to France, made up of two Federalists, Pinckney and John Marshall, and of one republican, Elbridge Gerry. Its composition gave little hope to peace advocates.

The commissioners arrived in France just when her international position was improving. Austria had signed peace preliminaries with Bonaparte. Abandoned by her strongest Continental ally and suffering from a long economic depression, England sent back Lord Malmesbury to Lille to discuss a settlement. The conference dragged on into September 1797, but without success.

Also the French Executive Directory had, in the interim, been purged of American friends. A triumvir, of which the venal Barras was the intriguing genius, became the controlling power, and Talleyrand, as unprincipled as Barras, was the choice for the Ministry of Foreign Affairs. Intrigue was the forté of this former churchman, and greed his sovereign passion. During his stay in America, he had become acquainted with the clandestine activities of French agents to restore French dominion in the western hemisphere, [39] a plan he had no intention of surrendering now that he was head of the Foreign Office. Thus, with the general situation changed, the Directory was little disposed to discuss peace terms with the American envoys.

The failure of the mission is history. The fault lay with both sides. If the intention of the American administration was to restore good relations, a different type of commission should have been sent. To have selected as envoy Charles Pinckney, whom the French had already refused to receive as successor to Monroe, was in itself an act of defiance. Equally so was the choice of Marshall, a warm partisan of the Jay Treaty. On the other hand, if the aim of the Directory was the restoration of friendship with the United States, it should have avoided littering the way with such demands as a *douceur* and a loan. This shady business, labeled the X.Y.Z. affair, was interpreted in the United States as a gross insult, and yet every public-minded citizen knew that the American government was then paying tribute to the Deys and Beys of North Africa.

The publication of the X.Y.Z. documents raised the war spirit to an imminent point. For the Federalists these documents were a prized weapon against the Republicans. The president's promise that he would not send another minister to France, unless assurance was given that he would be received with the respect and honor due to a free and independent nation, had wide support.

The nation was readied for war. On July 7, 1798, an act of Congress officially terminated the alliance with France. Placed in command of the army, Washington appointed three major generals, among whom developed an unsavory rivalry for precedence. Hamilton finally gained priority of rank. [40] Writing in retrospect more than a decade later, John Adams said that Hamilton's rise to second in command, that is, successor to

Washington, was in the general scheme of the British faction. It "was determined to have a war with France, and Alexander Hamilton at the head of the army and then President of the United States."[41] War, reckoned the Federalists, would restore Anglo-Saxon unity, forestall talk of peace between England and France and provide the sought-for opportunity of silencing the republican opposition.

Riding on the wave of indignation that had been sweeping the country since the disclosure of the X.Y.Z. demands, the Federalists pushed through Congress a set of laws commonly known as the Alien and Sedition Acts. Suffice it to say here that they were directed against foreigners, and against free speech and free press. They were meant to stop the diffusion of ideas that sounded subversive to Federalist ears, to nullify the First Amendment of the Constitution and, by giving more power to the executive, to undo the system of checks and balances. Passed in an atmosphere of Gallophobia, the laws were in the nature of a *coup d'état* aimed at the American political structure. They were intended for a war crisis that failed to come,[42] and were similar to the repressive measures of Pitt's government against the British reform movement.

4

France retaliated against America's war measures by confiscating enemy goods on neutral vessels. And she declared American ships to be lawful prize if they did not carry a list of the crew. American shipping losses increased.

The calculations of the American warhawks proved incorrect. For on both sides of the Atlantic cool-headed and informed observers cautioned against the consequences of Franco-American tension. Talleyrand anticipated a *rapprochement,* even as he refused to negotiate with the three envoys. He persuaded Gerry to remain after dismissing his two colleagues. Notwithstanding the unpopularity it might cost him, the American envoy felt morally bound to stay as long as the door was kept open.[43] Volney warned that French representatives in America were impairing the good will of her citizens.[44] And Louis Guillaume Otto, who had served the French minister in Philadelphia, submitted a report criticizing the Directory's American policy. French agents, he wrote, had misunderstood the character of the American nation when they thought they could drive a wedge between the people and the governing body. That had only united Americans. Franco-American relations, he continued, were further strained by mistakes at home, such as the refusal to receive Pinckney and the disrespect shown to America's neutrality. Otto recommended a realistic course. The common interests of the two nations required their combined resistance to British plunder.[45]

Of more immediate effect was the report of Victor Marie Du Pont to Talleyrand, dated July 16, 1798. Victor was the son of Pierre Samuel Du

Pont de Nemours, founder of the well-known House in Delaware. Appointed French consul general in Philadelphia, he arrived in May 1798 during the excitement provoked by the X.Y.Z. affair. He bluntly told Talleyrand that the piratical conduct of French privateers in American waters was one of the major causes of the country's gradual estrangement. To avoid a breach he proposed that all commissions of privateers in the Antilles be revoked, that all territorial violations on the American coast be disclaimed, that France propose a revision of the laws against neutrals and finally, that the American government be informed of the French intention to treat its envoys with dignity and honor. Du Pont added that he was voicing the opinions of America's republican leaders. Talleyrand forwarded the report to the Directory with his counsel for reconciliation. [46]

For he was apprehensive of the final outcome of his grand design with regard to French power in the West. He had visions of a French empire, even larger than the one that had been lost to England. He hoped to reconquer Canada and to persuade Spain to cede Louisiana and Florida. From this massive base France would press upon Mexico and Latin America to the south and on the United States to the east. But the plan was doomed to failure if war broke out between France and the United States. The Anglo-Saxon allies would then divide the coveted territories. Great Britain would take Santo Domingo, and the United States, Louisiana and Florida.

Such an event had to be avoided. Even before Du Pont submitted his memoir, Talleyrand had written cordially to Gerry as he was about to sail home. [47] The Directory, too, made indirect overtures for peace. Talleyrand contacted William Vans Murray, American Minister at the Hague, recommending the elimination of misunderstandings.

The Directory gave convincing evidence of its desire for peace. It put a stop to the issuance of letters of marque in the colonies; it declared that those already issued would be ineffective thirty days after the publication of the decree; it lifted the embargo on American vessels and it ordered the release of American prisoners. The new policy was featured in the American democratic press as proof of French sincerity. [48]

The Adams administration might have taken longer to defrost if articulate and forthright Americans at home and abroad had not pressed it to accept the French olive branch. Barlow was one of these Americans.

Chapter XIII
Voices of Peace

The hot debate in America between Anglophiles and Francophiles reached an alarming state by the spring of 1798. Federalists disseminated grim predictions should Great Britain be subjugated. Invasion, devastation, violation of wives and daughters, contamination of Anglo-Saxon purity—such was the fate that would befall the nation. To reinforce anti-French sentiment, turbulent bands called "the friends of order," went about searching for Gallic sympathizers and advocates of peace. Incredible charges were leveled at Jefferson. He had sold himself for French gold, some said. His ambition, said others, was to be the viceroy of the Directory in its colony of the United States, and he protected the most disreputable American Jacobins. Still others likened him to Cromwell or Robespierre. [1]

Republicans, on their side, depicted Britain's savage record in Bengal and Ireland and recalled the New England witch hunting. They acknowledged that the French Revolution was attended with violence, but so was every revolution, they asserted, including the American. [2]

The Alien and Sedition Laws were poorly executed. Their strictest enforcement was in areas that were thoroughly Federalist, as in New England, or in states like New York and Pennsylvania where Republicanism threatened the supremacy of Federalism. Of an approximate twenty-five persons indicted under the Sedition Law hardly a dozen were brought to trial. [3] A few newspapers were suppressed, and several editors jailed. But these were isolated cases. The conviction which attracted national attention was that of Matthew Lyon, a congressman from Vermont, who was the particular object of Federalist scorn. [4] The net effect of the Sedition Law was an increase of republican newspapers and their circulation. The Alien Law, counted on to strip the Republicans of the foreign vote, had the opposite effect. [5] The Federalists paid dearly for their miscalculation.

In the tempestuous atmosphere news arrived that the three American commissioners had been rebuffed by the Directory. Could the impending war be prevented? Only a small number believed it was possible.

1

A Quaker, George Logan, arrived in Paris on August 7, 1798. He was of an old Pennsylvania family, a physician, a gentleman farmer, a defender of the principles of 1776 and an active supporter of Franco-American amity. He was also an agrarian democrat, believing in social and political equality and in the perfectibility of man's nature. [6] Severely on the side of peace, he crossed the Atlantic to prove to French authorities that a breach with the United States would be a calamity to both nations and a triumph for British intrigue.

He happened to come at a propitious time. Talleyrand had assured Gerry of French desire for reconciliation, and the pro-Americans in the Directory were sounding the disposition of the Adams administration. Logan had meetings with Talleyrand and three Directors. Whether the conferences had the effect of dissipating misunderstanding cannot be said. At any rate, Logan thought so. The French government removed the primary American grievances, and presented him, before his departure, with copies of the decrees embodying the concessions. For the people of Paris, his biographer tells us, he "became the pivot on which French policy swung around." [7]

Back in the United States, he had interviews with the Secretary of State, with General Washington and with President Adams. To each he conveyed the hope of the Directory for a settlement. He was considered an impudent intruder, although Adams listened to him with a certain satisfaction. His unofficial assurances tallied with what the president learned through regular diplomatic channels. [8] "I saw marks of candour and sincerity in this relation that convinced me of its truth," [9] Adams later acknowledged.

Other private and trustworthy communications in support of peace reached America. In Paris Logan had met a number of his countrymen who were so alarmed by the war delirium that they were doing everything possible to dispel it. Adams admitted that in the winter of 1798 and 1799 a flood of letters poured in from Americans in France, all with a similar purpose.

Three examples are in order. Nathaniel Cutting of Brookline, Massachusetts, American Consul at Le Havre, wrote that France was sincerely disposed to negotiate. [10] From Richard Codman, a Boston merchant highly respected in the Federalist Party, came the advice that "the moment is extremely favourable for an accommodation." A reconciliation could be brought about, "which ought to be desired by all true friends to both countries." [11] A similar aim prompted the long letter Jefferson received from Fulwar Skipwith, Consul-General in Paris. We may conveniently omit his references to the undiplomatic conduct of two of the American commissioners in Paris and to the unpopularity of Adams in France. Relevant to Skipwith's object were his means of effecting a Franco-American rapprochement, such as the modification or cancellation of the Jay Treaty and the extension of a loan to France should she ask for it. [12] He also enlisted Barlow's aid in drafting a memorial to the Directory, recommending a course of action that would restore friendly relations. The Directory should send to Philadelphia a plenipotentiary who was respected for his moderation and integrity, value the rights of neutrals and permit free trade between France and friendly nations. [13]

2

In the American colony in Paris, Barlow was the most active in promoting peace between the two republics. It was not because he was a citizen of both, but because he believed that their hostility would liquidate their common principles and ease the return of despotism. His thoughts roamed over many peoples. His was a mind liberated from the confines of particularism.

He had been back from Algiers less than a month when the three American commissioners arrived in Paris. From Gerry he learned of the strained atmosphere at the conferences and of the provoking French demands. He was also informed that the three envoys were in disagreement on the course to follow. Pinckney and Marshall held fast to the instructions. Gerry was inclined to make the French request for a loan an opening for further talks. After nearly a month of negotiation, Pinckney and Marshall decided to go home. Gerry chose to stay.

Barlow felt frustrated. He no longer had influential friends in the French government through whom he could intercede in the deepening crisis. He also lacked confidence in the Adams administration and in the peaceful intentions of the two Federalist emissaries. Their coolness to the French government caused it to suspect, to cite Skipwith's words to Jefferson, "that their mission was virtually destined to the court of Louis XVIII, and not for the French republic." [14] Gerry, for his part, seemed to lack initiative.

Considering the facts that came to him from separate sources, Barlow concluded that the commission had never been intended for working out an understanding. Behind its appointment he discerned a threefold design: to conciliate American public opinion by pretending to desire a settlement; to lay the failure to the French government and, with national security as the argument, to prove the need of an alliance with Great Britain.

He was alarmed by the thickening war clouds. He dreaded to think of the effect the commissioners' reports might have in Philadelphia, unless evidence was heard from the other side. On February 24, 1798, he informed Senator Abraham Baldwin that he would soon impart to him what he believed to be the causes of misunderstanding between

France and America, and the way to remove them. He referred, in broad terms, to the president's "many blunders" and his persistence "in making more." [15]

The letter he promised Baldwin, the best parts of which he also sent to Jefferson, was dated March 1, 1798. Studying Franco-American relations since 1789, he noted that their breakdown had begun before the Jay Treaty. Actually it climaxed a series of acts, starting with Washington's appointment of Gouverneur Morris as Minister to France. For three years, Barlow wrote, he misled the president with respect to the principles and events of the Revolution, insulted the French nation and as far as possible betrayed it. After his recall, he was commissioned by Washington "as a secret agent to the cabinet of London, to transact business so apparently hostile to the interests of France" that it "sharpened the edge of resentment here more than the whole of Jay's Treaty."

The recall of Monroe was fraught with difficulties. He had neutralized French indignation and would have continued to do so, had he remained. But Pinckney was sent to take his place, to "the astonishment of all our friends and the exultation of the court of London."

Barlow turned to the presidential election of 1796. The French had hoped for the success of Jefferson, and in that hope was proof that they did not want to quarrel with America. The victory of Adams, however, drove them to extremes just short of war. Here Barlow vented his views of the man. He "had the least pretensions to prudence"; he chose "to play the bully"; his offer to negotiate was simply a pretense; and his language with regard to France was that of a madman.

Barlow was hard on the president. Adams, to be sure, was conservative in a Federalist way. He favored the rule of an elite, was quite out of sympathy with eighteenth-century philosophy, and was inimical to French revolutionary principles. Granted, too, he lacked political astuteness, for he bristled like a porcupine when he should have been gracious, and he exploded at a low voltage point. For all that, he was intensely devoted to what, in his conviction, was good for America. He placed his private interests below the needs of his country. And he was given to yield to stubborn facts when they acted as a solvent of prejudice.

Let us return to Barlow's narrative of the developing enmity of the two republics. Not the president alone, but also speakers in Congress outraged the Executive Directory; newspapers libeled the French republic. Barlow conceded that the wrongs from which stemmed French displeasure might have been misconstrued in the stormy climate of the Revolution. But the feelings were there nonetheless.

He proposed several ways to improve relations. The three commissioners should be replaced by Monroe or Madison. The president should voice friendly sentiments for France and "the highest respect for the principles of the revolution, the magnanimity of the nation and the sacrifices they have made in the cause of liberty." Like Skipwith, Barlow put forward the possibility of a loan and the reconsideration of the treaty with Great Britain.

He scarcely counted on the publication of the letter. [16] But Matthew Lyon printed it as a pamphlet with slight editing, [17] in violation of an alleged promise to Baldwin. Federalists rushed to arms and fired volleys of calumny at the author. [18] He was damned, called a Jacobin, a democrat, an infidel; his letters were intercepted and mutilated before they were printed. Federalist newspapers, in unison, pronounced him guilty of treason, of vindicating French conquests and sanctioning plots against American independence. In the preface to its reprint of the letter, *The Connecticut Courant* cried out: "Another Traitor! Americans—attentively read and contemplate the following infamous and unparalleled display of treachery and meanness, and let him whose indignation it does not rouse blush at this want of feeling." [19]

The Commercial Advertiser of New York wrote:

> Those who recollect what Mr. Barlow once was—those who once respected and loved him for his amiable disposition, his talents, and his supposed *piety*, will exclaim, 'Oh, how fallen!' They will discover new evidence, if possible, of the accursed demoralizing powers of that modern French philosophy which has made of Europe a charnel house, and which Mr. Barlow has long been known to have embraced with enthusiastic ardor. But who could have expected from him such displays of hatred for his native country. Who would expect that Joel Barlow would become the slanderer of Washington and Adams. The true lover of his country will mourn that so many of her children are become her most unnatural foes, and aim with patricidal arm the fatal dagger at her breast. [20]

The above editorials were consistent with a letter Noah Webster addressed to Barlow. Webster was candid, if anything. Instead of being alarmed by the embittered dispute between the two republics, as Barlow was, he looked upon it as "a subject of real congratulation." In fact, he said, the friendship of the French government was "dangerous to our peace and prosperity." The alliance of 1778, "an evil at the time," subsequently turned into "the greatest scourge inflicted on our country. French hostility alone can save us from ruin." The claim that the French were pursuing liberty provoked him. Their profession was contradicted by their actions. They plotted against peoples, insinuated themselves among the unlettered, diffused among them disobedience to their governments and encouraged them to plunder the wealthy. This, said Webster, was the "cowardly system of Jacobinism." He attributed Barlow's politics to a loss of religious faith. The well-bred man of early days became in France "a rude, insulting, dogmatical egotist," who spoke contemptuously of the American president and senate. It was the effect of atheism and licentious example. By "divesting yourself of religion," Webster lectured his classmate, "you have lost your good manners." [21]

The furor raised by Barlow's letter had the unforeseen consequence of crystallizing opinion on the issue of war and peace. His censure of the Federalist administration gained credibility among Republicans, especially since its publicity by Matthew Lyon was made a cause of his persecution under the Sedition Law. Never had Barlow expected, even in his most optimistic moments, that his private views would set people discussing the nation's foreign policy.

At least a year passed before he learned that his letter had inflamed feelings in the United States. Meanwhile he pleaded the cause of peace among American statesmen. He confided to Oliver Wolcott that the repeal of the embargo on American shipping would soon be forthcoming.[22] To his former friend, James Watson, senator from New York, he wrote on good authority that the Directory was ready to name a negotiator. To show its good intentions it withdrew all commissions to privateers in the West Indies. The senator, who was linked with prominent Federalists in receiving shipments of munitions the government had purchased in England, was in no mood to read about the peaceful intentions of the French. He replied in anger that their concessions were their way of concealing their heinous object of conquering America. He lost his composure. In a letter to Wolcott, he accused Barlow of acting the role of a French spy.[23]

On October 2, 1798, Barlow addressed a letter to George Washington. In the recesses of the ex-president's heart was an ineffable desire that some opening might be found through which responsible persons of the two nations could dialogue and reach an understanding. But he was in want of evidence for crediting the possibility of peace. Barlow's letter provided the basis for believing that it could be realized.

A copy of the letter went to Baldwin with instructions to publish it if it failed "to calm the frenzy of him [Washington] and his associates." The purpose was to inform Americans "that one of their chiefs at least has had a warning in proper time and from an unsuspicious quarter."[24]

Barlow set out to show that a settlement of the differences between the two republics was feasible. He gave two reasons: one, neither had an interest in going to war and two, the French government had signified its desire for a reconciliation. He cited three examples of the Directory's sincerity: it contemplated a just indemnity for spoliations on American shipping; it had in view a change of the laws with respect to neutrals; it had contemplated sending an emissary to the United States after Gerry's departure, had it not feared an unfriendly reception. Barlow therefore appealed to the old statesman to use his prestige in behalf of an accommodation.[25]

Washington forwarded the letter to President Adams with his comments. "From the known abilities of that gentleman," he remarked, "such a letter could not be the result of ignorance in him; nor from the implications which are to be found in it has it been written without the privity of the French Directory." Washington recollected the services Barlow had rendered his country in Algiers. He went on to say that if, in the opinion of the president, the letter could be a means of restoring peace on honorable and dignified terms, he, Washington, would respond according to instructions as to its tenor.

In weighing the president's reply to Washington, two facts must be taken into account. Fixed in his mind was Barlow's letter to Baldwin, with its disparaging words concerning him. Also, the American minister at the Hague, with sanction from home, was at the time discussing with Talleyrand's agent the terms of a settlement. Under the circumstances Adams looked upon Barlow as an impudent intruder and held him in contempt. His smoldering resentment burst into obloquy. Only infrequently, he wrote to Washington, did one meet "with a composition which betrays so many and so unequivocal symptoms of blackness of heart. The wretch has destroyed his own character to such a degree that I think it would be derogatory to yours to give any answer at all to this letter. Tom Paine is not a more worthless fellow." The comparison was a sort of excommunication. Finally he said: "The infamous threat which he has debased himself to transmit to his country to intimidate you and your country . . . ought to be answered by a Mohawk." [26]

The facts of history in time helped Adams triumph over his prepossessions. Reflecting a decade later on the peacemakers and the peace drive, he assessed Barlow's letter in praiseworthy terms. He called it "elaborate, elegant and ingenious," and its author was transformed into a respectable authority, though without credentials or responsibility to America or France. [27] Contrary to his earlier outburst, Adams said that he "gave all the attention and consideration to General Washington's and Mr. Barlow's letters." [28]

3

The issue of war and peace nearly ignited civil strife. In the rank and file people cried out against a conflict with France. Its loudest advocates were well-placed Federalists whose strength lay in their official following and in their control of Congress, but not in public opinion. Consequently they had reason to doubt that the mass of the people would follow them into a war, even in their New England stronghold.

They realized toward the end of 1798 that they had made an error in timing. Congress should have declared war after the departure of Pinckney and Marshall from France. That was the occasion psychologically, but the timely juncture had passed. According to George Cabot, people could no longer be convinced that peace was much more to be feared than war. [29] From his standpoint war would have enabled the Federalists to root out the democratic opposition. But they had missed the chance.

On February 18 the president nominated William Vans Murray, then Minister at the Hague, to be Minister Plenipotentiary to the French Republic. He did so on the strength of a letter from Talleyrand, saying that a minister from the United States would be honorably received. The nomination signified a sharp turn in America's foreign policy and led to a Franco-American rapprochement. Before that was achieved a split occurred in the Federalist Party.

The torrent of abuse that had fallen on Barlow after the publication of his letter to Baldwin proved to him that American journalism and party politics could descend to the same depths as in Europe. To be charged with not knowing his country was disagreeable enough. But to be called a traitor was painful. And who were among the maligners? His Yale classmates—including his old friend Noah Webster, whose political credo was summed up by a journalist in these words: By good government he means "the Hamiltonian administration; by good order, submission to the administration; and by peace, peace with England and war with France." [30] All Barlow could do at a distance was to return to pamphleteering, an art he had already practiced with signal success.

His answer to the assailants was a substantial and modestly entitled pamphlet, *Two Letters to the Citizens of the United States*. [31] It was not only a fair statement of his principles; it also had a tone of urgency and immediacy. To his old Hartford friend, Dr. Hopkins, whom he sent a copy of the first letter, he wrote that its sentiments were those "in which we have been nourished; for which we have sacrificed a *hundred thousand* lives, and *two hundred millions* of dollars; in the peaceable enjoyment of which we have been extremely happy & prosperous for about 18 years, and I know no good reason why we should give them up so soon, because a few of our fellow citizens, our former fellow labourers, choose to be kings & nobles, & ride upon our necks." [32]

The *Two Letters* struck first at Federalist accusations. The charge that he favored France against his own country was false, for he had protested against the French piratical practices with respect to American vessels. His sense of justice, he said, would never allow him "to sanction maritime plunder from any quarter, or even to approve the least restriction on trade."

He then inquired into Federalist domestic and foreign policies. Studying the American situation, he was alarmed by the increasing concentration of financial power. It had started with Hamilton's funding system, on the promise that the accumulating national debt would be extinguished. Ten years of experience, however, proved just the opposite. The debt kept growing, and the American government was borrowing at higher interest rates. He concluded that Hamilton's funding system was "one of the most memorable pieces of imbecility and impudence that ever was imposed upon a nation." The higher the national debt the clearer it was that the nation had sold itself. He had in mind the experience of Great Britain. The Federalist administration was striving to attach the United States to Great Britain by humiliating commercial treaties as well as "by seeking precedents in every thing among the worst of her follies." If the Federalists succeeded in imposing their system they would pattern it on that of decrepit old England. In a broad sense Barlow resumed his earlier polemic against Burke. There were two differences, however. He was arguing the case of America instead of that of France, and he directed his arguments not at Burke but at the Americans who took him as their model.

He distinguished between two types of Federalism. One was a mode of government suitable to the interests of the financial and mercantile aristocracy of America. It was democraticidal. The other was a principle of political and administrative organization, applicable advantageously on national and international scales. A combination of the federal and democratic principles was the *sine qua non* for the firm establishment of liberty and unity in the United States. Their achievement was subject to these conditions: The nation should be liberated from the national debt, otherwise it would alienate the western territories; the residence of the federal government should be centrally located; a uniform state religion should be avoided; a system of roads and canals was essential to link the states and frontier areas; the youth should be educated in republican principles, for education was not a family, but "a civil and even a political concern"; finally, a militia should replace a standing army. The program was a far-reaching one.

America had many advantages over Europe, Barlow pointed out with pride. There the people were held in obedience by a superstitious veneration of one man or family, by a standing army and a state religion. Taxes and wars made their burdens even more oppressive. America, however, was free from such restraints and encumbrances. She was also favored by geography. A wide ocean secured her against European interference. Futhermore, America's debts to Europe, argued Barlow, were "a powerful defensive weapon" against plunderers of her commerce. The American government had but to sequester the properties of the piratical creditor nations. The method was the most pacific and effectual that had ever been at the disposal of any government. All it had to do, as a precaution, was to issue a declaration of neutrality, define the rights of neutrals and give notice that property taken from American citizens by any power would be compensated by an equal amount taken from the subjects of that power, found within American jurisdiction. If that was confiscation, so was the seizure of American property on the high seas. Forestalling the argument that sequestration would impede the getting of credit abroad, he said that manufacturers were eager not only to extend it to Americans but even to overstock their warehouses.

What should be done if the subjects of the offending power did not have sufficient properties to compensate the losses of American citizens?

In that event, he replied, all commercial intercourse should be suspended with that power. He conceded that such a measure would cause considerable hardship. But it would avoid still greater hardship through war.

Failure to use the method of sequestration against England, he claimed, turned out to be expensive to the United States. In the first place, it was a sacrifice of character to wrong an old friend, namely France, and indirectly aid an inveterate enemy. Then it caused a rift with France that cost America at least sixty million dollars. Finally it prompted the start of a navy which he likened to a "terrible scourge" that would ultimately take its toll. The naval system, he wrote, "has been the ruin of every nation that has hitherto adopted it; . . . It is the system put in suction, which never can stop, or moderate its action, till all that feeds it is exhausted."

As a means of defense, a navy was less powerful than sequestration. America was essentially an agricultural nation and would continue to be so for a long time. As consumers of "European manufactures, their debts to manufacturing nations would therefore go on increasing," so that sequestration could be highly serviceable as a method of security.

He believed that great changes were near both within nations and in their foreign relations. The accelerated movement of ideas would climax in a new order of things. But much depended on America, he held. By uniting with other neutrals she could modify the law of nations and free commerce from the tyranny of contraband. Unhappily, with the Jay Treaty she had turned her back on neutrals. But she could recapture their confidence by asserting and maintaining the rules of international intercourse. Once war ceased to preoccupy France, the two nations could initiate an era of peace.

Barlow shared the eighteenth-century view that human betterment was "a truth of the utmost importance in its practical tendency." Every legislator should bear this maxim in mind and aid in creating the conditions for national happiness and international harmony. The two were interrelated. The mutual dependence of men was universal and "a permanent source of reciprocal confidence." He saw nations moving toward a confederation, which he preferred to name the *United States of Europe*. At this point he entered the realm long ago explored by others, from the early Greeks to Henry IV and Rousseau. The confederation he anticipated was contingent upon an increasing number of republics and liberated states. Their kindred interests would pull them together; their common objectives were peace and freedom. Two of their functions would be the guarantee of neutral trade and the arbitration of differences arising from it. They would enforce their decisions by withholding all commercial relations with the recalcitrant party.

Since Barlow's primary concern was the respect of the rights of neutrals in war time, he called upon the French to preface their fourth constitution with a declaration of the rights of nations, of which he prepared a draft. [33] It stipulated a revision of the maritime code, and it broadly defined the rights of nations, the neutrality of a vessel and the meaning of a blockade. We shall pass over the complexities of this branch of law and notice only those articles which obliged the French republic to abolish the system of privateering and invited the other powers to work out a mode of arbitration. The principles to be observed were first, that the flag of a neutral protected the cargo irrespective of its origin, and second, that a nation remaining neutral, while its neighbors were at war, retained the rights it had before the war began. England would of course oppose such rules, but France could act alone. With her immense resources, she could withstand a naval war with her rival. In this way she would become the benefactor of nations.

Barlow also drew up a program for a maritime convention that would be open to every nation willing to participate. The objectives were to determine the rights of neutrals, to provide for their guarantee without going to war and to set up an international court of justice. Should a guilty power fail to pay damages, the court would place it under the "Ban of Commerce," that is, the members of the convention would be forbidden to trade with it. Since the defiant country would very likely be dependent on commercial intercourse, a ban would be more effective than armed force.

Needless to say, the framers of the French constitution paid no heed to Barlow's draft declaration. It was, however, his answer to the accusation that he had been acting one-sidedly in his efforts to restore Franco-American amity.

He wanted to prove to Frenchmen that peace with the United States would be economically advantageous. They were misled, he told them in an anonymously published article, if they still believed that French trade with America had not increased since her independence. He produced a statistical table based on the figures of American customs, which showed that in 1797 her trade with France was larger than with England. It would continue to grow, he was certain, if Franco-American commercial relations returned to normal. [34]

Before these facts were made public, Barlow assured Abraham Baldwin that with the arrival of new American plenipotentiaries the chance was favorable for an amicable understanding. [35] He apparently had some exclusive knowledge, for nine months later a convention was signed, ending the cold war between the United States and France.

The effect of the *Letters* on Franco-American relations cannot be gauged. Undeniably they were instrumental in enlightening many. They are of course dated. They belong to the large ephemeral literature spawned by the controversy between Federalists and Republicans. Yet they are among the best of these writings. They lack the rasping tone, the caustic temper and vituperative vocabulary usually the hallmarks of polemics. They are instead an example of wisdom aged in experience and presented in distinguished prose. The editor of the New Haven edition of the *Letters* was so convinced by their reasonableness that in a prefatory note he made the following offer to prospective buyers: "If in all the heavy volumes that load your shelves, in the *Defence* [sic] *of the American Constitutions* [by John Adams], you find enough of solid matter to balance a dozen pages of this pamphlet, return the pamphlet to the bookseller, and he will return your money."

Chapter XIV
Looking at Tomorrow

The fourth French constitution for which Barlow had vainly drafted a declaration of the rights of nations was accepted overwhelmingly at the end of 1799. It legally sanctioned the dictatorship of Napoleon. Less than three years later, a fifth constitution made him consul for life with the right to appoint his successor. After more than a decade of revolution France had made a complete circuit. Absolutism came back in more efficient form. Yet, the revolutionary principles remained embedded.

In contrast with France, the United States chose the course to republicanism and democracy. By the time the fourth French constitution was adopted, the Federalist Party was losing its grip on power. It was going through an internal, agonizing struggle. Led by Hamilton, the faction had counted on war to impose an arbitrary government. But its hope was shattered by the rising anti-war sentiment and by the ensuing decision of President Adams to negotiate. The party split. Its downfall was the consequence of the policy that had amplified its unpopularity. A test was the election of 1800, in which, despite an odious smear campaign, [1] Jefferson became President.

Napoleon and Jefferson were the embodiments of incompatible systems. The one made war the instrument of despotic power. The other counted on science, industry and peace as the media of attaining the rule of the common man.

1

Barlow was disheartened. His trust in France to initiate his cherished aim had dwindled, though he still had at heart "the conservation of republican principles & the prosperity and harmony of the two republics." [2] With Bonaparte at the helm, Barlow saw a gloomy shadow on the horizon. "Bonaparte has thrown back the progress of civilization & public happiness about one age," he confided to Fulton in August 1802. "He has revived the ideas of false glory which were losing ground very fast." Fortunately the example of America continued to be irresistible. [3] European liberals and reformers looked upon her as a model of good government. [4] This was in line with what he had said earlier to Aaron Baldwin: "I believe that liberty will be maintained in that country [U.S.], if not established in Europe." [5]

The longer he observed the ascent of Bonapartism, the more he shrank from it. Its system of public instruction brought back old forms of education. The Legion of Honor was of a piece with the Consulate. Both were plain impostures. Barlow could not abide the bustling observance of Bonaparte's birthday. It was all deception—high masses and *Te Deum's*, bells ringing, cannon firing; "more powder burnt than would serve to conquer half of Europe, & this to conquer only the French people." [6] The dream of a republican France turned into a nightmare.

Of all Bonapartist enactments the most shocking was the restoration of slavery and the slave trade in the French colonies. It was "the first instance in modern times," Barlow remarked, "where slavery had been established by law." And what was the logic behind this outrageous legislation? "No colonies without slavery; no merchant marine without colonies; hence no commerce, save a wretched coastal trade." The reasoning was false, he pointed out to Ruth and Fulton. For American commerce in 1801 "was more than five times greater, in proportion to our internal wealth, than that of any nation in Europe & we have no colonies." [7]

Slavery in French colonies caused him to reflect on slavery in the United States, which he hoped would be forgotten lest it "became the greatest scourge to our country." The initial step could be made in recently acquired Louisiana. Congress would thereby set an extraordinary example for eradicating slavery altogether in the United States as well as in Spanish America. "If this opportunity is lost," he wrote to Alexander Wolcott, "we never shall have another so good for banishing by gentle & easy means a most alarming calamity from a great portion of the earth." And further in the same letter: "A race of hereditary masters cannot be a race of republicans, or of just men. As well might you expect it from a race of slaves. Indeed, where this distinction is established, the true principles of society and just government cannot long exist. It is vain to expect it." [8]

Barlow epitomized the anti-slavery sentiment of eighteenth-century America and Europe. The nature of his thought resembled Jefferson's and Paine's, Condorcet's and Brissot's; and his argument was as dynamic as that of the abolitionist societies in America, England and France.

2

Personal problems occupied Barlow in Paris. Ruth's health concerned him deeply for many years. And he was in need of adequate living quarters which, with the growth of the capital's population, were becoming increasingly difficult to find. The inflationary spiral under the Directory had boosted rents and real estate values. Spacious, elegant properties, however, sold at far less than their original cost, and a person with fluid capital could profitably invest in them. In fact Barlow had already been doing that.

Unable to locate a suitable lodging, even with the diligent help of Thaddeus Kosciusko, he decided to purchase a mansion at 50 *rue de Vaugirard*, opposite the Luxembourg gardens. It had everything a gentleman of ease could want—apartments, dozens of rooms, servants' quarters, stables, carriage houses and a cellar large enough to hold hundreds of casks. He bought it with the object of ultimately reselling it. Meanwhile, it would serve him as a residence. Fulton lived here with the Barlows in an almost idyllic relationship.

Henry Redhead Yorke, a former acquaintance and Paine's old friend in England, visited the new owner of the mansion and was impressed by its magnificence. A tour of it showed him that it was destitute of furniture, excepting four rooms. Yorke was of the opinion that the prospect of disposing of the property was Barlow's reason for continuing his stay in France. Actually other considerations, apart from Ruth's poor health, detained him, such as business matters, which took him to England and the illustrations for his *Columbiad*. Host and visitor talked of politics. Barlow, Yorke tells us, was extremely guarded in his remarks, but what escaped his lips was "full of gall." Since Napoleon's seizure of power, he had developed "the most profound contempt" for the French republic, its rulers and its people. He seemed to show a greater regard for England. He confessed to Yorke that every year he had been expecting the bankruptcy of the English system. But when Pitt came forward with the income tax and the country submitted to it cheerfully, he became convinced that the nation could carry on for decades. Barlow spoke of Pitt in surprisingly flattering terms. He had "saved the old fabric [the English constitution], if it be worth saving."

The conversation turned to the Treaty of Amiens. It could be permanent, Barlow believed, if there was a change in the French government. But with Bonaparte at its head, peace could not endure. He was surrounded by hungry generals and soldiers. Was Bonaparte secure? Yorke asked. More so than his predecessors, Barlow answered. How would it all wind up? Barlow saw two possiblities: either a complete subjugation of Europe by Napoleon or a civil war in France that would end in the restoration of royalty. His final advice to the privileged orders therefore was "to be on their guard, and remain quiet."

There is a ring of veracity in the interview. Barlow, we know, was disillusioned with France. History, moreover, showed that the British institutions had more stability than he had believed. Yorke was convinced as he terminated his story that Barlow's "inclinations are completely alienated from Europe, which he considers as undone, and he expresses the most fervent anxieties for the hour of his departure from it." [9]

That hour came about three years later, during which he was preoccupied by other interests, a few of them of a private nature. He had also committed himself to complete the translation of Volney's *Ruins* that Jefferson had begun but could not finish. Jefferson's part of the work amounted to a little more than half of the book, which he sent to the author with the geologist William Maclure. Barlow completed the remaining portion to Jefferson's delight. "I am glad you were able to engage so fine a writer of English to translate your work," he wrote to Volney. "A better hand you could not have found." [10] Published in Paris in 1802, the translation was intended to replace two other versions that were considered defective.[11]

The *Ruins* provoked controversy in the United States. Clergymen likened it to heathenism—which in their dictionary was synonymous with atheism. Among its severest critics was the chemist and theologian, Joseph Priestley, who had already found fault with Edward Gibbon's account of the spread of Christianity. But Priestley's arguments against Gibbon were enmeshed in inconsequentials. [12] His answer to Volney was no more clarifying. It was ill-tempered and littered with undignified reflections on the author's character. [13] Volney at first refused to be drawn into a personal polemic. When at last he broke his silence, his reply was both a summation of his principal ideas and a reminder to his assailant that in matters of doubt and uncertainty the sensible procedure was to leave the door open for new evidence. For this was the way to freedom and discovery. [14]

Shortly after the publication of the translation Jefferson, seconded by Madison, revived an earlier proposal to have Barlow write the history of the United States. Derived from the most indisputable sources, it would be an antidote to Federalist narratives. [15]

3

Barlow's friendship with Jefferson had seasoned since their meeting in Paris in the late 1780s. With respect to fundamental issues they were of one mind. Jefferson had been as pleased with Barlow's reply to Burke as he was with his *Two Letters*. "Nothing can be sounder than the principles it inculcates," he wrote to Barlow with regard to the second print. "You have understood that the revolutionary movements in Europe had, by industry and artifice, been wrought into objects of terror even to this country, and which was perfectly unaccountable, and during the prevalence of which they were led to support measures the most insane." He was referring to the Alien and Sedition Acts and the war measures. He assured his friend that the people were recovering from their fright as its instigators were losing ground. [16]

Months before the election of 1800, Barlow looked to Jefferson's rise to the presidency. It would erase factional frontiers, he believed, and revitalize the principles of the American Revolution. He was encouraged in the prospect of victory by the increasing republican strength in Federalist strongholds. [17] With the election over, Barlow mapped out in a letter to Senator Baldwin a course of action for the forthcoming administration. It should promote domestic manufactures, encourage agriculture, further internal improvements and systematize the most advanced ideas of education. Jefferson, he recalled, had "labored at this to some advantage while governor of Virginia, and I should hope he might do it to a more extensive effect as president of the U.S. . . . I dwell on these subjects with great anxiety, because America, tho young, is growing old in wrong habits & prejudices, which have not yet become inveterate, but will soon if not corrected. It depends on this generation, perhaps on that one man, to say whether America shall rise to real greatness & true glory, or retrograde & dwindle into the ape of every error that has hitherto degraded & tormented the human race." [18] A new road was not only possible, but accessible, if leadership had a correct sense of direction.

Barlow and Jefferson had common ideas on the art of government and foreign policy. Both were disquieted by concentrated power. Consequently, they adhered to the federal principle by which the states reserved to themselves the powers they had not surrendered to the central authority. They wanted a government that was rigorously frugal and simple. The savings of the public revenue would be applied to the discharge of the national debt. For they denied the Federalist saying that a public debt was a public blessing. They preferred a militia to a standing army, and a small navy for protecting the American coasts to a large, expensive one. All in all they looked to an improved America in every aspect of life. They were eighteeenth-century men, in that they had an abiding faith in progress, in the ultimate triumph of reason and in the unfettered freedom of expression. Science was in "insurrection," to cite Jefferson's metaphor, opening fresh highways for the advance of mankind. Viewing the European scene, they both concluded that the best foreign policy for America was free trade with all nations and no political alignment with any. And both hoped for the eventual fulfillment of the French revolutionary principles. [19]

Barlow was extremely pleased with the political climate in the United States after Jefferson's taking office. "All seems prosperous and happy in America," he wrote to Ruth from England. "People were never more united, the new President quite the ton; in danger of being spoiled by adulation but seems to behave with wonderful dignity." [20] Again to Ruth four days later, "Jefferson's character as a statesman, uniting honesty with talents, stands higher in England than that of any other man now living. . . . The present administration is gaining a great & solid reputation & universal confidence." [21] Even in Federalist Connecticut, he learned from Jefferson, Republicans were gradually winning ground.

The news about his native state might have turned his thoughts to the politics of his classmates and early literary associates. All of them, save a few, we showed earlier, continued to be rooted in traditions and were supporters of the Federalist program. One may recall, for example, Timothy Dwight, looked upon as the pundit of the Connecticut aristocracy. Of him the *Aurora* said that he "is propagating the doctrines and promoting the ecclesiastical schemes of Calvin and Knox. The clergy follow his opinions and plans in sermons, prayers and newspapers." [22] The bonds between Barlow and his early fellow literati had worn to shreds.

He was thoroughly displeased with Connecticut politics. "It is a little strange," he wrote to Alexander Wolcott, "that a people so enlightened, as we used to call ourselves, should have carried on a long war and made such immense sacrifices for a thing they did not want, and that they can have been brought up by two or three men to such a pitch of frenzy as to be as fierce now for slavery as they were twenty years ago for freedom. . . . I never heard of men more jealous of a new mistress than they are of their new theory, that despotism is the only government fit for mankind, & the sooner the American people can be brought into that happy state of ignorance which renders them fit for such a government the better it will be for them." But he trusted that this state of things was of short duration. [23]

The Republicans were well on the way toward vindicating his confidence, he learned from home, and were steadily entering the New England legislatures. The returns for governor in Connecticut showed that they were moving ahead, even though the Federalist candidate was enjoying popularity. Besides, thought Barlow, the votes for governor, especially in his state, were a bad barometer for measuring political sentiment. [24] New data reaching him made him sanguine of success on a national scale. Congressional elections in Rhode Island, Vermont and New Hampshire gave assurance that the Republicans would soon sweep their rivals out of office. Even the New Hampshire Governor came dangerously near being turned out. "Candid Federalists acknowledge," wrote the president, "that their party can no longer raise its head." Federalism as a concept of government was becoming odious.

4

Save for frightening symptoms in Ruth's condition, which compelled her to spend nearly six months at Plombières, Barlow was enjoying ease in his mansion on *rue de Vaugirard*. Guests came and went; present at dinners were Fulton and Paine, Volney and Kosciusko. Barlow and Paine were heard venting their aversion for Napoleon. [25] Other visitors were the Swans and Livingstons, and the Dutch Minister, Schimmelpenick, a source of political and diplomatic secrets. At Helen Williams's crowded teas Barlow met such English celebrities as the Opies, Kemble of the Drury Lane Theater and Sir Francis Burdett, the young Baronet and liberal member of Parliament. Salon society generally bored Barlow, as it has bored many others. The evening of April 30, 1802, however, he and J. H. Stone found themselves in deep discussion on epic poetry in relation to republicanism. Could the former inspire the latter was a question that engaged Barlow's attention, for this was precisely the time he was working on the *Columbiad*. Stone's conjecture that Virgil was a republican would be hard to prove, answered Barlow, for the reason that in epic poetry it was difficult "to inculcate republican principles *in action*." He went on to explain: "To make a strong picture of heroic achievements it seems necessary to single out particular heroes, and give them to wield the sword of whole nations, or at least of whole armies. This is not only an indirect praise of absolute command, or *despotism*, but it throws all subordinate agents of victory into the shade, & holds up to view an inequality of merit which does not exist in fact." He had little respect for the Roman epic poets. Virgil was a fawning flatterer of despots, shown by his *Georgics, Pastorals* and the sixth book of the *Aeneid*. And Lucan's *Pharsalia* could scarcely support the thesis that epic poetry could serve to implant republicanism in the minds of men. Actually it was anti-epic, Barlow observed, [26] and, as others termed it later, a metrical chronicle.

Barlow was confessing, perhaps unwittingly, that epic poetry had long ceased to be the vogue in literature. Though the epic form continued to fascinate littérateurs, its only useful yield was an increasing number of translations of early heroic poems. Neither the American and French Revolutions nor Bonaparte's ventures inspired like poetry of undying fame. With all his travels, Bonaparte could no more be a Ulysses than Josephine a Penelope.

Let us return to Barlow's social life in Paris. In August 1802 Congressman John Dawson of Virginia arrived, bringing letters from Jefferson and Abraham Baldwin and the treaty with France that the Senate had ratified. Barlow invited Dawson to stay with him, probably to learn details of American politics, for Jefferson had written him privately that the congressman was "fully informed and worthy of confidence." [27] In November Robert Livingston took up his duties as minister to France, which turned out happily for Barlow. The American minister, a wealthy man, succeeded Barlow as the financial backer of Fulton's experiments with the steamboat. [28] In the spring of 1803 Livingston and Fulton formed a partnership to construct a boat of specified dimensions that would be powered by steam. Monroe reappeared in 1803 to join Livingston in negotiating the purchase of New Orleans and the Floridas. Napoleon, however, determined to sell all of Louisiana. The purchase was an unexpected pleasure to Barlow, although he had known something of the backstage bargaining.

Among the bits of news he sent his wife was that Tom Paine was returning to the United States.[29] The same Yorke who had visited Barlow also called on Paine and drew his portrait on the eve of his departure. His name, we are told, was as odious in France as in England and America. To pronounce it in public was like tapping a sewer of obscene vocabulary. Yorke learned after some trouble that he resided on rue du Théâtre Français, a dilapidated part of Paris. What a contrast with Barlow's elegant residence! Paine's single room was filled with boxes of books and manuscripts, all labeled according to subject. Once he identified his visitor, he received him with the usual warmth. Like Barlow, he had been disenchanted with France. "This is not a country for an honest man to live in," he said to Yorke, "they do not understand anything at all of the principles of free government. . . . You see they have conquered all Europe, only to make it more miserable than it was before." Republicanism remained only in America, "the only country for such men as you and I. . . . I have done with Europe and its slavish politics."[30]

In the eyes of democratic republicans France under Napoleon was no longer a cynosure but a Gehenna. Barlow, as much as Paine, looked forward to an escape to the United States.

Of basic importance in Barlow's program of America's development was a national system of education. It was in fact his preliminary to a good order. In this respect his thought paralleled Rousseau's, Diderot's and Helvetius'. A resemblance is noticeable between his and their views on education, especially the trust in its efficacy to change circumstances and men. In common with Helvetius, for example, Barlow held that a nation's strength and happiness depended on the perfection of the science of education.

He had come to this decision while fighting the battle for Franco-American amity. Seen in this context, it may be read both as an answer to the war faction and as a supplement to his program for a progressive United States. The primary object of education, as he conceived it, was stated by him December 28, 1798, in remarks on General Ira Allen's account of the provision Vermont had made in that connection.

> The subject of public instruction is in all countries extremely interesting to me, as it is necessarily the most rational foundation of hope or fear relative to the future prosperity of nations; but it assumes the highest interest when applied to a new people, where prejudices are not deeply rooted; where most things are yet to be created & few to uncreate; and where the public mind is already so far enlightened as to comprehend the propriety of adopting a rational & extensive system. It is certain that if we wish to preserve the principles & practice of liberty where they are now enjoyed, to extend them to places where they are not known, or to improve them where they are partly understood, we must proceed by instruction. This is not only the most pacific, and the most legitimate way of changing or ameliorating the condition of man, but it is the most energetic & the most

effectual.

The attainment of that aim, he acknowledged, was far from easy. Prejudices, deep-rooted practices and vested interests would impede improvements of the establishment. Still he looked to a fortunate occasion "for founding a new system in a new country, to grow up with a whole people, to form their habits, enlighten their understandings, stimulate their enquiries, & concentrate their opinions on all the great objects which go into the composition of national happiness."

He trusted that America would follow this line of development. There was little in the English and German universities for his country to copy, and even less in elementary education as it was carried on in Europe. A new system could not be built on timeworn patterns. He was so gratified with Vermont's new approach that he proposed to outline a general plan of public instruction. [31]

The plan grew into his *Prospectus of a National Institution*. The project slowly shaped itself in his mind over a period of nearly eight years, and he mentioned it to Jefferson and to Abraham Baldwin. An immense field was open for the renovation of the United States. He sounded the warning that "if you suffer the present generation to pass away without putting them in the right path, and familiarizing them with sound principles, the chance is lost, your nation will degenerate & mankind will perhaps never be compensated for your unpardonable neglect." Then, after a few observations on the meliorative function of the sciences of chemistry and mineralogy, he remarked: "Sound reason in this country has no enemy but ignorance,—in other countries it has all sorts of abuses, reasons of State, religions of State, privileged orders, with all their wealth & power. Education, my friend, I mean instruction generally diffused among the great mass of the people, is the only means of retaining what we have got, & of acquiring more, of public happiness, liberty & peace." [32]

He seems to have recovered the enthusiasm of the previous decade. He had then rested his hopes on France and taken up the cudgels against Burke. But France had gone the wrong way. America alone could be the inspiration, provided she took the road to a better social order. This was perhaps a dream, the sort of dream that lured many people to American shores. With Jefferson as president, the prospect seemed bright, in Barlow's vision.

Animated by the outlook he was anxious to go back home. But he was delayed by a business affair and the drawings and plates for the *Columbiad*. The business related to a cargo seized by the British, for which he was claiming compensation. This required his going to England, where ten years earlier his name had been anathema to the British authorities. To avoid any possible annoyance, he traveled incognito and took the precaution of notifying the American minister in London that he was traveling on business. But all measures to avoid recognition were in vain. Somehow the news got about that he was in London. Horne Tooke and Sir Francis Burdett knew it, which meant that all London radicals were informed. Before long he was merrily dining with them. His old publisher, Joseph Johnson, joined them, and Barlow reported to his wife that he had grown "fat, careless & happy. He took me by the hand, shaking his sides, & the first word was 'well you could not get me hanged, you tried all you could.' " [33] He had spent nine months in prison for having published subversive literature.

Barlow also performed services for Fulton during his brief visit to England. He made some inquiries regarding an economical engine for the steamboat, and he talked at length with the mathematician, scientist, inventor and radical, Earl Stanhope, about the practicality of the water wheel in propelling boats. Stanhope and Fulton later projected a canal with a new system of inclined planes and improved locks.

Barlow and Fulton were sharing one another's problems. While the one concerned himself with pistons, cylinders and coal consumption, the other turned his artistic talent to making sketches for the *Columbiad*. By early July 1802 Fulton had done eight drafts; two more were still unfinished. His drawing of the Mohawks was the best thing Barlow had ever seen. In a prefatory note to Fulton, Barlow wrote: "You designated the subjects to be painted for engravings; and unable to convince me that the work could merit such expensive and splendid decorations, you ordered them to be executed in my absence and at your expense."

The publication of an elegant edition necessitated the help of artists and engravers. Barlow first employed the American historical and portrait painter, John Vanderlyn, who had studied in Paris; and then he turned to Robert Smirke, a member of the British Royal Academy, who was engaged for three possible reasons. First, he painted in monochrome which was best adapted for engraving; second, he was experienced in designing illustrations for books and finally, his political opinions were similar to Barlow's. Smirke was commissioned to do a series of ten pictures. For a frontispiece Fulton decided to use his portrait of Barlow. The edition proved to be costly, amounting to about ten thousand dollars. [34]

Barlow was all this time preparing for his homeward journey. He was disposing of his property and transferring his funds to the United States. With regard to Ruth's health he decided to consult doctors in England where she showed surprising improvement. They spent the winter of 1804 in London and, despite the inclement weather, enjoyed their stay. Fulton came to see them, and old friends helped to make evenings convivial. The English radicals had lost their bite, but they remained principled. Of them can be said what Barlow once said of himself: "I never have & never shall deviate from the broad & noble interests of my country and mankind." [35]

The Barlows sailed home early in the summer of 1805 and landed in New York in August. The voyage was long, stormy and full of tormenting seasickness. Still it was comforting to be back on native soil after an absence of seventeen years.

Chapter XV
Proposed Roads to Tomorrow

The face of America had changed somewhat during Barlow's absence. The population had increased from nearly four to approximately five and a half million. And it had spread out, especially westward. Kentucky, Tennessee and the Northwest had 109,000 inhabitants in 1790; Ten years later its population reached 377,000. Agriculture, fishing and trading were the primary occupations. Manufacturing was on a small scale, carried on in the home or in small shops. The application of technology to industry was only beginning. The textile industry was in its infancy. Shipbuilding, iron and paper manufacturing, however, had grown. The largest advances were in shipping and foreign trade. The domestic market expanded, but slowly. The opening of the Ohio-Mississippi waterway after the purchase of Louisiana stimulated the export of western produce. An immediate effect was to quiet the agitation of the settlers.

During the same time, the nation grew more prosperous. The mounting demand for American goods, a result of the European war, brought wealth into the country. Prices rose as capital accumulated. The abundance of savings served the progress of American industry after 1815. In Barlow's native New England about seventy power-driven textile mills were in operation in 1810. But they turned out only two percent of the cloth produced domestically. [1]

Life continued in the old routine way. Most families lived on farms, cultivated the land the way it had been done for generations, used the same tools, grew the same crops, ate homemade foods and wore homespun. City residents formed but a tiny number of the population.

America had also changed politically and socially. A Bill of Rights had been added to the Constitution. The freedoms it guaranteed to the individual, however, contrasted, at least in spirit and philosophy, with the suffrage limitations in the old states. The new ones to the west were singularly free of such restrictions. Two political parties had come into being whose diverse outlooks were evidence of economic and social cleavages. Class demarcations were far from clear, though they were apparent. The wealthy had grown wealthier during the war years in Europe, and while a little of the prosperity had trickled down to small farmers, artisans and laborers, the gap between rich and poor was greater than it had been before the Revolution.

The Federalist Party never recovered from its defeat in 1800. Before passing out of history, its leading die-hards plotted the dissolution of the Union. The idea of secession had been raised in the Federalist press in 1796 and 1797. By 1800 it became a threat. To save its settled way of life, warned upper Federalists, New England would be forced to establish a Northern Confederacy. [2]

There was intrigue during the administrations of Jefferson and Madison. A number of Federalists corresponded secretly with British agents with the insensate hope of drawing New England closer to Great Britain. Others favored luring Aaron Burr into the conspiracy, with the prospect of adding New York State to the Confederacy. But Hamilton frowned on the design. [3] The seccession movement ultimately went to pieces. It never had popular backing. It was a coterie at best, stubbornly standing its ground before the relentless march of events.

The same disposition to pursue their own advantage impelled the Federalists to oppose the purchase of Louisiana. Its acquisition, they realized, would lower the value of eastern lands and increase the Republican majority. [4] Barlow was revolted by this opposition. He could think of "no instance recorded in history of so palpable a display of passion, contradictory and degrading to the human character." [5]

1

Federalism succumbed slowly, especially in Connecticut. Here invective broke loose upon Barlow's arrival. His right to American citizenship was questioned, for by public act it was declared that he had recognized himself a citizen of France. With an allergy to facts, publicists asserted that he had been elected a deputy to the French Convention, at the bar of which he had appeared to renounce the Christian faith and to profess his belief in atheism. To cap it all, articles filled with shocking absurdities were published under his name in British and American newspapers.

The slander saddened him. For a time he felt lonely, a stranger in the land he had helped to gain independence, and unwanted in the place of his birth. Webster met him in this mental state and reported to their mutual friend Judge Stephen Jacob in Vermont:

"I have seen our old friend Barlow. He is still a little convalescent, chiefly by means of Bonaparte's harsh remedies for new philosophy; but I think his *constitution* so much impaired that a radical cure is impossible. He feels himself in an awkward situation—a downcast look, at least when I saw him, marks great depression of mind, or consciousness of something wrong at bottom." [6]

Republican strides in the stronghold of Federalism lifted his spirit. He was comforted by the tribute paid him at a welcoming reception in New Haven. About one hundred and fifty Republican legislators and other citizens met on October 29, 1805, to honor him for his "distinguished talents and patriotic services." In his reply he spoke with joy of the improvements he had observed everywhere in the country. Much, of course, remained to be explored, particularly in the immense field of political science, by which he meant the education of the people in the ways of governing. He professed deep faith in America's promise and in the success of her system. A vast domain had been added; settlers were taking up western lands; bars to equality were giving under pressure; people were living better; the voters had given Jefferson's second administration a clear mandate; and a feeling of optimism pervaded. Still more, America was charged with a lofty mission. "Our country must now be considered as the depository & the guardian of the best interests of mankind—all good men in Europe view it in that light. I hope we shall be duly sensible of the importance of this sacred deposit, & that our patriotism, without diminishing its energy, may at all times partake of the broad & peaceful character of general philanthropy." [7]

It was in the manner of a peroration, spoken with earnestness. For he had come back with the expectation of furthering scientific research and philosophical speculation, of fostering literary and artistic taste and promoting instruction in all fields of knowledge.

A parenthesis is in order here to describe his movements for renewing friendships and choosing a place to live. Though he was the most versatile son of Yale, he could hardly expect it to receive him cordially. It was under the iron rule of the intolerant Timothy Dwight. Nor could he look forward to a warm reception by his one-time Hartford friends. The intellectual ties had been sundered. Consequently Barlow had little inducement to settle in Connecticut.

He was drawn southward, to Washington. The president wanted him nearby for several reasons. With Barlow's aid he could better feel the pulse of European politics and decide on the country's best course in its relations with the great powers. He also counted on Barlow to write a history of the United States from the democratic republican standpoint.

In the matter of America's relations with Europe, conditions had worsened. Great Britain had gained control of the seas by the victory of Trafalgar. A month and a half later the battle of Austerlitz gave Napoleon mastery of the continent. As a result America was caught between the blockading decrees of the two foes. How could America defend her neutral rights? There is some indication that the question was put to Barlow, but we have no way of knowing his answer. A memorandum in an unidentified hand argued that America should declare her right to carry to any port, save in the case of blockade, articles of neutral origin, save contraband of war. She should, moreover, define the right of search and visits at sea and restrict the impressment of American seamen to the ports of the belligerent countries. We cannot say whether Barlow had any part in drafting the recommendations. But he had the memorandum in his hand. On the back of the folder containing it are the words, "Barlow valuable." [8]

He had his own motives for making Washington his place of residence. He had political ambitions. And he looked forward to the adoption of his educational program. The president was for it. And so was the indefatigable Senator George Logan. The senator had extended the Barlows a cordial invitation to stay with him in Philadelphia. [9]

2

Barlow's project of a national institution was the fruit of much study and consultation. Its roots went back to the scientific and philosophical societies of the seventeenth and eighteenth centuries. A more direct inspiration was the Institute of France, established during the French Revolution to promote science, literature and art; and to some degree, the University of France, created to maintain uniformity in the educational system Napoleon had erected. Auxiliary ideas on education came to Barlow from individuals he had met abroad and from the American pioneer geologist and social reformer, William Maclure. Scotch-born, he probably had early imbibed some of the thinking of the Scotch Jacobins. Maclure and Barlow had much in common. They were deeply interested in the history of the French Revolution, and each had amassed a substantial library; they shared the conviction that the American and French Revolutions had hastened the progress of freedom and civilization. [10]

They were both apprehensive of the harmful effects of the division of labor and technology, but neither one found a solution to the problems they foresaw. Maclure subsequently sought the answer in Owen's community of New Harmony. Barlow was confident that science would eventually "open the way" to a perfected order. [11] Significantly, he did not revert to the possibility of collective ownership he had suggested in *Advice to the Privileged Orders*. He came to rely instead on education and research stimulated by a national university and ancillary institutions.

They had differences of opinion, too. Maclure rejected Barlow's plan of a national institution for the reason that the knowledge it would disseminate and the influence it would radiate were of far less moment in the United States than "the equal distribution of knowledge as well as the equal distribution of property which increases the sum of general happiness." This view he derived from an analysis of social classes. Society, said Maclure, was divided into rich and poor, into buyers and sellers of labor. Happiness and intellectual progress depended on an equilibrium of the two extremes. Otherwise the rich would retain a monopoly of knowledge while the poor would be kept in ignorance. Institutions of higher learning, he wrote, were for the children of the wealthy, thereby fortifying their monopoly of knowledge, much as the banks and the rich monopolized property. An increase of the knowledge of the rich was also "an increase of general misery." Instead of establishing new universities or improving the old, he wanted schools for children to teach them, as he put it, "things not words, common sense in place of indefinite sound." [12]

Barlow was not converted to Maclure's social philosophy. He conceded that distinctions of wealth were not only more harmful than distinctions of rank, they also impaired the body politic and eroded the democratic institutions. Barlow had no objection either to Maclure's schools or to the Pestalozzian education he supported. In fact he was in communication with Joseph Neef, a former colleague of Pestalozzi in Paris. To his way of thinking, that type of school and educational method could neither rule out institutions of higher learning nor invalidate their worth in promoting science and fostering an intellectual climate. In the long-range view they would even prevent national disturbances and the rise of despotism.

Anticipations like these were probably in Barlow's mind when he wrote out his plan for a national university. At Jefferson's request he drafted a bill to be presented to Congress, and Senator Logan became a member of a committee that was to consider it. To win public support, Barlow published the project, entitled *Prospectus of a National Institution to be Established in the United States,* and had friends put it "into good hands." [13] A copy went to Madison with the request "to encourage it among your friends." "I may mistake the true interest of the country," said Barlow. "But it appears to me that this project embraces one of the most essential of them." [14]

The *National Intelligencer,* the administration's organ, paid tribute to the author of the *Prospectus.* [15] The writer of the encomium caught the true meaning of the National Institution. Its objective was promoting republicanism in America and projecting its growth by enlisting the aid of outstanding talents in science, mechanics, art, literature and industry.

The aim was reminiscent of Henri de Saint-Simon's. His *Letters of a Genevan* in 1802 charted the global development of mankind, planned by scientists, artists and industrialists, for the purpose of improving humanity. [16] The ultimate realization of both projects required the unity of all the disciplines.

The object of the National Institution was to map the young nation's advance. The country was vast, much of it unexplored; its products varied; its people of diverse origin, with different manners and propensities and with a proneness to diverge and separate. The function of science, art, literature and political economy was to cultivate a harmony of interests and to serve government in creating a better national life.

Barlow believed that once the country was out of debt the better part of the revenue would be diverted to public improvements. To that end the National Institution would "prepare the way for the government to act on those great objects with intelligence, economy, and effect," and "aid its operations when it shall be ready to apply its fund to that purpose." [17] Planning and research should begin at once in order to be ready when the government was disposed to start.

Worthy of notice was Barlow's tribute to the French National Convention for its far-seeing legislation. He recalled the educational reforms and the Institute that Napoleon modified because he feared the novel ideas political science might produce. The fact was, declared Barlow, the French Revolution had taken long strides in the field of education. The Convention's plans "on this subject were great, and in general good; much good indeed has grown out of them, though they have not been pursued by the government during its subsequent changes, in the manner contemplated by the projectors." To substantiate his claim he named the many educational and scientific establishments credited to the Convention. [18]

A quick survey of science in general caused him to conclude that it was still in its infancy. Several of its branches, for example, chemistry, mechanics and hydraulics, recorded some progress; but anatomy and medicine had advanced only slightly. Political economy, government, history, literature and philosophy were so little methodized that they scarcely deserved to be called sciences. Little or no standing was given to them, even though they had been the objects of investigation by such eminent men as Locke, Berkeley, Pope, Hume, Robertson, Gibbon, Adam Smith and Blackstone. Yet no subjects of study were more properly suited to the United States. Here was in process a republican experiment combining the federal and democratic methods. The world still had to be persuaded that her system was "the greatest improvement in the mechanism of government that has ever been discovered, the most consoling to the friends of liberty, humanity and peace." [19]

Barlow counted on the National Institution to aid the success of the experiment. His plan called for a central university and related universities, colleges and educational bodies throughout the land. A normal school was also contemplated. The National Institution would have laboratories, libraries, apparatus for the arts and sciences, gardens for botany and agricultural experiments and a printing press that would publish the results of research as well as text books for the nation's elementary schools. Research would be encouraged by scholarships and correspondence. The Military and Naval Academies would be connected with the Institution as would the Mint and Patent Office. In fact, no aspect of knowledge would be beyond its attention. Considering its many objects and its comprehensive organization, a historian likened it to the House of Solomon of Bacon's *New Atlantis.* [20]

Barlow's bill had a checkered history. Influential men of both parties favored it, and so did the administration. But advocates of state rights and state institutions opposed it. Logan introduced a bill into the Senate that was substantially like Barlow's. It passed on a second reading, was referred to a committee, amended on the third reading and sent to a select committee which never reported it. Friends subsequently made a heroic effort to save part of the plan by organizing the Columbian Institute for the Promotion of Arts and Sciences. The Institute languished and finally closed its doors in the Jacksonian period.

3

Both the *Columbiad* and the *Prospectus* were meant to focus attention on the coming glory of America and mankind. The first forecast a prosperous, peaceful world order that:

> *Makes patriot views and moral views the same,*
> *Works with enlighten'd zeal, to see combined*
> *The strength and happiness of mankind.*

The second traced the course of that goal.

The epic poem was a life's work that had developed in the author's mind over a period of about thirty years. The *Vision of Columbus* was its first draft, the revision began in Paris. By the middle of 1802 only two of the ten books remained to be finished. They were completed while the illustrations and engravings were being done. The *Columbiad* was finally published in Philadelphia in 1807.

Two epics, with the same title, had already appeared in America. One was by a certain Richard Snowden. [21] Another, in blank verse, was attributed to the Irish immigrant, John Daly Burk, who succeeded Freneau as editor of the *Time-Piece*. It was "a republican poem," in Freneau's judgment, which held the promise of immortality. [22] This was of course an overestimation.

A comparison of the *Vision of Columbus* and the *Columbiad* reveals significant contrasts. They are explainable, first, by the French revolutionary events, and then, by the changes wrought in the author's views. He became a dyed-in-the-wool republican, hostile to the race of kings. Also during the rewriting of the poem he was approaching philosophical materialism. The *Columbiad* was a longer poem and maturer than the *Vision of Columbus*. Apart from having two thousand more verses, the argument ran along different lines. The new version glorified peace instead of war; the improvement of civilization was linked to the advancement of science rather than to faith; and man replaced Providence at the wheel of progress. Symbolic of the author's changed trend of thought was the dedication of the poem to Robert Fulton. Also credit for

French aid to America went, not to the Bourbon monarch, as in *The Vision*, but to the *philosophes*, "the Gallic sages."

The principle object of the revised poem was stated in the Preface.

> *I wish to encourage and strengthen in the rising generation a sense of the importance of republican institutions, as being the great foundation of private and public happiness, the necessary aliment of future and permanent ameliorations in the condition of human nature.*

In the author's opinion the subject of the *Columbiad* was superior to that of the celebrated epics. It had a special direction, a "political tendency." The real purpose of the *Iliad* was to implant in young minds the divine right doctrine, to make plunder honorable and to teach that war and conquest were the noble pursuits of peoples. In the *Aeneid* the poet "wrote and felt like a subject, not like a citizen." The example of Napoleon might have flashed through Barlow's mind when he said that Virgil's object was "to increase veneration of the people for a master . . . and to encourage the great system of military depredation." [23]

Barlow claimed a grander scope for his poem. Its aim was to instill a love of liberty, to cast disfavor on conquest and the havoc of war, to exalt republican principle and to show that the betterment of society was a disputed objective because organized liberty was little practiced. Consequently the war scenes and descriptions of battles were relegated to a minor position.

The first five books of the *Columbiad*, save for some small alterations, remained the same as in *The Vision of Columbus*. Forlorn and despondent, Columbus is saved from utter dejection by Hesper, the guardian genius of the Western Hemisphere, with the prophecy of the glories that would garland his name. Book V in both poems brings us news of the volunteers and the death of Montgomery.

At this point the *Columbiad* deviates from *The Vision*. In book VI the scene shifts from the death-riddled British prison ship to Washington crossing the Delaware, and then to Burgoyne, a British Xerxes, like him defeated by inferior, valorous numbers. Here the poet asks:

When shall the applause of men their chiefs pursue
In just proportion to the good they do,
On Virtue's base erect the shrine of fame,
Define her empire, and her code proclaim?

Book VII goes on to the surrender of Cornwallis. Fittingly the poet introduces the alliance with France, the role of French philosophy in bringing the old world to the new, and the inspiration of the American Revolution. As the fate of Cornwallis seems sealed, Barlow exclaims:

Sad field of contemplation! Here, ye great,

Kings, priests of God, and ministers of state,
Review your system here! behold and scan
Your own fair deeds, your benefits to man!

● ● ● ● ● ●

You choose to check his toil, and band his eyes
To all that's honest and to all that's wise.

Book VIII begins appropriately with a Hymn to Peace, quite similar to that of the *Vision*, but longer. The patriots are exhorted to preserve the liberty they won. It faced a dire threat from slavery and the slave trade. Cries Atlas to Hesper:

Enslave my tribes! what, half mankind imban,
Then read, expound, enforce the rights of man!
Prove plain and clear how nature's hand of old
Cast all men equal in her human mould!

The cultivation of art, science and commerce is the opening theme of Book IX. Hesper predicts the progress of society and the coming of perpetual peace. All scientific inventions and geographical discoveries pointed that way. Systems of government similar to the American would extend to the whole earth.

Finally, in Book X the vision embraces all people. A general congress of nations meets to establish the political unity of mankind. This may explain why Barlow was once termed a "precursor of the League of Nations." [24]

The golden age was not in the past, asserted Barlow. The notion that the social state of man was not meliorative had mischievous implications. It suggested that he was retrogressing; it discouraged efforts at political and social improvement; it served as a defense of every type of tyranny and oppression; it instilled a belief that ignorance was better than knowledge; and it justified the idea that war and violence were better than peace and industry. Yet mankind's striving to forge ahead showed the very opposite. [25] The period of great prosperity, the poet declared, lay ahead. With the help of the highest achievements in art, science and industry, men will enjoy abundance and live by mutual aid.

The poem is painfully didactic. It labors industriously to inflame Americans with the bright future of the young republic. It prods the verses to exhibit the gathering energy of the country and its confidence "to lead all nations, lighten every land." It voices an awakened national consciousness. Its intense love of country is blended with the spirit of international brotherhood.

The *Columbiad* is more a discourse on progress than an epic. As poetry it is dull and waxlike. The lines seem laboriously worked out, as if the poet worked with a thesaurus. Grace of expression is woefully lacking, as is brilliant fancy. It is an extravagance of declamation without flashes of great art. It is, in the judgment of a literary historian, "sonorous, metallic, rhetorical." Among its principal defects are "forced description, manufactured sentiment, sublimity generated by pasteboard and starch." [26]

On the other hand, the poem excels in political and philosophical reflections. Here the author was quite secure with his storehouse of knowledge and breadth of experience. These attainments set him far above contemporary American bards and ranked him higher than a large number in Great Britain at the time. In the opinion of the *Edinburgh Review*, the poet deceived himself if he had any aspiration to be an American Homer. His style was cumbersome, and he mistook "hyperbole for grandeur." However, said the critic, in comparison with the rhymesters of the day he was a giant. As "a philosophical and moral poet, we think he has talents of no ordinary value." [27]

The *Columbiad* was an earnest example of the literary flowering in America. But it never had a large audience, despite its reprints. The first edition was too expensive for the average book-buyer. Individuals privately spoke well of it. Josiah Meigs wrote that "your poem is too honestly Republican for the noble bloods of your country." [28] Noah Webster at first intended to praise it, but its "atheistical principles," to cite him, caused him to remain silent. [29] *The Monthly Anthology and Boston Review* said that it was, "in its present state, a very uncommon production and one which, considering its general plan and the singular conformity of character in all its parts, forms a sort of epoch in the literature of our country." [30]

Adverse opinion came from two separate sources. A reader of Chatham County, North Carolina, mildly reproved the poet for having omitted Paine from the constellation of American revolutionaries. The answer was a blend of respectability and opportunism. Paine, wrote Barlow, had disgraced his public character by his almost "habitual drunkenness." Those who knew him only in private life, who had either not read his writings or chose to forget them "would be highly offended to see his name treated with any respect or approbation." Barlow's hasty strokes were hardly satisfactory, even to himself. He hoped, he said, to set the record straight in the history of the United States he was working on, where Paine would receive "strict and ample justice . . . as one of the most able and efficient defenders of our rights." [31] The history was never written.

Barlow's estimate of Paine was in a letter to James Cheetham, the abusive journalist from New York, who requested information for the life of Paine he was writing. This was the wrong time to publish such a biography, ran the reply. Paine's "own writings are his best life, and these are not read at present." Barlow went on to admonish Cheetham that dwelling on the unpopular aspects of Paine's life to the exclusion of his estimable traits of character might make the book a best-seller, but it would pervert the truth. The biographer "should give us Thomas Paine *complete*, in all his character, as one of the most benevolent and disinterested of mankind, endowed with the clearest perception, an uncommon share of original genius, and the greatest breadth of thought." He should be ranked "among the brightest and most undeviating luminaries of the age in which he has lived, yet with a mind assailable by flattery . . . with a mind, though strong enough to bear him up and to rise elastic under the heaviest hand of oppression, yet unable to endure the contempt of his former friends and fellow laborers, the rulers of the country that had received his first and greatest services." [32]

The sharpest criticism of the *Columbiad* arrived from his old friend, Bishop Grégoire. His letter addressed to the author quickly reached the public and caused controversy. [33] What aroused the Bishop's displeasure? As he neared the last pages of Book X he read these verses:

Beneath the footstool all destrucive things,
The mask of priesthood and the mace of kings,
Lie trampled in the dust; for here at last
Fraud, folly, error all their emblems cast.

He then looked at Smirke's illustration with the inscription "Final destruction of prejudices," that Fulton had designed. There he beheld lying in a heap, together with swords, scepters and crescent, such objects as miters, crosiers, censers and a crucifix. The engraving, he declared, was "an attack against all Christian societies . . . an act of intolerance, of persecution, which offends God and man." It reminded him of the anti-Christian acts of the French Revolution. He granted that Barlow's manner was different, but the final results were the same, irreligion, immorality and social disorder.

American clergymen applauded the bishop for having added refined fuel to their assaults on leading Republican "infidels." But they were hasty in enjoying the triumph. For the same year that his letter was published, Barlow's *Letter to Henry Grégoire in Reply to His Letter on the Columbiad*, appeared in pamphlet.

It was a disarming refutation. [34] A person's religion, replied Barlow, depended on a chain of circumstances beyond his control, such as his place of birth and the teachings of the sect to which he adhered. He, Barlow, was born a Puritan, and to a Puritan Catholics were idolaters. He made use of no cross except the mystical one of mortifying his sins. Had Puritans answered a call for a crusade and reconquered the tomb of Christ, "they would have trampled on the cross with as fervent a zeal as they would upon the crescent." The use of emblems was a relative matter. One sect might consider those of another as predilections of a dangerous tendency and honestly desire their destruction without any hostility to the sect's fundamental doctrines. It was in this sense that the crucifix and other symbols of Christianity were tossed on the heap of prejudices.

The bishop, continued the answer, had apparently mistaken the meaning and motive of the poem. Taken as a whole, with the preface and notes, it was more moral, more consistent with what the bishop acknowledged to the spirit of the Gospel and more energetic in denouncing oppression in every shape "than all the writings of all that list of Christian authors of the three last ages," whom Grégoire considered "the glory of christendom."

Barlow took up the defense of the French revolutionaries against their critic. The primary cause of their hostile acts against the Church was not their lack of faith, but "the complicated ceremonials of their worship," the countless varieties "of pomp and circumstance" that were incorporated "with the vital principles of faith and practice." The exterior of the edifice had been so shellacked with deceit that to remove it without injuring the system required a more discriminating eye and a steadier hand than the times could afford. It was not surprising therefore that the revolutionaries brought down the entire structure.

The reply was met with silence, as Barlow had foreseen. "I do not expect this letter to Grégoire will be read," he wrote to his friend Stephen Jacob in Vermont. "The Tories will not print it. They are afraid the truth should be known." [35]

A second letter from the bishop was cordial and apologetic in a way.[36] But it did not disarm Barlow's slanderers. *The Monthly Anthology and Boston Review*, for example, which had praised the *Columbiad*, changed its tune. It demoted Barlow to the rank of indifferent poets, sorry politicians and bad philosophers. [37] Benjamin Rush, after reading the bishop's letter, wrote exultingly to John Adams, "It is a masterly performance and exposes with great eloquence the folly and madness of infidelity." [38]

Friends congratulated Barlow on his reply and hoped to get it into the press. But their efforts were in vain. A letter from Philadelphia said that "It is full, smooth, forcible . . . It has surpassed my expectations."[39] Madison praised it both for its content and the spirit that emanated from it.[40]

Publishing the *Columbiad* was very expensive. Even if the entire first edition sold, it would not pay for itself. Barlow calculated that it would not cover half of the approximate ten thousand dollars it cost. [41] It was reissued in three separate editions, without the illustrations. But it never became popular.

The fault lay not only in the poem, but also in the spirit of the age. The "inordinate and universal pursuit of wealth as a means of distinction," as Barlow expressed it, derogated from regard for scientists and men of letters. [42] Even so, contemporaries esteemed Barlow. In 1807 he was elected to the Military Philosophical Society. Two years later the

American Philosophical Society made him a member, and the University of Georgia conferred on him the degree of Doctor of Laws. At a dinner given in Washington to Captain Lewis on the success of his expedition, he honored the explorer in a poem of nine stanzas. It probably had a warm reception in the crowded dining room, but it needed more than applause to stamp it with immortality.[43] And it incited John Quincy Adams to write a parody which, if better known in its day, might have sunk his standing among political thinkers and littérateurs.[44]

One of Barlow's other public appearances merits some notice. At the commemoration of July 4, 1809, he delivered an oration[45] which surprised even good friends. "I was doubting what you would say, equal to your own reputation, on so hackneyed a subject," Jefferson wrote him afterward, "but you have really risen out of it with lustre, and pointed to others a field of great expansion."[46] The speaker forecast a radiant America. It had been fated by Providence. The predestined course of the country, drawn with sureness, might have struck a welcome note in listeners who counted on self-interest as the vehicle to the nation's future. But Barlow had other media in mind. Men had to be taught to evaluate the most promising means of the country's growth. To leave it unplanned would amount to repeating the errors of Europe. The new generations had to be prepared to assume the responsibilities of leading the country in the right direction, by way of public improvements and public instruction. These were the nation's best investment. He then recapitulated what he had formulated in his *Letters from Paris*. America was better suited than other nations to work out her great promise. Her democratic system had been tested and proved invulnerable. A wide ocean protected her against the belligerent powers. Her vast resources awaited development. Within her boundaries at least two hundred million people could live in peace and comfort.

This was his vision of America's future. It epitomized the principal ideas of his literary work.

Chapter XVI
Mission to Napoleon

1

"Kalorama" (Greek, meaning "fine view") was the name of Barlow's estate in Washington. Its history dated from 1750 when it was built with imported British bricks. The house with about thirty acres had passed through several hands before Barlow bought it. Jefferson had tried in 1802 to interest Barlow, describing it as "a most lovely seat adjoining this city, on a high hill, commanding a most extensive view of the Potomac."[1]

Here is how Barlow portrayed the property to a friend:

> I have here a most delightful situation; it only wants the improvements that we contemplate to make it a little paradise. It is a beautiful hill, about one mile from the Potomac and 200 feet in elevation above tidewater, with Washington and Georgetown under my eye and Alexandria eight miles below, still in view, the Potomac reflecting back the sun in a million forms and losing himself among the hills that try on each side to shove him from his course. If you have a plan of the city I can show you my very spot. Look at the stream called Rock Creek, that divides Washington from Georgetown. I am just outside the city on the Washington side of the Creek, just above where it takes its last bend and begins its straight, short course to the Potomac. My hill is that white circular spot.[2]

He bought it for $14,000, or for about half of its cost, according to Jefferson's estimate. Remodelling was made at the suggestions of Benjamin Latrobe, the architect, and Robert Fulton helped embellish the house and grounds. Jefferson advised on gardening and the planting of fruit trees.

The estate was elegant, quite a contrast to the Connecticut farm where Joel had grown up. To be sure the approximate thirty acres of Kalorama were but a fraction of his father's one hundred and seventy in Redding. But the houses on the properties were just incomparable. Kalorama was palatial, tastefully equipped, with nothing of the old farm's rusticity. It was a landmark and a show place. According to its historian,

"It at once became and for more than a century continued to be the resort of all that was choicest in American society and the Mecca of foreign travellers and visitors." [3]

Here Barlow installed his library, regarded then as one of the most valuable in the country. Here he finished writing the *Prospectus of a National Institution*. And here Abraham Baldwin was buried.

Much of Barlow's time was spent gardening, tree planting and pruning in the orchard, laying out paths and planning wings to be added to the house. It was all in the style of a gentleman farmer.

At the housewarming the fashionable of Georgetown and Washington were present. In the crowd of guests were army and navy officers, the Madisons and the Gallatins, the French Minister and the British Minister.

Kalorama soon became the meeting place of the highest men in the administration. "Many and long were the councils around the library fire or on the veranda at Kalorama," we are informed, "when President, Secretary of State and host wrestled with the knotty international problems, often with the sympathetic British envoy Erskine, or with the sarcastic minister of the most incomprehensible French Emperor, present. It is safe to assert that no important political issue of that time was ever decided without the expressed opinion of Joel Barlow." [4]

The impression was current that once Madison was elected President, Barlow might be named Secretary of State. But filling cabinet vacancies is too frequently determined by political wire pulling rather than by the competence of the appointees. Madison's first choice was Albert Gallatin, but a senate cabal opposed him because he was foreign-born. A strong bloc forced the president, in the interest of party unity, to appoint the wealthy Baltimore politician, Robert Smith. But he was notoriously unsuited and his bungling of the foreign policy compelled Madison to oust him in 1811.

Failure to get the nomination disappointed Barlow. Perhaps Madison's plausible explanation gave him temporary satisfaction.[5] For among the public figures of the day, he was undeniably the best qualified to head the State Department. He had proved himself an able diplomat in the North African crisis; he was versed in the politics of the European belligerents; he spoke several languages; had many personal and useful connections in foreign governments; and enjoyed high respect as a *littérateur*. Perhaps his fidelity to French revolutionary principles and his advanced views on education and the function of government made him a *persona non grata* to conservatives in Congress.

Though his political ambition had been checked, he continued to be a loyal supporter of the administration. This was illustrated by his withering reply to Robert Smith's diatribe against the president. [6] He ridiculed the ex-Secretary, recalled the intrigue that had put him into the cabinet and derided him by saying that he lacked the vigor of mind "to support an argument, even on the right side of the question." Barlow vindicated the Non-Importation Act Smith had opposed even though it was the most sensible measure at the time, considering Congressional opposition to an embargo, and then went on to accuse him of having recklessly upset the president's negotiations with England for the repeal of her orders in Council.

Barlow's answer exemplified his legal acumen, sustained polemical power, trenchant analysis and mastery of style. Roused to indignation, the old pamphleteer turned out a devastating attack on one of the most inept politicos ever elevated to a high post. The president and friends of the administration were grateful.

2

In 1804 appeared the first volumes of John Marshall's *Life of Washington*. The subject, the author and the size of the work compounded to give it prominence. Its partisan character was obvious from the start, despite the claim that it had been compiled from authentic records, Washington's papers among them. It was zealously Federalist, hostile to the French Revolution in the spirit of Gouverneur Morris, pro-British à la Hamilton, anti-republican and anti-democratic in the manner of Fisher Ames. Besides, it was badly proportioned and hastily written in parts. It understated or ignored Jefferson's views on foreign and domestic policies, yet Hamilton's tax and financial programs were treated at length. It praised the defenders of the Jay Treaty, but scorned the democratic-republican clubs. They were "pernicious societies, claiming to be the people." Their toasts to the Mountain and the revolutionary tribunal were impending signs that the spirit which had triumphed in France, "and deluged it with the blood of its revolutionary champions, might cross the Atlantic, and desolate the hitherto safe and peaceful dwellings of the American people." Already, the author warned, "were principles familiarly proclaimed which, in France, had been the precursors of that tremendous and savage despotism, which, in the name of the people, and by the instrumentality of affiliated societies, had spread its terrific sway over that fine country, and had threatened to extirpate all that was wise and virtuous." [7]

Jefferson was outraged by Marshall's narrative. He called it a "party diatribe," a "five-volumed libel" and an "abuse" of Washington's papers. He assailed the author's partiality, "displayed in lavishness of praise on certain military characters, who had done nothing military, but who afterwards, and before he wrote, had become heroes in party, altho' not in war; and in his reserve on the merits of others who rendered signal services indeed, but did not earn his praise by apostasising in peace from the republican principles for which they had fought in war."[8]

To countervail Marshall's Federalist partisanship, he counted on

Barlow to do the history of the United States, covering more or less the same ground. Jefferson had in fact urged the writing of it as early as May 3, 1802, saying, "Mr. Madison and myself have cut out a piece of work for you which is to write the history of the United States, from the close of the war downwards. We are rich ourselves in materials, & can open all the public archives to you; but your residence here is essential, because a great deal of the knowledge of things is not on paper, but only within ourselves, for verbal communication." He then referred to Marshall at work on his *Life of Washington*, "principally with a view to electioneering purposes. But it will consequently be out in time to aid you with information, as well as to point out the perversions of truth necessary to be rectified. Think of this, & agree to it." [9]

As the project became more pressing, Jefferson returned to it. Writing on January 9, 1804, while Barlow was still in Paris, he said "that federalism is in its last agonies, & that we want nothing more than for you to come home & write its history. A more instructive lesson can never be offered to our country, and this is the spot where alone it can be written. Marshall is engaged in writing a libel on republicanism under the mask of a history of Genl. Washington. The antidote is reserved for you." [10]

Barlow agreed to write the history after returning to America. Every possible help was given him. Precious documents and boxes of rare, printed matter were lent him, and personal reminiscences of active participants in events were made available. He was offered manuscript notes on the American Revolution in the South. [11] On August 1, 1808, he inquired of Jefferson what had been the secret causes of the Whiskey Insurrection and asked for evidence on an alleged Tory plot to make Washington president for life at the expiration of Adams's term of office. [12]

Work on the history was extremely slow for reasons that can be surmised at best. Perhaps it needed more time and reflection than Barlow had estimated; perhaps he was sidetracked by domestic and international problems. It is possible, too, that he was temperamentally unsuited to stay on an assignment of prolonged investigation. In any case, the history advanced at a snail's pace. It did not even have a plan as did his contemplated story of the French Revolution. All we have of it is bare fragments. [13]

A piece which seems to have neared final shape sketched the unparalleled beginnings of the first English settlements as companies of adventurers, independent of each other. Since their object was neither conquest nor plunder, they had no need either for great generals or wise legislators or "a high order of priesthood." Their principal enemies were the unsubdued elements of nature, the surmounting of which required courageous effort and honest industry.

Barlow laid the foundation of most of the American institutions to two cirmcumstances. First, the colonists brought with them the ideas of

English liberty. This was "a greater advantage than any other colonies ancient or modern have possessed." Second, their dependence on the English crown gave them protection against other powers and served them as a common arbiter.

Such was the situation of the colonies before their independence. Uniting among themselves, they first had to recognize that they were all equal and then to substitute for the English government one which Barlow described as an "imperfect union," that is, a confederation; "they assumed indeed the name & style of *The United States*; but they were not in fact united by any other tie but the sentiment of common danger."

He apparently intended to treat with some thoroughness the motives which prompted the adoption of the federal constitution. In 1808 when he visited Monticello, he copied Madison's unrevised notes on the Constitutional Convention of 1787 that had been entrusted to Jefferson. The celebrated body apparently arrested his interest, for he remarked: "The causes that led to the adoption of the New Constitution must be developed with great clearness.—Chais's [sic] rebellion was only a visible symptom of the hidden disease," by which he meant the distinctions of wealth. As a symptom, however, it was productive "because it led us to discover the remedy," that is, more democracy.

In the light of the stray pieces and comments, one can justly regret that he failed to write the history. It might have opened new lines of research and inspired generations of historians.

Jefferson was impatient with the extreme slowness of the work and appealed to Barlow to get on with it. "You owe to republicanism, and indeed to the future hopes of man, a faithful record of the *march* of this government, which may encourage the oppressed to go and do likewise. Your talents, your principles and your means of access to public and private sources of information, with the leisure which is at your command, point you out as the person who is to do this act of justice to those who believe in the improvability of the condition of man; and who have acted on that behalf, in opposition to those who consider man as a beast of burden made to be rode by him who has genius enough to get a bridle into his mouth." [14] When he learned that Barlow had been appointed plenipotentiary to France, he asked sorrowfully: "What is to become of our past revolutionary history? Of the antidotes of truth to the misrepresentations of Marshall?" [15] Barlow answered that he hoped to write the story after his return. [16]

3

In the five or six years before the departure of the Barlows for France a cloud seems to have spread over their relations with Fulton. Early in 1806 they received word of their friend's betrothal to a wealthy widow in London. The news came upon them "like a shipwreck" to cite Barlow.

Ruth was lacerated, he reported, "constantly in tears, unable to eat or sleep, and relapsing into bodily sufferings without her usual flow of spirits to support them."

Possibly she had become infatuated with the younger man. He was handsome and irresistibly charming. He was about six feet in height, with a slender, well proportioned figure, strong features, large, expressive eyes, and an abundance of dark, curly hair. He was cheerful, cordial, kind and devoted, and he was uncommonly creative. Perhaps she counted on marrying him to her sister, Clara Baldwin. The engagement blighted the hope.

Barlow read in the news a loosening of bonds that had tied him to his friend for many years. The prospective bride, he answered, undoubtedly had all the excellence Fulton had described. Here he introduced a *but*, bearing a load of argument. Her English education, habits, feelings and pattern of life made her ill-adapted to live happily in America. Nor would Fulton be happy living in England. His cast of mind was American; his services were needed in his native land and his heart belonged to the Barlows. Another consideration was the widow's children, brought up in affluence and ease. Children should be had when the parents are young and poor, so that they might be brought up to labor.

The dreams of one ménage for three vanished. It could not comfortably house a fourth person of different tastes and background. Barlow put it in these terms: "Young and old, rich & poor, gay and sober, urban & sylvan, Thames & Schuylkill cannot harmonize so as that one soul shall animate the whole." One more thought passed through his mind. *The Canal* had to be finished, and that could be done only together, under one roof, in the same ideal conditions in which it had been begun. [17]

We do not know the circumstances that put an end to the betrothal. Anyhow, Fulton informed his friend that he had settled his affairs in England and would return to America.

Before very long he transferred his affection to Harriet Livingston, a cousin of his partner. After their marriage, a coolness imperceptibly came over their relations with the Barlows. The two families set up a common ménage in Kalorama, but that proved to be utopian. Ruth and Harriet found themselves incompatible. Other reasons, according to Fulton, were the difficulty of pursuing his study of mechanics in Washington, the desire of having his own home and, perhaps more decisive, his intense interest in the steamboat business centered in New York.[18]

Fulton's attachment to the Barlows survived the separation. He kept them abreast of his doings, and informed them of the first successful voyage of the Clermont. He watched over the literary rights of his friend, whose major works he contemplated publishing. While Barlow was abroad, he wrote him that as an investor in the unincorporated Middletown Cloth manufactory, he risked his entire fortune for any of its losses.[19] Also Fulton provided in his will that the $7,000 due him from Barlow's estate were not to be claimed during Ruth's lifetime.

An occurrence that cast gloom over the Barlow household was the death of Abraham Baldwin in March 1807. The loss left a void in their lives. He had been their adviser and confidant, and he had been dedicated to the improvement of America. In the obituary Barlow wrote for the *National Intelligencer*, he noted Baldwin's enduring achievements, among them the founding of the University of Georgia. [20]

4

The most vexing problem of Jefferson's and Madison's administrations arose from the necessity of defending the nation's neutral rights. This grew progressively troublesome as the European war continued. England's intention was to drive Americans from the seas, to have "the *permanent dominion of the ocean,* and the *monopoly of the trade of the world,"* as Jefferson wrote to Madame de Staël. "To secure this, she must keep a larger fleet than her own resources will maintain. The resources of other nations then must be impressed to supply the deficiency of her own." [21]

Napoleon would have doubtlessly pursued a similar plan had he controlled the sea. He revealed his true objective by the exacting rules he laid on neutral trade and by the confiscation of neutral ships and cargoes in French ports.

Each of the two powers counted on economic weapons to bring the other to submission. England aimed at preventing the outflow and inflow of goods through French ports; France hoped to ruin England's industry and commerce by closing her large market on the continent. Both methods were injurious to American trade.

Blockading decrees emanated from the respective sides. From 1803 to 1806 British Orders in Council set regulations for trade between neutrals and enemy colonies, shut up French colonial and Channel ports and closed the mouths of German rivers. Napoleon's reply was the Berlin decree on November 21, 1806, which proclaimed the British Isles in a state of blockade and cut off British trade with the Continent. England retaliated with another set of orders that forbade all trade between France and her satellite states, commanded the impressment of seamen, and stopped ships from entering or coming out of the ports of France, her allies and colonies, from which British vessels were excluded. Thereupon Napoleon issued the Milan decree, declaring good prize all vessels that had been searched by the British, or had paid duties to the British government, or were bound to or from an English port or her colonies.

Subsequent orders by Napoleon only irritated Americans to the point of imminent war with France. His Bayonne decree subjected to confiscation American vessels going to France, Holland, North Germany and Italy for the reason that the American Embargo was in force. His Rambouillet decree ordered the seizure of American ships entering

France, Spain or Italy as long as the same measure was applied to French ships in America. In 1809 he excluded American merchantmen from France, Spain, Naples, Prussia, Sweden and Russia on the ground that they were British in disguise. He doubled duties on colonial goods in February 1810, and the following month he seized all American ships in French and allied ports in retaliation for America's Non-Intercourse Act, although no French vessel had been confiscated by the United States. He then proceeded to set up a system of special licenses for American ships and to impose heavy duties on American and colonial products. He set a model of deception with his fictitious repeal of the Berlin and Milan decrees in the summer of 1810. [22]

Confronted with the restrictions and depredations of the two powers, the American government had to choose between war and peaceful coercion. Jefferson preferred the second course, so that the Embargo Act was passed, prohibiting American ships from sailing to foreign ports. According to Henry Adams, it was at once a defensive and punitive measure aimed at England and France and a delaying action until the country's debt was paid and its strength increased. [23]

The embargo caused an explosion of protest in the mercantile community in New England. To the argument that it was wiser and, in the long run, more effective in bringing the two warring states to terms by keeping vessels, cargoes and seaman at home, opponents of the act answered that it curtailed personal liberty and the rights of property. They calculated that it was more profitable to risk the loss of a number of ships than to have them and their cargoes rot in home ports. An estimate by Boston Federalists put the American net drop in income, exclusive of that on freight, at $10,800,000, on a total export value of $108,000,000. [24]

Though the estimate seemed extravagant, it was accepted as a true representation of the damage. Apart from causing discontent, the embargo was difficult to execute. Shipowners could not be kept from chancing to run the blockade. The government had to replace the embargo by the Non-Intercourse Act which permitted trade with all countries except Great Britain and France. The president was authorized to suspend its application to either country that withdrew the restraints on American vessels. To evade the law, each of the two belligerents tried the artifice of prevarication, that is, informing the American government unofficially that it had complied with the provisions, on condition that they remained in force against its foe.

The American administration was not deceived. If Madison publicly credited an unconfirmed report from France that she had revoked the obnoxious decrees, it was owing not to naive credulity but to a calculated belief that he needed the verbal exemption with which to press his case against Great Britain. The time seemed propitious for an arrangement. American observers in England were reporting the disastrous effect of the Non-Intercourse Act on trade and manufacturing. Stocks were accumulating; unemployment was growing; distress was spreading, and with it unrest, so that troops had to be sent to manufacturing towns. Parliament was petitioned for the withdrawal of the Orders in Council. But the ministers refused to yield. [25]

Though grossly offended and deeply angered by England's arrogance and her violent action against American shipping, Madison would have welcomed an accommodation. But her policy, regarding America, was, in his words, "monopoly and piracy." [26] It meant denial of America's independence and a check to her economic growth. For this reason, he proclaimed on November 2 that non-intercourse would go into effect against Great Britain on February 2, 1811, unless she gave up the Orders in Council before that date. Also in February of the same year, he named Barlow envoy to France. The Senate approved the nomination on February 27, 1811, by a vote of twenty-one to eleven.

Opponents of Barlow put forth the following arguments: He had not settled his account with the Treasury, relative to expenditures in negotiating treaties with the North African states; he had become rich in France by improper means; his predilections were for France, for he was a French citizen; as a poet, "dealing in visions," he was "ill qualified for the business of the world" and finally, he lacked the business knowledge necessary to make claims for the restitution of American property in France. [27]

These objections had also been raised by the Federalist press and by General Samuel Smith of Maryland who strongly desired the appointment. But they were answered by Henry Clay and especially by a foremost Federalist, Timothy Pickering. Clay produced evidence showing that Barlow's accounts at the Treasury had been finally closed and then pointed out that French citizenship was simply an honorary title that had been conferred on other foreigners, including Washington. Pickering's answer was more comprehensive. Suffice it to say that he refuted the charge of Barlow's prepossession for France. He had lived there long enough, said Pickering, "to be disgusted" with the system of government and hence "had been the more inclined to return to his native country." The point that Barlow was a visionary poet who had become wealthy by some unknown means evoked the reply that this was proof of his understanding "the world as well as Poetry." The Federalist senator had high regard for the nominee's ability and his extensive studies, including international law, so essential for a diplomat. To be sure, he had been enthusiastic over the French Revolution, but so had many of his countrymen, and like them had come to a sober understanding of it. Pickering censured Barlow's role during the cold war between France and the United States, even recalled his letter to Abraham Baldwin, but in his opinion, "Mr. Barlow now entertained very different sentiments respecting the French." Considering the appointee's many qualities, he concluded that "he was as fit, and indeed more fit than any other person whom the President could nominate."

Barlow was a bipartisan choice. His Federalist brother-in-law, Henry Baldwin, wrote him on June 11, 1811, that "influential Federalists do not hesitate to give their decided opinion that you are the fittest man that could be put by. Those only abuse you who would abuse everybody appointed by Mr. Madison and everything he does." Baldwin ended the letter: "You go on your mission with as much of the public confidence as any other man could possess in these times and with a great prospect of acquiring additional fame." [28]

Why did the administration consider Barlow's mission important? The reason seems to be that it was part of the tactical maneuver to plot a firm and proper course between the warring powers. Madison desired to win concessions from Napoleon that would vindicate his distinction between the two belligerents and justify extreme measures against the greater aggressor. At the same time he was deeply disappointed with Napoleon's double-dealing and strongly suspicious of his promises.

Both disappointment and suspicion were the keynote of the instructions handed to Barlow. He was to seek the removal of the license system, to demand a reduction, if not the abolition, of the heavy duties on American imports, to get reparations for the seized American ships and cargoes, to put a stop to French piracy against American shipping, which involved obtaining authentic evidence of the abrogation of the Berlin and Milan decrees, and finally to arrive at an understanding with France on the admission of American vessels to French ports. The whole tone of the instructions "was that of protest," [29] according to Irving Brant.

Five months intervened between Barlow's appointment and his departure. Behind the delay was a sense of uncertainty on the part of the president as to the real intentions of Napoleon. No official confirmation of the repeal of the Berlin and Milan decrees had been received. Linked to this state of doubt were increasing French outrages against American commerce. The French minister in Washington was told firmly that the patience of the United States had worn thin. It was a grave error on the part of Europeans, Monroe said to him, to consider Americans peddlers of pepper and ginger. "The immense majority of citizens do not belong to this class, and are, as much as your Europeans, controlled by principles of honor and dignity." [30] British obduracy finally convinced Madison that the success of his policy depended on good relations with France. But France had to reciprocate or face American retaliation. In the middle of July a report reached Washington that American vessels sequestered in France since November 2, 1810, had been released. Barlow then received the order to depart. He and his party, consisting of Ruth, her half-sister, Clara Baldwin and Thomas Barlow, the adopted nephew, sailed on the frigate Constitution on August 11, 1811, and arrived in Paris

September 20. He again occupied the large house on rue de Vaugirard. Old friends, among them Volney and Helen Maria Williams, welcomed him.

Barlow seems to have sensed the difficulties of his assignment. In fact he was doubtful of its positive value. He confided to his friend, Henry Dearborn, Secretary of War under Jefferson: "I go with great reluctance on every account. The prospect of rendering any essential service to the public is by no means brilliant. . . . There is a faint idea of negative good, that is, preventing in some degree the mischief that might otherwise be done, & this is all that can be promised from the mission."[31] To Fulton he wrote that he was going with a heavy heart. "I have left my country, possibly & why not probably forever. But if such should be the result it will not be my fault, that is, the fault of my inclinations or wishes. I go with an ardent wish, but without much hope of doing good, & with the full intention, tho with a feeble hope of living to return." [32] The dejected state of mind might have caused him to leave with Fulton a list of his works to be published in two volumes in the order he had indicated.

The Emperor's absence delayed the start of negotiations. Meanwhile Barlow impressed on the Duke of Bassano, the Foreign Minister, the urgency of his business. The Duke was amiable and said that the Emperor was inclined to do everything to maintain good relations with the United States. On November 10 Barlow submitted a memorandum to the effect that should America's trade be excluded from the French and other ports, contrary to the repeal of the Berlin and Milan decrees, she would be compelled to reopen trade with the British territories. He requested that the Emperor order the prompt execution of the announced repeal. He then proposed three measures to improve Franco-American relations: restoration of American ships and cargoes to their owners; indemnity for confiscated properties, acknowledged to be American; a new commercial treaty between the two countries, based on reciprocity. All Barlow could gain for the time being was a modification of the rules regarding goods brought by American vessels, but he could not get the Duke to sign a prepared declaration respecting the above terms. [33] Business was further deferred by the Emperor's projected trip to Russia.

The thesis long held authority that Barlow had been duped by the French Foreign Minister and Napoleon. [34] But it has since been assailed with fresh evidence, portraying an astute plenipotentiary, persistent in his demands, cold and expansive, according to the occasion, hardheaded as a questioner and unyielding in his claims. [35] The documents show that during the many interviews he had with the Duke, he neither deviated from his instructions nor allowed himself to be distracted by irrelevant talk. On the contrary, he forced the Foreign Minister into a state of anxiety over the American policy, so much so that he was eager to get Napoleon's authority to conclude a commercial treaty with the

United States.[36]

Illustrative of Barlow's stubborn adherence to his course was the way he obtained confirmation of the repeal of the Berlin and Milan decrees. Upon receiving word from the American representative in London that Great Britain would not budge from the Orders in Council until she had authentic evidence of the revocation of the French restrictions, he asked the Duke for a written declaration to that effect. The Duke went pleading to Napoleon, and the result was the St. Cloud decree, predated to April 28, 1811. It was a formal statement of the nonexistence of the decrees, with regard to the United States, since November 1, 1810. Barlow at once saw through the lie. The fact was that the decree had not been published at the time of its date. To Madison he wrote on May 12, 1812, that in his opinion the decreee "was created last week expressly for this occasion." Furthermore, that in answer to his request for a copy of the official decree, he had been referred to some notes in the *Moniteur*, which, not being official, as he told the Duke, would only serve to stir American opinion against France. In effect he coerced the Foreign Minister not only to produce the St. Cloud decree, but also to provide him with a copy which he rushed to London just when British merchants and manufacturers were pleading with Parliament for the repeal of the Orders in Council.[37]

Nor was Barlow more pliable in his dealings with Baron von Dalberg and Jean Baptiste Petry, both of whom had been charged with the negotiations when the Duke departed for Vilna. Dalberg reported that the American was hard to handle. To the suggestion of a commercial treaty he replied that more immediate issues needed settling beforehand. The reply coincided with Madison's suspicion whether the idea of a treaty "be not meant to gain time, and be guided by events."[38]

Barlow did not relax his pressure on the French Foreign Ministry. Though the United States had been at war with England since June 1812, he already spoke of pacification with England and of a war against France. He even hinted the possibility of his recall. Petry warned his superior toward the end of September 1812 that there was no time to lose to prevent hostilities with the United States. The Americans were slow in coming to a decision, he said, but once they did they pursued their object until they obtained satisfaction.[39] The question had reduced itself, according to Petry, to a treaty *or* a war with the United States. In November, the French Minister in Washington learned that an agreement could have been reached quickly, if Barlow had not stood firm on the question of indemnities.[40]

The negotiations had apparently reached a deadlock by October 1812. Barlow's position was clear: He held to his instructions, and he was bent on a new commercial agreement between his country and France. The French, on the other hand, were dilatory, making promises but hesitating to commit themselves. The reason lay undoubtedly in the campaign in the East on which the Emperor had embarked. Still the problems in the West were grave enough to need immediate consideration. How to avoid hostilities with America was a question that troubled the French Foreign Ministry. Taking all circumstances into account, the Ministry finally decided to continue the talks with the American envoy in a new environment. Since the Foreign Minister was already in Vilna, Barlow was asked to join him, with the inducement of completing the negotiation of a treaty. Was the invitation a maneuver to gain time, as Madison probably suspected? Barlow looked upon it as a genuine approach to expediting the business. [41] Seen in this light, it was impossible to decline the invitation without risking the loss of everything he had worked to achieve during his mission. Consequently he and Thomas set out on October 26 on the long and difficult journey of 1430 miles from Paris to Vilna. Shortly afterwards Petry was ordered to proceed to the same city.

Chapter XVII
Failure of a Mission

1

Barlow's early ambition had been to write the great American epic. He finally lived one in its stead, in two months rather than in ten years. It was the odyssey of one who, for love of country, went through torrential rains and rivers of mud, through blinding storms and blood-congealing frosts, over gore-soaked fields and snow-piled roads, through scenes so distressing that upon reaching his destination he cried out: "O God! O God! What did you make mankind for? I want to know. A creature endowed with so much intellect, foresight, calculation, prudence—and uses them so little." [1]

The tale of the odyssey is told by him in letters to Ruth, through whom he channeled his reports to Washington. Except for a few stops at inns, he and Tom ate, slept, read and wrote in the carriage. On November 5 they arrived in Berlin, nine days after starting from rue de Vaugirard. The going was very slow and tedious. "It is one of the worst seasons of the year & of the moon, & this is one of the worst moons & worst years for rain & roads that have been known."[2] Berlin impressed Barlow favorably, but he could not stop to tour it. He still had twelve more days of travel to Vilna.

Conditions worsened the farther he went. After crossing the Vistula, he estimated that he had covered 735 miles in eleven days over miry roads. They were bleak days. "Saw the sun, the blessed sun, this morning for the second time since the rue de Vaugirard," he wrote on November 9. "Then but half an hour."

Two days later he was in Königsberg, "eleven hundred and ten miles from the rue de Vaugirard." Recording the mileage seemed to register a mood of loneliness. The rain continued, but not a speck of frost, which was unusual for the season. He amused himself by improvising a rhapsody on mud.

"It is thick or thin, black or brown, according to circumstances, through all the kingdom of Westphalia. Saxony is a quagmire, but the Devil's own hasty pudding is in the great basin of 140 miles from Thorn to Konigsberg, from the Vistula to the Pregel. The horses legs are the ladles that stir it up. The carriage wheels whirl it over your head in a black rainbow that moves as you move, and seems to be intended, like the brilliant one of Noah, as a sign, but not a sign that God will not drown the world again, but on the contrary that he will drown it again, which I verily believe he intends to do, notwithstanding his covenant with our grandfather."[3]

From the Danish Minister to France, also on his way to Vilna, Barlow learned something about privations he would encounter in Lithuania. He consequently armed himself with cases of Madeira, Bordeaux and rum as well as sugar, coffee, rice and spices. Fortunately he also bought a pelisse, for beginning November 13 the cold was so severe that a bottle of water froze solid inside the carriage.

On November 18, after a journey of more than twenty-two days, he was met at the gates of Vilna by a dragoon the Duke had sent to escort him to his lodgings. The mounted guide, he informed Ruth, conducted the carriage as fast as he could; "but it is impossible to conceive the embarrassment of the streets, choked up with at least a thousand wagons and carts, crowding to get through the town, all loaded with sick & dying soldiers, remnants of luggage & all sorts of relics of glorious war."

The devastation he saw on his way to the Lithuanian capital tormented and sickened him. Numerous villages burnt or houses unroofed, fields untilled, hundreds of wagons with wounded—sights that wrenched the nerves and hearts of hardened men. "All cultivation is totally neglected this year," he wrote November 18, "so that if there had been any inhabitants they could not have subsisted. We met perhaps this day before arriving at Vilna 600 waggons of sick, dragging on thro' the rain, mud and snow or dry frost, as the case may be; not covered waggons, bien entendu, but open, naked planks laid upon wheels. . . . It grows worse & worse & worse & worse the nearer you approach to the theatre of glory." A person coming from Moscow to Vilna, Barlow was told, had counted twenty-five thousand dead horses. The number of dead men could not be determined; they were generally buried. He estimated that "about one million out of the nine hundred millions alive & singing psalms last May have perished in six months in this glorious Russian War." [4]

Staying in the war-torn city raised insoluble problems. Lodging and provisions were unobtainable, unless they were procured in advance. Thanks to the Duke, Barlow's quarters had been reserved for him. They were not "very convenient," Thomas reported to Clara, but "the best the town afforded. . . . We found it very difficult to get things the most necessary such as beds to ly [sic] on & things convenient for a decent table & . . . that which was fit to eat." [5] Were it not for Barlow's hospitality the ministers of Denmark, Austria and Baden might have been forced to live in their carriages. All had to do their own housekeeping. Barlow and the Danish minister made a common kitchen and dined together. There were the usual diplomatic receptions at the Duke's, and parties attended by envoys and beautiful Polish women. But the splendor was missing.

When Barlow arrived in Vilna he was still sanguine about the success of his mission. He has "never been their [French] dupe," Ruth wrote to Dolly Madison November 10, "but well understanding his character he has endeavored to parry their strokes, & thinks he shall have them at last." [6] Hopes grew barren as news trickled through the censorship that the Emperor was hard pressed and compelled to fall back. After the horrible episode in the crossing of the Berezina, the retreat became a disorganized flight, and he had to be defended by a battalion or he might have fallen into the hands of Cossacks. Once he felt he was out of danger he secretly left his army and hastened west in a closed carriage. Barlow learned from sundry sources that the Duke had met him outside Vilna and provided him with an escort. He was in Warsaw on December 10, where, according to a report, he summoned several high officials and said to them: "I have not been beaten by the enemy, but I could not fight the elements. In the space of a few days I lost 36,000 horses by the cold. Till the *6th* of November I was master of Europe. It is not the same now." He announced his intention of assembling another huge army against the Russians. [7]

Napoleon was not exaggerating. Heavy frosts had set in, writes Eugene Tarlé, which completely crushed the remnants of the Grand Army. "Their tattered uniforms, their torn shoes no longer protected them from the cold." He cites from Marshal Berthier's report to the Emperor: "A frost of 35 degrees and the abundant snow that covers the ground brought about the disaster of the army which is no more." For dozens of miles the roads to Vilna "were littered with corpses. Soldiers built shelters with the corpses of their comrades, piling them like logs."[8]

For the diplomats the disaster meant journeying about three hundred and twenty miles to the Polish capital during one of the coldest spells in history. When he arrived Barlow learned that Napoleon had fled the city. "The Emperor arrived at Vilna 12 hours after I left it," he informed Ruth on December 13. "He past us on the road 4 days after, when we were asleep in a post house. When we came to Warsaw he had past here 24 hours for Paris." [9] His optimism was sagging, and he could not hold back the confession that the long, harrowing journey had been in vain. "Perhaps all these movements will do no harm to our affair," he wrote again the same day, "tho it is pretty clear that the trip to Vilna has done no good." [10]

Deeply disappointed, he distracted himself with amusing accounts of things and persons. He found diversion, for instance, in the incongruity between the hard sounding Polish names and their beautiful female bearers and in drawing the attire of Louis, the coachman. "He has on him, besides the under & ordinary covering of flannel waistcoats & other things, two pantaloons, one of them over his boots, then a pair of fur boots over them, that come a foot above his knees; then a fur bag that takes in both his feet & legs & knees; then three great coats & a woolen blanket belted around his waist; then another woolen blanket tied round his neck & chin, & round his shoulders to hold down the yard-long capes of his three great coats; then a great thick fur cap that lappets under his chin, and covers all the flat parts of his face & fringes his nose; then a pair of thick fur mittens to cover his buckskin gloves. Nothing of him but his nose can come within some inches of the external air." [11]

It was forced gaiety. However much he tried to focus on the burlesque, he could not erase from his memory the gruesome things he had seen and heard. They made an indelible imprint on his thought, brought inconsolable grief over man's incapacity to keep from destroying himself. The droll sketch of the coachman's portable barricade against the frost was succeeded by a report of shocking figures on Napoleon's Grand Army and what remained of it. "The latter will be to the former as 1 to 8 or 1 to 10, as to the men. But not one to one hundred as to horses; in artillery, out of the 1500 fine pieces that past the Nieman there is scarcely one left." The disaster was complete.

The figures bespoke ghastly scenes that might have challenged even a Daumier. Barlow must have exercised strong restraint as he portrayed them to Ruth. According to a Polish count, "there were now lying in the fields, marshes, rivers and roads between Vilna & Moscow one hundred and fifty thousand carcases of horses lately of the French & allied armies, & perhaps fifty thousand bodies of men unburied. Not half of them killed in battle, but dropt dead with sickness, famine & frost." The Polish army of 74,000 men was almost annihilated. [12]

2

The facts mangled his emotions. They aroused feelings of hatred and revenge for "the immensity of the mischief." Barlow sought refuge in imagination, and the result was a bitter, scorching poem, "Advice to a Raven in Russia."

Escaping the terrifying tragedy might have redressed his drooping spirit. His last two letters to Ruth described the itinerary of his homeward trek. He planned to go first to Warsaw and then to Cracow to see the mines, perhaps also to look into the dungeon at Olmutz where Lafayette had been kept. Love for sightseeing had never left him. But cruel winds and frosts had set in. After November 28 the "thermometer fell to 45° below zero (Fahrenheit), and temperatures of 30° to 40° were common." [13] It was hardly the time to risk a long journey. Barlow, however, had no choice. He mustered his courage and arrived in Warsaw

December 12, having covered about 320 miles over deep snows in a bitter cold. "I never travelled in such cold weather before," he wrote to Ruth the following day. "We ran three nights without stopping." And the thought recurred to him, "how many soldiers, sick, wounded & well have been frozen to death within the last ten days. Probably many thousands." [14]

An earlier letter assured Ruth that he was enjoying "vulgar health." The piece of news was probably meant to allay her worries, for she knew that he had been under insufferable strain. Apart from his relentless pressure for a Franco-American agreement, which turned out to be very doubtful, he had to bear up under conditions that would sap the energies of younger and hardier men. Living in a carriage for days on end, sleeping on straw at post houses and traveling in the most inclement weather—these hardships inevitably sapped his strength. He caught pneumonia and ran a high fever. The illness had advanced beyond medical relief when he reached the village of Zarnowiec on December 21. Here he died five days later.

The afflicting news stunned Ruth. Fortunately Clara was with her. Thomas intended to have the body embalmed and brought to the United States. But the mountains of snow prevented it. Besides, the Cossacks were advancing so rapidly that there was no time to lose. Barlow had to be buried at Zarnowiec instead of at Kalorama, to Ruth's sorrow.

Heavy with grief, she could not sail home until September 1813. In New York she was warmly received and housed by the Fultons. But she decided to go back to Kalorama where everything reminded her of her Joel. Sometime before her death in 1818, she had a pillar erected in the Zarnowiec church, which inspired Helen Maria Williams to write:

Far o'er the cheerless space the traveller's eye
Shall this recording pillar long descry,
And give the sod a tear where Barlow lies,
He, who was simply great, & nobly wise;
Here led by patriot zeal he met his doom
And found amid the frozen wastes a tomb. [15]

The news of Barlow's death was received with mixed feelings in America. Critics and foes of the administration counted it "A divine interposition between us and the disgrace and ruin, which might otherwise have been brought upon us by a *formal* alliance with the French despot." [16] A Federalist Congressman "supposed Barlow had concluded a treaty offensive and defensive, between France and United States, and gone to the Devil to get it ratified." [17] Friends of the government mourned the loss. Americans in Paris sent Ruth their esteem and regard for the deceased countryman. [18]

Two publications in French were calculated to preserve his memory in his second homeland. One, by Pierre Samuel Du Pont de Nemours, underscored his efforts to knit relations between the Philosophical Society in Philadelphia and the Société d'encouragement de l'industrie nationale in Paris. [19] Another, by his friend, the German littérateur Konrad Engelbert Oelsner, an acute observer of French revolutionary events and participants, referred to him as "a man of genius and a friend of humanity, who did credit to his century." [20] Ruth's reply to Oelsner cited these lines from *King John*:

> *Grief fills the room up of my absent child,*
> *Lies in his bed, walks up and down with me,*
> *Puts on his pretty looks, repeats his words,*
> *Remembers me of all his gracious parts,*
> *Stuffs out his vacant garments with his form;*
> *Then, have I reason to be fond of grief.* [21]

3

Barlow labored many years to become America's epic poet, but failed. Neither *The Vision of Columbus* nor *The Columbiad*, for all the polish he gave them, rose to eminent heights. As a poet Barlow will be remembered, not for these two long compositions, but for "The Hasty Pudding," done in Chambery, and "Advice to a Raven in Russia," [22] written in Vilna. The first is steeped in homesickness and love of country; the second, in grief over woe-whelmed humanity and in rage over the war-hungry monster.

The poet's long-standing dislike of Napoleon grew into an aversion during the eastward journey. The conqueror appeared to him as "this king of woes." The devastation, the misery and the countless slain he had come upon, stamped themselves on his mind, caused him deep pain and finally burst forth in impassioned verse.

The "Advice to a Raven in Russia" is dyed in wrath. From the first verse to the last it discharges blazing anger at the conqueror in pursuit of inglorious ends, who havocked whole nations and strewed countless dead over many lands. Says the poet to the raven as if in reproof:

> *Black fool, why winter here? The frozen skies,*
> *Worn by your wings and deafen'd by your cries,*
> *Should warn you hence, where milder suns invite,*
> *And day alternates with his mother night.*
>   *You fear perhaps your food may fail you there—*
> *Your human carnage, that delicious fare,*
> *That lured you hither, following still your friend,*
> *The great Napoleon to the world's bleak end.*

*You fear, because the southern climes pour'd forth
Their clustering nations to infest the north,
Bavarians, Austrians, those who drink the Po
And those who skirt the Tuscan seas below,
With all Germania, Neustria, Belgia, Gaul,
Doom'd here to wade thro slaughter to their full,
You fear he left behind no wars, to feed
His feather'd cannibals and nurse the breed.
Fear not, my screamer, call your greedy train,
Sweep over Europe, hurry back to Spain,
You'll find his legions there; the valiant crew
Please best their master when they toil for you.
Abundant there they spread the country o'er
And taint the breeze with every nation's gore,
Iberian, Lusian, British widely strown;
But still more wide and copious flows their own.*

    *Go where you will; Calabria, Malta, Greece,
Egypt and Syria still his fame increase,
Domingo's fatten'd isle and India's plains
Glow deep with purple drawn from Gallic veins.
No raven wings can stretch the flight so far
As the torn bandrols of Napoleon's war.
Choose then your climate, fix your best abode,
He'll make you deserts and he'ill bring you blood.*

    *How could you fear a dearth? Have not mankind,
The slain by million, millions left behind?
Has not CONSCRIPTION still the power to wield
Her annual faulchion o'er the human field?
A faithful harvester! or if a man
Escape that gleaner, shall he scape the BAN?
The triple BAN, that, like the hound of hell,
Gripes with joles to hold his victim well.*

    *Fear nothing, then, hatch fast your ravenous brood,
Teach them to cry to Bonaparte for food;
They'll be like you, of all his suppliant train,
The only class that never cries in vain.
For see what natural benefits you lend!
(The surest way to fix the mutual friend)
While on his slaughter'd troops your tribes are fed,
You cleanse his camp and carry off his dead.
Imperial scavenger! But now you know,
Your work is vain amid these hills of snow.
His tentless troops are marbled through with frost
And change to crystal when the breath is lost.
Mere trunks of ice, tho limb'd like human frames,*

And lately warm'd with life's endearing flames.
They cannot taint the air, the world impest,
Nor can you tear one fibre from their breast.
No! from their visual sockets as they lie,
With beak and claws you cannot pluck an eye.
The frozen orb, preserving still its form,
Defies your talons as it braves the storm,
But stands and stares to God, as if to know
In what curst hands he leaves his world below.

Fly then, or starve; tho all the dreadful road
From Minsk to Moskow with their bodies strow'd
May count some Myriads, yet they can't suffice
To feed you more beneath those dreary skies.
Go back and winter in the wilds of Spain;
Feast there awhile, and in the next campaign
Rejoin your master, for you'll find him then,

Notes

Introduction

1. See Martha Orenstein, *The Role of Scientific Societies in the Seventeenth Century* (Chicago, Ill., 1928).
2. Brooke Hindle, *The Pursuit of Science in Revolutionary America* (Chapel Hill, N.C., 1956), pp. 67–74, 141–145.
3. Eric Hobsbawn in *The [London, England,] Times, Literary Supplement*, January 25, 1968, p. 80.
4. It had at least six answers, one by John Adams, *Thoughts on Government*.
5. The best selection from this large volume of verse is by Kenneth Moore, *Songs and Ballads of the American Revolution*. The rare first edition of 1855 was reissued in 1964.
6. Moncure D. Conway, ed., *The Writings of Thomas Paine* (New York, N.Y., 1908), IV: pp. 484–487.
7. Three volumes of Freneau's poetry were issed by Princeton University in 1902. See Fred Lewis Pattee, ed., *The Poems of Philip Freneau, Poet of the American Revolution*. See also Jean H. Hagstrum, "William Blake Rejects the Enlightenment," Theodore Besterman, ed., *Studies on Voltaire and the Eighteenth Century* (Geneva, Switzerland, 1963), XXV: pp. 811–828.
8. *Adventures of Ideas* (New York, N.Y., 1947), p. 36.
9. Bernard Bailyn, *The Ideological Origins of the American Revolution* (Cambridge, Mass., 1967), pp. 26–28.
10. *Studies in Philology*, 1931, XXVIII: 235–251. *Modern Philology*, 1934, XXXII, pp. 157–177.
11. Louis Trénard, "La diffusion du Contrat Social, 1762–1832," *Publications de l'Université de Dijon*, 1963, XXX: pp. 432, 438. According to Daniel Mornet's analysis of the catalogues of 500 private libraries of French liberal bourgeois, in the latter half of the eighteenth century, the *"Contrat Social"* was listed only once, while "La Nouvelle Heloïse" was listed 165 times. *"Revue d'histoire littéraire de la France,"* 1910, XVII: pp. 467–468.
12. Paul Merrill Spurlin, *Montesquieu in America, 1760–1801* (Baton Rouge, La., 1940), pp. 258–261.
13. *O Strange New World* (New York, N.Y., 1964), p. 431, n.39.
14. It was translated and published in London in 1763.
15. Ray Forrest Harvey, *Jean Jacques Burlamaqui, A Liberal Tradition in American Constitutionalism* (Chapel Hill, N.C., 1937).
16. *The Principles of Natural and Politic Law* (London, England, 1763), II: pp. 87–91, pp. 92–97.
17. Joseph J. Spengler, "The Political Economy of Jefferson, Madison and Adams" David Kelly Jackson, ed., *American Studies in Honor of William Kenneth Boyd* (Durham, N.C., 1940), pp. 49–50. See also John Adams, *Works* (Boston, Mass., 1851), IV: pp. 287, 290, 427–8; VI: pp. 65, 270–271, 279–281.
18. Spengler, pp. 8–9.
19. Richard Frothingham, *The Rise of the Republic of the United States* (Boston, Mass., 1872), pp. 118–120, note.
20. Durand Echeverria, *Mirage in the West. A History of the French Image of American Society to 1815* (Princeton, N.J., 1957), pp. 74–77, 149–154, 240–244; Samuel Bernstein, *Essays in Political and Intellectual History* (New York, N.Y., 1955), pp. 63–64.
21. [Cornelius de Paw], *Recherches philosophiques sur les américains* (London, 1771). The first edition appeared in Berlin, 1768–1769.
22. The following publications were among the best known of the anti-slavery literature:
 Ralph Sandiford, *Brief Examination of the Practice of the Times* (1729).
 Benjamin Lay, *All Slave-Keepers Apostates* (1735).
 John Woolman, *Some Considerations on the Keeping of Negroes* (1758).
 Anthony Benezet, *An Epistle of Caution and Advice Concerning the Buying and Keeping of Slaves* (1754).
 Observations on the Inslaving, Importing and Purchasing of Negroes (1760).
 Short Account of That Part of Africa Inhabited by the Negroes, With Respect to the Fertility of the Country, the Good Disposition of Many of the Natives, and the Manner by which the Slave Trade is Carried On (1762).
 A Caution and Warning to Great Britain and Her Colonies, in a Short Representation of the Calamitous State of the Enslaved Negroes in the British Dominions (1767).
 Some Historical Account of Guinea . . . with an Enquiry into the Rise and Progress. of the Slave Trade (1771). (This most ambitious. work was plagiarized by John Wesley in his *Thoughts on Slavery* [1774].)
 Benjamin Rush, *Address to the Inhabitants of the British Settlements in America upon Slave-Keeping* (1773). For additional titles of anti-slavery pamphlets in preindependence years see Bailyn, *op cit.*, pp. 232–246.
23. Moncure Daniel Conway, ed. *op. cit.*, I: 4–9.
24. See the useful lecture of J. Franklin Jameson, *The American Revolution Considered as a Social Movement* (Boston, Mass., 1956), reprinted.
25. Jackson Turner Main, *The Social Structure of Revolutionary America* (Princeton, N.J., 1965) pp. 41–42, 66–67.
26. See Stephen T. Riley, "Dr. William Whiting and Shays' Rebellion," *Proceedings of the American Antiquarian Society*, (October 1956), pp. 119–166.
27. The manuscript is dated 1797. It was published for the first time in 1922 by Samuel Eliot Morison, with a foreword on the author.
28. Mary Caroline Crawford, *Social Life in Old New England* (New York, N.Y., 1914), p. 161.
29. Richard L. Bushman, *From Puritan to Yankee* (Cambridge, Mass., 1967), p. 231.
30. Walter F. Prince, "An Examination of Peters's Blue Laws," *Annual Report of the American Historical Association*, 1898, pp. 97–138.

Chapter I

1. The texts of the address and of the president's answer were published in *The Annual Register or a View of the History, Politics and Literature for the Year 1792* (London, England, 1799), II: pp. 73–75. For the French texts see *Le moniteur (réimpression)*, XIV: pp. 593–594; also *Convention nationale, Journal des débats et des décrets*, No. 70: pp.

213

450–451. The answer is also cited in Henri Grégoire, *Mémoires* (Paris, France, 1837), I: pp. 416–418.
2 Victor C. Miller, *Joel Barlow: Revolutionist, London, 1791–1792* (Hamburg, 1932), pp. 44–45; also cited in the *Trial of Thomas Hardy for High Treason* (London, England, 1795), II: p. 60.
3 These biographic facts are in *The Trial of John Frost* (London, England, 1794).
4 A copy of the covering letter he included is in the Barlow Papers, Pequot Library, Southport, Conn. It was cited in the *Trial of Thomas Hardy*, II: 43.
5 Miller, *op. cit.*, pp. 35–37; also *Second Report from the Committee of Secrecy of the House of Commons* (London, England, 1794), Appendix, pp. 37–38.
6 Miller, *op. cit.*, 4, notes pp. 12–13.
7 Barlow Papers, Harvard University Library, Box 1, letter undated. Cited here and hereinafter by permission of the Harvard College Library.
8 Charles Burr Todd, *The History of Redding, Conn.* (New York, N.Y., 1906), chs. 1–3.
9 *Ibid.*, pp. 174–177; see also James Hill, *Genealogy of the Hill Family from 1632, including a Biographical Sketch of Joel Barlow* (Norwalk, CT., 1879).
10 *The Hasty Pudding*. It was a mock-heroic and immensely popular. It had eight printings in 1796 alone. Subsequent editions continued to appear, three of them in 1797. We have followed the edition of 1815, Hallowell, Maine.
11 Mary Caroline Crawford, *Social Life in Old New England* (New York, N.Y., 1914), pp. 351, 356.
12 For the above facts we have relied on the detailed account of Theodore A. Zunder, *The Early Days of Joel Barlow* (New Haven, CT., 1934).
13 See Lous W. McKeehan, *Yale Science. The First Hundred Years* (New York, 1947), ch. 3.
14 Woodbridge Riley, "The Rise of Deism in Yale College," *The American Journal of Theology*, 1905, IX: pp. 480–482.
15 See Zunder, *op. cit.*, pp. 20–21.
16 Barlow Papers, Harvard, Box 1.
17 See Franklin B. Dexter, *Biographical Sketches of the Graduates of Yale College* (New York, N.Y., 1902), III: p. 642.
18 Barlow Papers, Harvard, Box 4.
19 *Literary Diary* (New York, N.Y., 1901), II: p. 284.
20 *Travels in North America in the Years 1780, 1781 and 1782* (Chapel Hill, N.C., 1963), II: p. 485.
21 It was published in New Haven the same year and reprinted a decade later.
22 The record of his early poetry is in Barlow's *Commonplace Book, 1774–1776*, Abraham Baldwin Papers, University of Georgia. The Barlow Papers, Harvard, Box 4, contain 7 stanzas of a poem, "To a Friend at Cambridge," written July 5, 1777, and 8 stanzas of a poem "To Mr. Abraham Baldwin," dated March 7, 1779.

Chapter II

1 *Miscellaneous Works* (Philadelphia, 1888), p. 38.
2 Barlow Papers, Harvard, Box 2.
3 *Ibid.*
4 Barlow Papers, Pequot Library, letter of December 26, 1779.
5 *Miscellaneous Works*, pp. 43–44.
6 Barlow Papers, Pequot Library, Buckminster's letters to Barlow.
7 Theodore A. Zunder, "Six Letters of Joel Barlow to Oliver Wolcott, Junior," *The New England Quarterly*, 1929, II, pp. 479–480.

8 Henley-Smith Papers, Library of Congress, Barlow to Buckminster, March 19, 1779.
9 Barlow Papers, Harvard, Box 2.
10 *Ibid.*, Box 4.
11 *Ibid.*, Box 1.
12 *The New England Quarterly*, 1929, II, p. 487.
13 Barlow Papers, Harvard, Box 1.
14 *Ibid.*, Letter to Ruth Baldwin, September 26, 1779.
15 *Ibid.*, Box 2.
16 *Ibid.*
17 See Leon Howard, *The Connecticut Wits* (Chicago, Ill., 1943), ch. 4.
18 Letter of April 18, 1780, to Colonel Jeremiah Wadsworth, cited in Zunder, *The Early Days of Joel Barlow*, p. 100.
19 Letters of April 20 and May 25, 1780, *ibid.*, pp. 101–102.
20 For Elizabeth's letters to him see Charles Knowles Bolton, *The Elizabeth Whitman Mystery at the Old Bell Tavern in Danvers* (Peabody, Mass., 1912).
21 Barlow Papers, The Huntington Library, Ruth's letters to Joel, cited with permission.
22 Unless otherwise indicated, references to their correspondence are the Barlow Papers, Harvard, Box 1.
23 Daniel Defoe, *An Essay Upon Projects* (1697) reprinted by Henry Morley, ed., *The Early Life and the Chief Earlier Writings of Daniel Defoe* (London, England, 1889), p. 152.
24 Barlow Papers, Harvard, Box 4, book 8.
25 W. J. Bell, *Early American Science* (Williamsburg, Va., 1955), pp. 8–9.
26 Cited in Zunder, *op. cit.*, p. 11.
27 Barlow Papers, Harvard, Box 4.
28 Letter of August 31, 1782, cited in Emily Ellsworth Ford, *Notes of the Life of Noah Webster* (New York, N.Y., 1912), I: pp. 54–55.
29 Barlow Papers, Harvard, Box 1.
30 *Ibid.*
31 See *e.g.* the letter of Elias Boudinot to Governor Livingston in New York, in which appears the following paragraph:
"As I know your Excellency is fond of Men of Genius and Literature, I beg leave to recommend him to your Notice. The Specimens of this Performance [*The Vision of Columbus,*] which have been communicated to Gentlemen of Taste in this City, have done him great honor." Mass, Hist. Soc. MS. letter, Philadelphia, PA., November 25, 1782.
32 Zunder, *op. cit.*, p. 142.
33 Barlow Papers, Harvard, Box 1.
34 *Ibid.*
35 J. T. Headly, *The Chaplains and Clergy of the Revolution* (Springfield, Mass., 1861), p. 208.
36 The last six stanzas appear in *ibid.*, p. 209.
37 Published in Hartford, 1782.
38 Zunder, *op. cit.*, p. 142.
39 Barlow Papers, Harvard, Box 1.
40 *Ibid.*, Box 4.
41 Charles W. Burpee, *History of Hartford County, Connecticut* (Chicago, Ill., 1928), I: p. 224.
42 Stiles, *op. cit.*, III: 14.
43 See her New Year's Day poem to the Barlows, Bolton, *op. cit.*, pp. 87–91.
44 Anson Phelps Stokes, *Memorials of Eminent Yale Men* (New Haven, CT., 1914), I: p. 134.
45 *The American Mercury*, January 17, 1785.
46 *Ibid.*, February 21, 1785.
47 *E.g., ibid.*, September 6, 13, 20, 27, 1784.
48 Doctor Watts, *Imitation of the Psalms of David, corrected and enlarged by Joel Barlow* (Hartford, CT., 1785), Preface.

49 *Op. cit.*, III: pp. 155–156.
50 Mass. Hist. Soc., Barlow to Livingston, July 21, 1785.
51 Eight editions of Beccaria's *Essay* appeared in England. Three appeared in the United States before 1800. It was on the shelves of library companies and college libraries. It was in the Hartford library and in two small Pennsylvania libraries. Harvard College had Italian, French and English editions. It was published in the *Worcester Gazette*, the *New Haven Gazette* and in the *Connecticut Magazine*. Copies were in the private libraries of Freneau and Buckminster. See Paul M. Spurlin, "Beccaria's *Essay on Crimes and Punishments* in Eighteenth Century America," *Studies on Voltaire and the Eighteenth Century*, XXVII, 1963, pp. 1489–1504, ed. by Theodore Besterman.
52 Barlow Papers, Harvard, Box 4. See also Milton Cantor, "Joel Barlow: Lawyer and Legal Philosopher," *American Quarterly*, 1958, X: No. 2: 165–174.
53 Barlow Papers, Harvard, Box 3.

Chapter III

1 From 1787 to 1789 the compiler Garnier published no fewer than 39 volumes of imaginary voyages and utopias. See Georges Pariset, *Etudes d'histoire révolutionnaire et contemporaine* (Paris, France, 1929), p. 242.
2 The first edition in two volumes had four subsequent reprintings. A fifth edition in three volumes appeared in 1788. An edition in four volumes, including a posthumous volume on the history of Virginia to 1688 and of New England to 1651, was published in 1800. The history sold so well that a thirteenth edition was issued in 1817. The first edition in two volumes had two French translations, in 1778 and 1780.
3 Edward Gibbon, *Essai sur l'étude de la littérature* (London, 1761), pp. 29, 31, 32.
4 *Essai sur la poésie épique*, (n.p., n.d.) pp. 2–4, 14–15, 30. An English translation was published in London in 1727.
5 Cited by Richard Payne Knight, *The Progress of Civil Society* (London, England, 1796), Preface.
6 "A Receipt to Make an Epic Poem," in Pope's *Selected English Essays* (1903), pp. 134–138, World's Classic Series; Freneau's recipe for composing epic poetry is in his essay, "On Epic Poetry," published anonymously in *The Daily Advertiser*, November 10, 1796, cited by Lewis Leary, *That Rascal Freneau. A Study in Literary Failure* (New Brunswick, N.J., 1941), p. 181.
7 *An Historical View of the English Government: From the Settlement of the Saxons in Britain to the Revolution of 1688* (London, England, 1818), IV: pp. 333–334. The first edition was in 1787.
8 Paul Hazard, *La révolution française et les lettres italiennes, 1789–1815* (Paris, France), p. 207.
9 Its first edition in Italian, in 1809, was in four volumes. It was translated by G. A. Otis and published in Philadelphia in 1820. The translation had at least fourteen American editions. A French edition appeared in 1812–1813.
10 His *Poetical Works* (Hartford, 1820), 2 vols. contain "M'Fingal" as well as other major and minor poems. For an estimate of Trumbull as a poet, see Howard, *op. cit.*, ch. II. See also Alexander Cowie, *John Trumbull, Connecticut Wit* (Chapel Hill, N.C.,1936).
11 Leon Howard, *The Connecticut Wits* (Chicago, Ill., 1943), the most extensive biography of Humphreys is by Frank Landon Humphreys, *Life and Times of David Humphreys* (New York, N.Y., 1917). See David Humphreys, *Miscellaneous Works* (New York, N.Y., 1804).

12 See his letter to Webster, June 6, 1788, published by Theodore Zunder in *American Literature*, 1929, I: pp. 201–202.
13 Howard, *op. cit.*, p. 93.
14 Grace A. Ellis, *Memoir, Letters and a Selection from the Poems and Prose Writings of Anna Letitia Barbauld* (Boston, Mass., 1874), I: p. 199.
15 Vernon L. Parrington, ed., *The Connecticut Wits* (Hamden, CT., 1963), Introduction, p. xiii.
16 Henry A. Beers, *The Connecticut Wits and Other Essays* (New Haven, CT., 1920), p. 11.
17 Cited by Leary, *op. cit.*, p. 183, from *The Daily Advertiser*, December 16, 1790.
18 In his "Poem on the Happiness of America."
19 *The Pennsylvania Democrat*, September 8, 1809, cited by Leary, *op. cit.*, p. 329.
20 Howard, *op. cit.*, p. 148.
21 Zunder, *op. cit.*, p. 220.
22 *The Vision of Columbus* (Hartford, CT., 1787), pp. 242–244, note.
23 James Woodress, *A Yankee's Odyssey. The Life of Joel Barlow* (New York, N.Y., 1958), p. 88.
24 Barlow to Jefferson, June 15, 1787, Coolidge Collection, 1787, No. 381, Mass. Hist. Soc.
25 Barlow sent 100 copies of the poem in sheets to Matthew Carey, bookdealer and printer in Philadelphia, at half a dollar a copy. But the account has apparently never been settled. More than a decade later Barlow wrote Carey from Paris to say that he had drawn on his account the balance of $93.55, covering the cost of the 100 copies plus interest for 10 years and 9 months. Barlow's letter, October 25, 1798, is in the Historical Society of Pennsylvania.
26 For a detailed study of the revisions Barlow made in the fifth edition, see Arthur L. Ford, *Joel Barlow* (New York, N.Y., 1971), pp. 68–73.
27 *Ibid.*, p. 94
28 Zunder, *op. cit.*, pp. 224–227.
29 *Ibid.*, pp. 230–231.
30 *The Monthly Magazine and British Register*, 1798, II: 250.
31 Barlow Papers, Harvard, Box 2.
32 George Warren Gignilliat, *The Author of "Sanford and Merton." A Life of Thomas Day, Esq.* (New York, 1932). Price had forwarded the manuscript to him at Barlow's suggestion. Lewis Leary, "Thomas Day on American Poetry," *Modern Language Notes*, 1946, LXI: pp. 464–466. Day's answer to Price, April 8, 1786, was published in *Proceedings of the Mass. Hist. Soc.*, series 2, 1903, XVII: pp. 339–341. David Erdman has pointed out that for his poem *America: A Prophecy*, William Blake had drawn on Barlow's epic Book V. David V. Erdman, "William Blake's Debt to Joel Barlow," *American Literature*, 1954, XXVI: pp. 94–98.
33 Barlow Papers, The Huntington Library. Barlow's letter to Day bears the date June 14, 1787.
34 F. L. Humphreys, *op. cit.*, I: p. 387, 397.
35 The above account and citations have been drawn from Luther O. Riggs, ed., *The Anarchiad: A New England Poem, Written in Concert by David Humphreys, Joel Barlow, John Trumbull, and Dr. Lemuel Hopkins* (New Haven, 1861), with Notes and Appendices; also Howard, *op. cit.*, pp. 180–200.
36 Parrington, *op. cit.*, Introduction, p. xi.
37 The address was published under the title, *An Oration Delivered At the North Church in Hartford at the Meeting of the Connecticut Society of the Cincinnati. July 4, 1787, in Commemoration of the Independence of the United States*.

(Hartford, 1787). In the Barlow Papers, Harvard, Box 4, is a copy of the *Oration* with revisions. He deleted four paragraphs in which he had expressed gratitude to Louis XVI and the commanders of his army and navy. Deleted, too, and this is significant for future reference, was a paragraph lauding John Adams for his *Defence of the Constitutions of Government of the United States of America.*

Chapter IV

1 Chester Whitney Wright, *Economic History of the United States* (New York, N.Y., 1949), pp. 179–180.
2 Joseph S. Davis, *Essays in the Earlier History of American Corporations* (Cambridge, Mass., 1917), I: p. 181.
3 Theodore Thomas Belote, *The Scioto Speculation and the French Settlement at Gallipolis, a Study in Ohio Valley History* (Cincinnati, OH., 1907), p. 16.
4 *Ibid.*, pp. 17–18.
5 Davis, *op. cit.*, I: p. 127.
6 For the facts on Duer's life we have relied on the account in *ibid.*, pp. 117–125.
7 MS. letter of Cutler and Sargent to Barlow, November 26, 1787, Scioto and Ohio Land Papers, Box 1, New York Historical Society.
8 Archer B. Hulbert, "Andrew Craigie and the Scioto Associates," *Proceedings of the American Antiquarian Society*, new series, 1913, XXIII: pp. 226–227.
9 Davis, *op. cit.*, pp. 140–146; Belote, *op. cit.*, pp. 18–20. Also E. C. Dawes, "The Scioto Purchase in 1787," *Magazine of American History*, 1889, XXII: pp. 470–482.
10 In re Barlow's appointment see Cutler-Sargent Correspondence, Massachusetts Historical Society.
11 Davis, *op. cit.*, I: p. 147.
12 MS. letter, Cutler to Sargent, January 3, 1788, Massachusetts Historical Society.
13 MS. letter, Cutler to Sargent, February 27, 1788, *ibid.*
14 Cited in Davis, *op. cit.*, I: p. 147.
15 *Ibid.*, I: p. 149, n. 2.
16 *Ibid.*, I, pp. 155–156, Craigie corresponded with Brissot in France. See *e.g.*, Craigie's letter, Oct. 7, 1790, Scioto and Ohio Land Papers, Box 2, French letters, New York Historical Society.
17 Lucy M. Gidney, *L'Influence des Etats-Unis d'Amérique sur Brissot, Condorcet at Mme. Roland* (Paris, France, 1930), p. 28.
18 Etienne Clavière and Brissot de Warville, *Considerations on the Relative Situations of France and the United States of America* (London, England, 1788). The real author was Brissot.
19 The English title of the revised edition is *New Travels in the United States of America* (London, 1792). Other editions were published in London and Dublin. A Dutch translation appeared in Amsterdam in 1794.
20 Barlow Papers, Harvard, Box 4, diary.
21 Washington, *Writings* (Washington, D.C., 1939), XXIX: pp. 503–504, 506–508.
22 Richard Platt to Winthrop Sargent, March 8, 1789, Mass. Hist. Soc.
23 Samuel Bernstein, *Essays in Political and Intellectual History* (New York, N.Y., 1955), pp. 63–65.
24 *E.g.*, Le Trosne, Baudeau, Morellet and Du Pont.
25 *Réflexions sur la formation et la distribution de la richesse.* It was first published in the Physiocratic Journal *Ephémérides du citoyen*, 1769–1770.
26 The best work on Mazzei is by Howard R. Marraro. See his *Philip Mazzei, Virginia's Agent in Europe* (New York, 1935); *Mazzei's Correspondence with the Grand Duke of Tuscany During His American Mission*, reprinted from *William and Mary College Quarterly*, second series, 1942, XXII; and his translation of *Memoirs of the Life and Peregrinations of the Florentine Philip Mazzei, 1730–1816* (New York, N.Y., 1942).
27 It was written in Italian and quickly translated into French. Two chapters were translated by Condorcet. Its French title is *Recherches historiques et politiques sur les Etats-Unis de l'Amérique septentrionale* (Paris, France, 1788).
28 For example, François Boissel's *Catéchisme du genre humain*, published in 1789; [Charles Robert Gosselin], *Réflexions d'un citoyen* (1787); [Saige], *Manuel de l'homme libre* (1787); Brissot de Warville, *Observations d'un républicain sur les différents systèmes d'administrations provinciales* (1787); Nicolas Collignon, *L'Avant-Coureur du changement du monde entier* (1786).
29 Bernstein, *op. cit.*, p. 65.
30 Jefferson, *Writings* (Washington, D.C., 1907), VII: p. 319.
31 Barlow Papers, Pequot Library.
32 Barlow Papers, Harvard, Box 1.
33 A copy of the letter in the Mass. Hist. Soc.
34 Theodore Belote, *Selections from the Gallipolis Papers* (Cincinnati, OH., 1906), p. 71.
35 The agreement to set up the company is cited in *ibid.*, pp. 48–52. A copy, with slight verbal differences, is in the Historical Society of Pennsylvania.
36 Belote, *The Scioto Speculation*, p. 27–28.
37 Belote, *Selections*, p. 73.
38 A biographic account of Playfair appeared in *The Gentleman's Magazine and Historical Chronicle*, 1823, XVIII: pp. 564-566, and in *The Edinburgh Annual Register*, 1823, III: pp. 332–334. His principal work against the French Revolution is *The History of Jacobinism, its Crimes and Perfidies* (Philadelphia, 1796). The book had a number of editions abroad, several of them in translation. It served as a text for American Francophobes. Playfair's first important publication on economics was *The Increase of Manufacturers, Commerce, and Finance, with the Extension of Civil Liberty, Proposed in Regulations for the Interest of Money* (London, England, 1785).
39 This was the theme of his major work, *An Inquiry into the Permanent Causes of the Decline and Fall of Powerful and Wealthy Nations* (London, England, 1805). A second edition was published in 1807.
40 *Ibid.*, 2nd edition, pp. 264–266.
41 Charles Burr Todd, *Life and Letters of Joel Barlow* (New York, N.Y., 1886), p. 69.
42 Davis, *op. cit.*, pp. 225, 236–237; see also the article of Henri Carré, "Les émigrés français en Amérique," *Revue de Paris*, 1898, VIII: pp. 311–340.
43 Letter of Barlow to Fitzgerald, January 4, 1790, New York Public Library.
44 Belote, *Selections*, p. 72.
45 *Ibid.*, p. 71.
46 Duer to Barlow, Nov. 4, 1790, Scioto and Ohio Land Papers, New York Historical Society.
47 Belote, *Selections*, pp. 67-70.
48 Barlow to Walker, April 10, 1791, The Historical Society of Pennsylvania.
49 Belote, *Selections*, p. 77.
50 Barlow Papers, Harvard, Box 2.

Chapter V

1 Barlow Papers, Harvard, Box 1. Letter of Jan. 1, 1790.

2 *Ibid.*, Letter of Jan. 2, 1790.
3 *Ibid.*
4 Cited in John Dos Passos, *The Ground We Stand On* (New York, 1941), p. 302.
5 The testimonial was printed by A. B. Shepperson, *John Paradise and Lucy Ludwell of London and Williamsburg* (Richmond, Va., 1942), pp. 382–384.
6 H. E. Scudder, ed., *Recollections of Samuel Breck with Passages from his Notebooks* (Philadelphia, PA., 1877), pp. 171–172.
7 Barlow Papers, The Huntington Library.
8 Barlow Papers, Harvard, Box 2. Letter of May 3, 1791.
9 Barlow Papers, The Huntington Library. Letter of November 15, 1791.
10 Barlow Papers, Pequot Library.
11 Barlow Papers, Harvard, Box 2. Letter of October 17, 1791.
12 *Ibid.*
13 The full title reads *Advice to the Privileged Orders in the Several European States, Resulting from the Necessity and Propriety of a General Revolution in the Principle of Government* (London, England, 1792).
14 The English text, in Barlow's hand, is in the Hanley-Smith Papers, Library of Congress.
15 *Discours à l'assemblée nationale, prononcé par William Henry Vernon au nom des citoyens unis de l'Amérique, séance du 10 juillet 1790.*
16 *Assemblée nationale: Journal des débats et des décrets*, July 10, 1790, No. 341: pp. 2–3.
17 *Journal politique national des états généraux et de la révolution de 1789*. The first series had 20 numbers; the second, 24.
18 *De l'état de la France présent et à venir* (London, England, 1790). It had three editions the first year.
19 Edmund Burke, *Works* (Boston, Mass., 1871), III: pp. 217–227.
20 *Life of the Right Honourable Edmund Burke* (London, England, 1878), 5th revised edition, p. 311.
21 *Ibid.*, p. 322. For a similar approach to the principal polemical writings see James T. Boulton, *The Language of Politics in the Age of Wilkes and Burke* (London, England, 1963), pp. 75–249. In an appendix Boulton surveys chronologically the development of the controversy concerning Burke's *Reflections* by listing 88 titles appearing from 1790 to 1793. The author makes no claim to the completeness of the list.
22 *Vindiciae Gallicae. Defence of the French Revolution and its English Admirers against the Accusations of the Right Hon. Edmund Burke* (London, England, 1791), Preface, pp. ii–iii, v.
23 Burke, *op. cit.*, III: pp. 243–244.
24 Alfred Owen Aldridge, *Man of Reason. The Life of Thomas Paine* (Philadelphia-New York, 1959), p. 141.
25 Burke, *op. cit.*, IV: pp. 16–17; VI: pp. 116–118.
26 Joel Barlow, *Political Writings* (New York, N.Y., 1796), pp. 253–255. The long note on Burke was reprinted by Freneau in *The Time Piece*, September 25, 1797, and in an American edition of Barlow's *Conspiracy of Kings* (Newbury, 1794).
27 Cited in Moncure Daniel Conway, *The Life of Thomas Paine* (New York, N.Y., 1909), I: pp. 300–301.
28 Aldridge, *op. cit.*, p. 161. See also by the same author, "The Rights of Man de Thomas Paine symbole du siècle des lumières et leur influence en France," in Pierre Francastel, ed., *Utopie et institutions au XVIIIe siècle. Le pragmatisme des lumières* (Paris, France, 1963), pp. 277–287.
29 Cited in E. P. Thompson, *The Making of the English Working Class* (New York, N.Y., 1964), p. 108.
30 From May 6 to May 27, 1791.
31 May 31, June 4, June 7 and July 7, 1792.
32 Jefferson, *op. cit.*, VIII: p. 224.
33 It appeared under different titles, in Boston, Philadelphia, Albany, London, Edinburgh and Glasgow.
34 Cited by Wendell Glick, "The Best Possible World of John Quincy Adams," *The New England Quarterly*, 1964, XXXVII: p. 14.
35 James Holland Rose, *Life of William Pitt* (London, England, 1923), II: pp. 21–22.
36 On Mary Hays, Helen Maria Williams and Charlotte Smith see B. G. MacCarthy, *The Later Women Novelists 1744–1818* (Oxford, England, 1947), pp. 79–82, 153–162, 187–189, 196–198.
37 C. Kegan Paul, *William Godwin: His Friends and Contemporaries* (London, England, 1876), I: p. 71.
38 *Advice to the Privileged Orders*, Introduction. All further references are to Barlow's *Political Writings* (New York, N.Y., 1796).
39 *Ibid.*, p. 29.
40 *Ibid.*, p. 33.
40 *Ibid.*, pp. 34–35.
42 *Ibid.*, pp. 36–40.
43 *Ibid.*, pp. 41–45.
44 *Ibid.*, ch. iii.
45 *Ibid.*, ch. iv.
46 *The History of our Customs, Aids, Subsidies, National Debts and Taxes, from William the Conqueror to the Present Year* (London, England, 1761).
47 *The History of the Public Revenue of the British Empire* (London, England, 1785–1790).
48 *De l'administration des finances de la France* (Paris, France, 1784).
49 *An Inquiry into the Nature and Causes of the Wealth of Nations*. It was published in 1776. The first American edition appeared in Philadelphia in 1789.
50 Specifically in Chapter 4, "Of Constitutions."
51 Raymond A. Preston, ed., *An Enquiry Concerning Political Justice and Its Influence on Virtue and Happiness* (New York, N.Y., 1926), II: Book viii. See also Samuel Bernstein, *Essays in Political and Intellectual History* (New York, N.Y., 1955), pp. 45–48.
52 Barlow, *Political Writings*, 110. Years later Barlow acknowledged a resemblance between his ideas in the *Advice* and Godwin's in *Political Justice*. But he opposed Godwin's system, saying that it was "wire-drawn and not adapted to the present state of society, nor to one of which we have any idea. I do not think that society can exist without a regular government, or with property in common." Cited by Milton Cantor, "The Life of Joel Barlow," doctoral dissertation, Columbia University, 143, n. 5.
53 *Ibid.*, p. 138.
54 Leon Howard, *The Connecticut Wits* (Chicago, Ill., 1943), p. 437.
55 Grimm-Diderot, *Correspondance littéraire, philosophique et critique* (Paris, France, 1829), I: pp. 272–273.
56 *Oeuvres philosophiques* (Amsterdam, 1772), I: separate pagination.
57 Meslier's severe attack on French society circulated in manuscript during the eighteenth century. It was published in full in 1864 in Amsterdam. A complete edition of his writings, *Oeuvres de Jean Meslier*, was issued in Paris in 1970.
58 Boissel's book had a second edition in 1792. It is of some interest that in a letter to Jefferson on March 21, 1788, Boissel offered to send him a manuscript copy with

permission to publish it in America, with the hope that it might persuade people to establish an order "which would forever protect the United States from the evils afflicting even the most enlightened peoples, and inevitably stemming from the homicidal, mercenary order." Julian P. Boyd, ed., *The Writings of Thomas Jefferson* (Princeton, N.J., 1955), XII: pp. 685–686.
59 Barlow, *Political Writings*, pp. 149–156.
60 See Arthur O. Lovejoy, *The Great Chain of Being* (Cambridge, Mass., 1942), pp. 185–203.
61 "A Free Inquiry into the Nature and Origin of Evil," in his *Miscellaneous Pieces in Verse and Prose* (London, England, 1770), pp. 295-296, 325–335.
62 In *The Fable of the Bees: Private Vices, Public Benefits*.
63 Victor C. Miller, *Joel Barlow: Revolutionist, London, 1791-1792* (Hamburg, 1932), pp. 4, n. 13; 21; 27, n. 79. The first edition of the *Advice* was disposed of in about four months. A second was printed in June 1792, and a third the following year. It appeard in German in 1792 and in French in 1794.
64 1796, VII: p. 321.
65 Barlow Papers, Harvard, Box 2. Copy of Jefferson's letter to Barlow.
66 *The National Gazette*, August 4, 1792.

Chapter VI

1 *Essays, Moral and Political* (London, England, 1832), pp. 79, 87–88, "On the Rise and Progress of Popular Disaffection."
2 For an account of these associations see Henry Jephson, *The Platform. Its Rise and Progress* (New York, N.Y., 1892), I: ch. 2.
3 *A View of the Causes and Consequences of the Present War with France* (London, England, 1797), p. 13.
4 *The Correspondence of the Revolution Society, with the National Assembly, and with Various Societies of the Friends of the People in France and England* (London, England, 1792), p. 3; Samuel Bernstein, *Essays in Political and Intellectual History* (New York, 1955), pp. 48–49.
5 *Second Report from the Committee of Secrecy of the House of Commons*, Appendix C; also George S. Veitch, *The Genesis of Parliamentary Reform* (London, England, 1913), pp. 200–207.
6 On Spence see Olive Rudkin, *Thomas Spence and His Connections* (New York, N.Y., 1927); Christopher Brunel and Peter M. Jackson, "Notes on Tokens as a Source of Information on the History of the Labour & Radical Movement," *Bulletin of the Society for the Study of Labour History*, No. 13: pp. 26–36.
7 John Binns, *Recollections* (Philadelphia, PA., 1854), pp. 45–46.
8 See *The London Corresponding Society's Addresses and Resolutions* (1792); also *A Vindication of the London Corresponding Society* (London, England, 1796?); Henry Collins, "The London Corresponding Society," John Saville, ed., *Democracy and the Labour Movement* (London, 1954), pp. 103–134; a history of the London Corresponding Society in *The Moral and Political Magazine of the London Corresponding Society*, July 1796, pp. 83–86; September 1796, pp. 180–181; October 1796, pp. 230–233. This history was left unfinished. See also Thomas Hardy, *Memoir* (London, England, 1832), pp. 10–16. For broader accounts of the popular societies see W. P. Hall, *British Radicalism, 1791–1797* (New York, N.Y., 1912); G. S. Veitch, *op. cit.*; P. A. Brown, *The French Revolution in English History* (London, England, 1918).
9 Lord William Auckland, *Journals and Correspondence* (London, England, 1861), II: pp. 423–424.
10 See *e.g.*, Thomas Moore, ed., *The Memoirs of Lord Edward Fitzgerald* (London, England, 1897); also Lucy Ellis and Joseph Turquan, *La Belle Pamela* (London, England, 1924), pp. 248–249.
11 Arthur Aspinall, ed., *The Early English Trade Unions* (London, England, 1949), Preface and pp. 1, 3, 4–21.
12 *Ibid.*, Preface.
13 A. Aspinall, *Politics and the Press* (London, England, 1949), p. 68.
14 See Thompson, *op. cit.*, pp. 112–116.
15 The general title of the series is *Liberty and Property Preserved against Republicans and Levellers: A Collection of Tracts.* See Samuel Bernstein, *Essays in Political and Intellectual History* (New York, N.Y., 1969), pp. 50–51, reprint.
16 Cited in Lionel D. Woodward, *Une anglaise amie de la Révolution Française* (Paris, France, 1930), p. 7.
17 Christopher Hill, "The English Revolution and the Brotherhood of Man," *Science & Society*, 1954, XVIII: pp. 289–309.
18 *A Collection of Addresses Transmitted by Certain English Clubs and Societies to the National Convention of France* (London, England, 1793), pp. 164–165.
19 *The Moral and Political Magazine of the London Corresponding Society*, September 1796, pp. 154–155.
20 *The National Gazette*, "Independence," July 4, 1792.
21 Written in 1794. See *The Complete Works of Robert Burns* (Philadelphia, PA., 1886), IV: pp. 14–16.
22 Moncule D. Conway, ed., *The Writings of Thomas Paine* (New York, N.Y., 1908), II: p. 472.
23 For surveys of peace projects see Elizabeth Souleyman, *The Vision of World Peace in Seventeenth and Eighteenth Century France* (New York, N.Y., 1941), and Shelby T. McCloy, *The Humanitarian Movement in Eighteenth-Century France* (Lexington, KY., 1957), ch. xii.
24 Louis Picard, *Le passé, le présent et l'avenir*. On Picard, see Louis Allard, *La comédie de moeurs en France au dix-neuvième siècle* (Cambridge, Mass., 1923), I: pp. 55–75, 65–68.
25 Georges Avenel, *Anacharsis Cloots, l'orateur du genre humain* (Paris, France, 1865), 2 vols.
26 L. Chevalley, *La déclaration du droit des gens de l'abbé Grégoire* (Paris, France, 1913); *Mémoires de Grégoire*, I: pp. 428–430.
27 Victor C. Miller, *Joel Barlow: Revolutionist, London, 1791–1792* (Hamburg, 1932), pp. 18–19.
28 Warner to Barlow, August 19, 1791, Pequot Library.
29 They are in the Barlow-Hayley correspondence, Pequot Library.
30 Cited in Jacobine Menzies Wilson and Helen Lloyd, *Amelia. The Tale of a Plain Friend* (New York, N.Y., 1937), p. 15.
31 P. W. Clayden, *The Early Life of Samuel Rogers* (Boston, Mass., 1888), p. 191.
32 *The Monthly Mirror*, April 1796, p. 326.
33 See his *Triumphs of Temper. A Poem in Six Cantos* (Kennebunk, Me., 1804), Preface, dated January 31, 1871; his *Poems and Plays* (London, England, 1788), III: pp. 109–112, 118–120, 125.
34 A revised edition, the fifth, appeared in Paris in 1793 and was so advertised in America. See *e.g.*, *The Argus*, or *Greenleaf's New Daily Advertiser*, January 27, 1796. See aslo Lewis Leary, "Joel Barlow and William Hayley; A Correspondence," *American Literature*, March 1949–January 1950, XXI: pp. 325–334.

35 John Johnson, ed., *Memoirs of the Life and Writings of William Hayley, Esq., the Friend and Biographer of William Cowper, Written by Himself* (London, England, 1823), I: p. 425. Barlow wrote Hayley on March 6 to thank him for his kind attentions. Ruth was grateful for the present of his writings and sent the tenderest regards to Hayley's young son. The letter is among Barlow's papers at The Huntington Library.
36 Clarke to Barlow, March 25, 1792, Pequot Library.
37 We have used the American edition, Newburyport, Mass., 1794.
38 For a good account of this period of the Revolution see Georges Lefebvre, *The French Revolution from its Origins to 1793* (New York, N.Y., 1962), ch. xii, trans. by Elizabeth Moss Evanson; Albert Mathiez, *La révolution française* (Paris, France, 1922), I: chs. x–xi. On Robespierre's opposition to the war, see Bernstein, *op. cit.*, ch. ii.
39 A revised edition appeared in Paris, 1793, and another in London, 1796. It had two American printings, one in Newburyport, 1794, and another in New York, 1796.
40 Leon Howard, *The Connecticut Wits* (Chicago, Ill., 1943), p. 289.
41 The translation was published in 1792 in London, Dublin and the United States.
42 Alexandre Tuetey, ed., *Correspondance du ministre de l'intérieur relative au commerce, aux subsistances et à l'administration générale, 16 avril–14 octobre 1792* (Paris, France, 1917), pp. 275–281.
43 *Causes qui se sont opposées aux progrès du commerce entre la France et les Etats-unis de l'Amérique, avec les moyens de l'accélérer et la comparaison de la dette nationale de l'Angleterre, de la France et des Etats-Unis en six lettres adressées à Monsieur le Marquis de la Fayette* (Paris, France, 1790).
44 The account is based on Howard C. Rice, "James Swan, agent of the French Republic," *New England Quarterly*, September 1937, X: pp. 464–486; *Dictionary of American Biography*; *Proceedings of the Massachusetts Historical Society*, XIII: pp. 209–210; Samuel Flagg Bemis, "Payment of the French Loans to the United States, 1777–1795," *Current History*, March 1926, XXIII: pp. 829–831.
45 Barlow Papers, Harvard, Box 1.
46 *Ibid.*, letters of June 10 and 18, 1792.
47 *Ibid.*, letter of June 25, 1792.
48 For these events see Lefebvre, *op. cit.*, ch. xiii.
49 Cited by Leon Howard, "Joel Barlow and Napoleon," *The Huntington Library Quarterly*, 1938–1939, II: p. 40.
50 Barlow, *Political Writings*, p. 160. *A Letter to the National Convention* had two editions in 1792. The first was published by Johnson; the second, by the Society for Constitutional Information. The first American edition appeared in New York, 1793, and a second, in 1795. A French translation was issued in Paris in 1792.
51 *Ibid.*, pp. 171–172.
52 *Ibid.*, p. 161.
53 *Ibid.*, p. 164, Barlow's italics.
54 *Ibid.*, pp. 166–169.
55 *Ibid.*, p. 170, Barlow's italics.
56 *Ibid.*, pp. 175–176, Barlow's italics.
57 *Ibid.*, pp. 177–197.
58 *Ibid.*, pp. 190–191.
59 *Dissertation sur la peine de mort* (Paris, France, 1782).
60 *Recherches philosophiques sur le droit de propriété et sur le vol considéré dans la nature* (Chartres, 1780), pp. 102–111.
61 *The Increase of Manufactures, Commerce and Finance, with the Extension of Civil Liberty, Proposed in Regulations for the Interest of Money* (London, England, 1785), p. 34.

62 M. Ray Adams, *Studies in the Literary Backgrounds of English Radicalism* (Lancaster, PA., 1947), p. 51.
63 Letter of November 3, 1792, The Huntington Library.
64 Cited by Lewis Leary, *American Literature*, 1949–1950, XXI: p. 333.
65 Cited in M. Ray Adams, *op. cit.*, p. 49.
66 Barlow Papers, Pequot Library. Portions of the *Letter* were cited at the trial of Thomas Hardy. See *Trial of Thomas Hardy for High Treason*, II: pp. 35–42.

Chapter VII

1 Georges Lefebvre, *The French Revolution from its Origins to 1793* (New York, N.Y., 1962) pp. 270–271.
2 *Le moniteur* (réimpression), XIV: p. 562.
3 Victor C. Miller, *Joel Barlow: Revolutionist, London, 1791–1792* (Hamburg, 1932), pp. 47–50.
4 For the above letters see Charles Burr Todd, *Life and Letters of Joel Barlow* (New York, N.Y., 1866), pp. 108–110.
5 Charles James Fox, *Speeches* (London, England, 1815), IV: pp. 445–447.
6 *Letters to Imlay* (London, England, 1879), p. 127.
7 Cited by M. Ray Adams, *Studies in the Literary Backgrounds of English Radicalism* (Lancaster, PA.), p. 58.
8 Letter to James Watson, August 24, 1793, Yale University Library.
9 See Charles Dufayard, *Histoire de Savoie* (Paris, France, 1930), pp. 262–269; Grégoire, *Mémoires*, I: pp. 418–421.
10 Albert Sorel, *L'Europe et la révolution française* (Paris, France, 1897), III: pp. 201–204.
11 Grégoire, *Mémoire en faveur des gens de couleur ou sang-mêlés de St. Domingue et des autres isles françaises de l'Amérique, adressé à l'Assemblée nationale* (Paris, France, 1789); *An Inquiry Concerning the Intellectual and Moral Faculties of Negroes* (Brooklyn, N.Y., 1810), trans. by D. B. Warden.
12 Grégoire, *Motion en faveur des juifs* (Paris, France, 1789) and *Essai sur la génération physique, morale et politique des juifs* (Metz, 1789); see also Ballin P. Grunebaum, *L'Abbé Grégoire et les juifs* (Paris, 1931) and Ruth F. Necheles, "The Abbé Grégoire's Work in Behalf of Jews, 1788–1791," *French Historical Studies*, 1969, VI: pp. 172–184.
13 Cited in Todd, *op. cit.*, p. 97.
14 *Ibid.*, p. 98.
15 General Doppet, *Mémoires politiques et militaires* (Paris, France, 1824), pp. 104–107.
16 *Journal des débats*, No. 152, February 17, 1793, pp. 217–218. A copy of the decree of the Convention making Barlow a citizen is in the New York Public Library.
17 It appeared in French in Chambéry in 1793, and in Italian in Nice the same year. It had English and American editions in 1795. It was reprinted in his *Political Writings*, pp. 199–235, in 1796. We have relied on this text.
18 Barlow, *Political Writings*, pp. 202–205.
19 *Ibid.*, p. 207.
20 *Ibid.*, pp. 208–212.
21 *Ibid.*, p. 230.
22 In the New York *Weekly Magazine*, January 1796, and soon thereafter in New Haven. It had eight printings in 1796 alone, and three in 1797. It was pirated by literary magazines and newspapers.
23 Frederick J. Turner, "Documents on the Relations of France to Louisiana, 1792–1795," *American Historical Review*, 1897–1898, III: p. 505.

24 Samuel Bernstein, *Essays in Political and Intellectual History* (New York, N.Y., 1955), p. 74

25 See Jefferson's long letter of August 16, 1793, to Gouverneur Morris, American minister to France, in *Writings*, IX: pp. 180–209.

26 Albert Laponneraye, ed., *Oeuvres de Maximilien Robespierre* (Paris, France, 1840), III: pp. 455–475.

27 Linguet, *Annales politiques, civiles, et littéraires du dix-huitième siècle*, 1777, I: 12–16. A similar apprehension was conveyed in 1783 by the Venetian ambassador in Paris to his home government. See R. R. Palmer, *The Age of the Democratic Revolution* (Princeton, N.J., 1959), I: p. 239.

28 The memoir was published in French and English by Douglas Brymner, *Report on Canadian Archives, 1890* (Ottawa, 1891), pp. 108–117. It was summarized by Turner, *op. cit.*, pp. 651–652.

29 The plans were summarized by Turner, *op. cit.*, pp. 491–503, 651–661.

30 Documents bearing on Clark's expedition were published by J. L. Jameson in the *Annual Report of the American Historical Association*, 1896, I: pp. 930–1107.

31 The plan was published in *ibid.*, pp. 953–954.

32 For these facts we have relied on Ralph Leslie Rusk's "The Adventures of Gilbert Imlay," *Indiana University Studies*, March 1923, X, no. 57: pp. 1–26.

33 See Imlay's letter to the Minister, April 22, 1793, cited in Rusk, *ibid.*, p. 20, n. 70.

34 Cited in Turner, *op. cit.*, p. 495. The plan is described in *ibid.*, pp. 494–496.

35 Mary Wollstonecraft, *Letters to Imlay*, p. 81.

36 Rusk, *op. cit.*, p. 24.

37 *Annual Report of the American Historical Association*, 1896, I: p. 952.

Chapter VIII

1 Georges Lefèbvre, "Le commerce extérieur, de l'an II," *La révolution française*, 1925, LXXVIII: pp. 133–134.

2 Pierre Caron, ed., *La commission des subsistances, de l'an II. Procès-verbaux et actes* (Paris, 1925), pp. 625 n, 668.

3 Rice, *op. cit.*, p. 471.

4 Caron, *op. cit.*, pp. 88, 102, 662–663.

5 For some of the data we have relied on Milton Cantor's doctoral dissertation, "The Life of Joel Barlow," 1954, Columbia University.

6 Knox Papers, Mass. Hist. Soc., Swan to Knox, December 21, 1793.

7 Elizabeth W. Latimer, ed., *My Scrap-Book of the French Revolution* (Chicago, Ill., 1903), p. 54.

8 Moncure D. Conway, ed., *The Writings of Thomas Paine* (New York, N.Y.), II: pp. 104–107.

9 The petition appears in full in *ibid.*, 107–109. A shortened version was published in Sampson Perry, *An Historical Sketch of the French Revolution* (London, England, 1796), II: pp. 515–516. See also Alfred O. Aldridge, *Man of Reason. The Life of Thomas Paine* (Philadelphia–New York, 1959), pp. 208–209.

10 W. H. Bruford, *Germany in the Eighteenth Century: The Social Background of the Literary Revival* (Cambridge, Mass., 1935), p. 181.

11 Sydney Seymour Biro, *The German Policy of Revolutionary France* (Cambridge, Mass. 1957), p. 817.

12 *Ibid.*, p. 248.

13 Barlow's biographic sketch and preface in Brissot, *New Travels in the United States of America* (London, England, 1794).

14 *Précis historique de la révolution française* (Paris, France, 1792).

15 Benjamin P. Kurtz and Carie C. Autrey, eds., *Four New Letters of Mary Wollstonecraft and Helen M. Williams* (Berkeley, CA., 1937).

16 Most of his letters to Americans were published in *Proceedings of the American Antiquarian Society*, new series, 1925, XXXV: pp. 272–451; his four letters to Barlow are in the Barlow Papers, Harvard, Box 2. Ebeling's letter to Stiles, June 26, 1794, was published in *Collections of the Massachusetts Historical Society*, 2nd series, VIII: pp. 270–275.

17 *Collections of the Mass. Hist. Soc.*, 2nd series, VIII: pp. 269–270.

18 The contemporary of Goldsmith and Smollett.

19 *De l'Allemagne* (Paris, 1860), pp. 118–119.

20 Joseph Dorfman in the *Political Science Quarterly*, 1944, LIX: pp. 83–100.

21 Barlow Papers, Harvard, Box 4.

22 See Jephson, *op. cit.*, I: pp. 172–179.

23 For the above data we have relied on the excellent study of François Crouzet, "Bilan de l'économie britannique pendant les guerres de la Révolution et de l'Empire," *Revue historique*, 1965, CCXXXIV: pp. 79–109.

24 It had 36 numbers, from November 20, 1797, to July 9, 1798.

25 Charles Edmonds, ed., *Poetry of the Anti-Jabcobins* (New York-London, 1890), p. 271.

26 *Ibid.*, p. 286.

27 Thomas James Mathias, *The Pursuits of Literature* (Philadelphia, 1800), *passim*. It first appeared in four parts from 1794 to 1797 and subsequently had many editions. The first American edition, cited here, was a reprint of the seventh English edition.

28 Henry R. Yorke, *Letter to the Reformers* (Dorchester, England, 1798), pp. 15–16, 39–40.

29 Robert Fellowes, *Address to the People on the Present Relative Situations of England and France, with Reflections on the Genius of Democracy and on Parliamentary Reform* (London, England, 1799), pp. 20–36

30 John Bowles, "Thoughts on the Origin and Formation of Political Constitutions" (1796) in *The Retrospect. A Collection of Tracts, Published at Various Periods of the War* (London, England, 1798), pp. 285–301,

31 William Sabatier, *A Treatise on Poverty, its Consequences and the Remedy* (London, England, 1797).

32 *An Inquiry into the State of the Public Mind Amongst the Lower Classes, and the Means of Turning it to the Welfare of the State* (Dublin, Ireland, 1798).

33 Hannah More, *Works* (New York, N.Y., 1835), V: p. 296. See also R. K. Webb, *The Political Working Class Reader* (London, England, 1955), p. 42.

34 No. I, February, 1798, pp. 6–7. *The Brazen Trumpet* had six numbers, from February 10 to March 17, 1798.

35 *Ibid.*, No. II: 41.

36 His best known work was an edition of Lucretius.

37 *A Reply to Some Parts of the Bishop of Llandaff's Address to the People of Great Britain*, 1798. See Sir Leslie Stephen, *History of English Thought in the Eighteenth Century* (New York, N.Y., 1962), I: pp. 373–375. For a portrait of Dr. Watson see Stephen's *History*, pp. 384–387; also Dr. Watson's controversy with Thomas Paine over his *Age of Reason*, pp. 388–392. Regarding this controversy, William Blake commented in 1797: "To defend the Bible in the year 1798 would cost a man his life. The Beast and the Whore rule without control. It is an easy matter for a Bishop to triumph over Paines attack, but it is not so easy for one who loves the Bible. . . .

I have not the charity for the Bishop that he pretends to have for Paine. I believe him to be a State trickster." David V. Erdman, ed., *The Poetry and Prose of William Blake* (New York, N.Y., 1965) pp. 601, 602.

38 See the excellent account of the persistent reform movement during the war years in Thompson, *op. cit.*, pp. 175–185.

39 Eugene Perry Link, *Democratic-Republican Societies 1790–1800* (New York, N.Y., 1942), pp. 126–127.

Chapter IX

1 London, England, 1792–93, 4 vols.
2 *Letters Containing a Sketch of the Politics of France from the Thirty-first of May 1793 till the Twenty-eighth of July 1794* (London, England, 1796), 4 vols. This series had a second edition in Dublin, Ireland, and another in Philadelphia, PA., in 1796.
3 For a list of such advertised publications in the United States see Anson Ely Morse, *The Federalist Party in Massachusetts to the Year 1800* (Princeton, N.J., 1909), pp 98–99, n. 3.
4 *Peace with the Jacobins Impossible* (London, England, 1794).
5 *The History of Jacobinism, Its Crimes, Cruelties and Perfidies: Comprising an Inquiry into the Manner of Disseminating, under the Appearance of Philosophy and Virtue, Principles Which are Equally Subversive of Order, Virtue, Religion, Liberty and Happiness* (London, England, 1796), 2 vols. Playfair's *History* at once had an American edition. Published in Philadelphia in 1796, it was a cue for William Cobbett, alias Peter Porcupine, to publish the same year his *History of the American Jacobins.*
6 *An Historical and Moral View of the Origin and Progress of the French Revolution; and the Effect it Has Produced in Europe* (London, England, 1794).
7 *An Historical Sketch of the French Revolution* (London, England, 1796), 2 vols.
8 This edition had illustrations designed by William Blake.
9 *A Discourse Delivered February 19, 1795, the Day Set Apart by the President for a General Thanksgiving Through the United States* (Boston, Mass., 1795).
10 See W. de Loss Love, Jr., *The Fast and Thanksgiving Days in New England* (Boston-New York, 1895), pp. 362–368, 372–377.
11 Sullivan's pamphlet, published anonymously, bore the long title, *The Altar of Baal Thrown Down: or, the French Nation Defended, Against the Pulpit Slander of David Osgood, A.M. Pastor of the Church in Bedford, A Sermon, par Citoyen de Novion* (Boston, Mass., 1795).
12 *The Independent Chronicle* (Boston, Mass.), October 2, 1797.
13 Barlow Papers, Harvard, letter to John Fellows. It was reprinted, with a wrong date, in *Gazette of the United States,* August 23, 1799.
14 See his *The Guillotine, A Democratic Dirge, A Poem* (Philadelphia, PA., 1796).
15 See *The Political Green-House for the Year 1798. Addressed to the Reader of the Connecticut Courant* (Hartford, CT., 1799). It was believed that Hopkins and Dwight were his collaborators.
16 *The Revolution in France, Considered in Respect to its Progress and Effects* (New York, N.Y., 1794). We have used the text in his *Collection of Papers on Political, Literary and Moral Subjects* (New York, N.Y., 1893).
17 Barlow's letter to John Fellows, May 23, 1795, cited in note 13.

18 George Gibbs, *Memoirs of the Administrations of Washington and John Adams, edited from the Papers of Oliver Wolcott, Secretary of the Treasury* (New York, N.Y., 1846), I: p. 135.
19 The original letter is in the Yale University Library; a copy is in the Barlow Papers, Harvard, Box 2. The italics are Stiles's.
20 Edmund S. Morgan, *The Gentle Puritan. A Life of Ezra Stiles 1727–1795* (New Haven, CT., 1962), pp. 457–459.
21 *Ibid.*, p. 456.
22 Cited by Elie Halévy, *La formation du radicalisme philosophique* (Paris, France, 1901), II: p. 201.
23 *History of American Jacobins, Commonly Denominated Democrats* (Philadelphia, PA., 1796).
24 *Ibid.*, p. 37
25 *The Independent Chronicle* (Boston), August 29, 1796; the entire statement was reprinted in *The New York Argus,* or *Greenleaf's New Daily Advertiser,* September 5, 1796.
26 John I. Johnson, *Reflections on Political Society* (New York, N.Y., 1797), pp. 13–15.
27 Gibbs, *op. cit.*, I, p. 161.
28 Barlow Papers, Harvard, Box 1.
29 Both notes and outline are in Barlow Papers, Harvard, Box 4.

Chapter X

1 Barlow Papers, Harvard, Box 1.
2 *Naval Documents Related to the United States Wars with the Barbary Powers: Naval Operations* (Washington, D.C., 1939), I: pp. 22–26.
3 *Ibid.,* pp. 38–39.
4 *Ibid.,* pp. 80–81; see also *American State Papers: Foreign Relations* (Washington, D.C., 1832), I: p. 529.
5 *Naval Documents,* etc., I: p. 83.
6 See Frank E. Ross, "James Leander Cathcart—Troublesome, Litigious Trifler,'" *Americana,* 1934, XXVIII: pp. 477–485.
7 *Ibid.*, p. 480. It may be said here that Cathcart was appointed consul to Tripoli in July 1797. In the same year O'Brien was named consul general to Algiers. For portraits of both Captains see H. G. Barnby, *The Prisoners of Algiers* (London-New York, 1966).
8 *Naval Documents,*etc. I: p. 89, pp. 107–115; Ray W. Irwin, *The Diplomatic Relations of the United States with the Barbary Powers, 1776–1816* (Chapel Hill, N.C., 1931), pp. 70–72. After September 5, 1795, sixty-five American prisoners were temporarily liberated, among them O'Brien and Cathcart.
9 *American State Papers: Foreign Relations,* Monroe to the Secretary of State, October 4, 1795, II: p. 722.
10 "The Diplomatic Journal and Letterbook of James Leander Cathcart, 1788–1796," *Proceedings of the American Antiquarian Society,* 1954, LXIV: pp. 340–341; also Barlow's statement, November 1, 1796, in Barlow Papers, Harvard, Box 3.
11 Barlow Papers, Harvard, Box 4.
12 In the Harvard University Library.
13 *Naval Documents,* etc., I: p. 140.
14 See Paul W. Bamford, *The Barbary Pirates, Victims and the Scourge of Christendom* (Minneapolis, Minn., 1792).
15 *Naval Documents,* etc., I: p. 141.
16 *Ibid.,* pp. 126, 136–137. For a fuller account of Donaldson's mission see Frank E. Ross, "The Mission of Joseph Donaldson, Jr., to Algiers, 1795–97," *The Journal of Modern History,* 1935, VII: pp. 422–433.

17 *Naval Documents*, etc., I: 132–133; also Cathcart's "Diplomatic Journal and Letterbook," *op. cit.*, LXIV: pp. 367–369.
18 Barlow Papers, Harvard, Box 1.
19 *Naval Documents*, etc., I: p. 138.
20 Barlow Papers, Harvard, Box 1, letter of April 26, 1796.
21 *Ibid.*, letters of March 14 and April 2, 1796.
22 *Naval Documents*, etc., I: p. 143.
23 *Ibid.*, 143–145; also Charles Burr Todd, "A Forgotten American Worthy," *Lippincott's Magazine*, 1880, XXVI: pp. 72–73.
24 Cathcart's "Diplomatic Journal and Letterbook," *op. cit.*, LXIV: pp. 389–390, 392.
25 *Naval Documents*, etc., I: pp. 163–165.
26 Barlow Papers, Harvard, Box 1.
27 Full letter in *Ibid.*; *The New Englander*, 1873, XXXII: 433–437; Todd, "A Forgotten American Worthy," *op. cit.*, pp. 79–83; *American Literature*, 1937–38, IX: pp. 443–448.
28 In the Barlow Papers at the Henry Huntington Library are a number of pieces relating to Barlow's efforts to ship the freed men to America.
29 Irwin, *op. cit.*, p. 75.
30 Barlow Papers, Harvard, Box 1, letter to Ruth, September 25, 1796; Barlow Papers, Pequot Library, Humphreys to Barlow, July 23, 1796.
31 *Naval Documents*, etc., I: p. 176.
32 Barlow Papers, Harvard, Box 1, letter to Ruth, October 9, 1796. Among the Barlow Papers, Peqout Library, is a draft in Barlow's hand of a treaty with the Bey of Tunis, consisting of 21 articles.
33 *Naval Documents*, etc., I: p. 191.
34 Barlow Papers, Harvard, Box 1.
35 *Naval Documents*, etc., I: pp. 199–201.
36 *Ibid.*, p. 183.
37 *Ibid.*, pp. 206–208.
38 *Ibid.*, p. 203.

Chapter XI

1 Albert Elmer Hancock, *The French Revolution and the English Poets* (Port Washington, 1967), p. 62.
2 On Boulanger, see John Hampton, *Nicolas Antoine Boulanger et la science de son temps* (Geneva, Switzerland, 1955). *Christianity Unmasked* was long attributed to Voltaire, but he denied it because the work led to atheism which he detested, he said. Charles Rihs, *Recherches sur les origines du matérialisme historique* (Geneva, 1962), p. 98, n. 219.
3 Barlow Papers, Harvard, letter to John Fellows, August 23, 1795.
4 Robert Niklaus, *The Age of the Enlightenment* (London, 1967), p. 403, eds. W. H. Barber, J. H. Brumfitt, R. A. Leigh, R. Shackleton and S. S. B. Taylor.
5 Jacques Proust, *Diderot et l'Encyclopédie* (Paris, 1967), p. 297, n. 1.
6 Charles François Dupuis, *The Origin of All Religious Worship* (New Orleans, 1872), p. 16.
7 *Ibid.*, p. 301.
8 *Ibid.*, pp. 304–306.
9 *Ibid.*, pp. 318, 319.
10 *Ibid.*, pp. 330–331, 337, 339.
11 Gilbert Chinard, *Jefferson et les idéologues* (Baltimore, MD., 1925), p. 38.
12 William Smith, ed., "Memoirs of My Life and Writings," in *The History of the Decline and Fall of the Roman Empire* (New York, n.d.), I: p. 93
13 *The Poor Man's Guardian*, December 6, 1834.
14 A. Cobban, *In Search of Humanity. The Role of the Enlightenment in Modern History* (London, England, 1960), p. 65.
15 Cited in *ibid.*, p. 106.
16 Pierre Bayle, *Oeuvres diverses* (The Hague, 1737), III *(Pensées diverses)*, pp. 51, 55, 73–74, 78, 91–92.
17 *Ibid.*, pp. 109–110, 113.
18 Barlow Papers, Harvard, Box 4.
19 *Ibid.*
20 *Ibid.*
21 *Ibid.*
22 *Ibid.*
23 *Ibid.*
24 Bernstein, *op. cit.*, p. 107.
25 Barlow Papers, Harvard, Box 2.
26 Barlow Papers, Pequot Library, Ruth Barlow to C. Colden, July 24, 1815.
27 Lewis Leary, *op. cit.*, p. 361.
28 Eleanore J. Fulton, "Robert Fulton as an Artist," *Papers of the Lancaster County Historical Society*, 1938, XLII, No. 3; also J. Franklin Reigart, *The Life of Robert Fulton* (Philadelphia, PA., 1856), p. 34 ff.
29 Frank Podmore, *Robert Owen* (New York, N.Y., 1924), I: p. 58; *The Life of Robert Owen by Himself* (New York, N.Y., 1920), pp. 49, 97.
30 See H. W. Dickinson, *Robert Fulton, Engineer and Artist* (London, England, 1913), pp. 27–28.
31 In the Barlow Papers, Harvard, Box 3, is a listing of over 100 paintings by West as well as other data, showing the vast extent of his work.
32 David Whittet Thomson, "Robert Fulton and the French Invasion of England," *Military Affairs*, 1954, XVIII: No. 2, p. 58.
33 Barlow Papers, Pequot Library, Southport, CT.
34 The draft is in the Barlow Papers, Pequot Library, Southport, CT.
35 Barlow Papers, Harvard, Box 2.
36 *Bulletin of the New York Public Library*, 1901, V: pp. 348–356.
37 Paul Mantoux, *The Industrial Revolution in the Eighteenth Century* (New York, N.Y., 1927), pp. 123–135.
38 See Lequinio's *Richesse de la république* (Paris, France, 1792).
39 Cited in C. Colden, *The Life of Robert Fulton* (New York, N.Y., 1817), pp. 25–26.
40 William Barclay Parsons, *Robert Fulton and the Submarine* (New York, N.Y., 1922), Ch. iv; Alice C. Sutcliffe, *Robert Fulton and the "Clermont"* (New York, N.Y., 1909), Pt. ii; Félicien Pascal, "Napoleon I contre les torpilleurs," *Revue politique et littéraire*, 1904, 5TH series, I: pp. 274–276; *The American Historical Review*, 1934, XXXIX: pp. 489–494.
41 Parsons, *op. cit.*, p. 32.
42 I came upon it in the Pequot Library, Southport, CT., and published it with an Introduction in *Science & Society*, 1944, VIII: pp. 40–63.
43 Parsons, *op. cit.*, chs. vi–x; Fulton's letter to Barlow, September 12, 1806, Barlow Papers, Pequot Library; also Charles William Vane, ed., *Correspondence, Despatches, and Other Papers of Viscount Castlereagh* (London, England, 1851), V, *passim*; and Robert Fulton's letters to the Right Honourable Lord Grenville, photostat copies in the New York Public Library.

222

Chapter XII

1. Beverly W. Bond, *The Monroe Mission to France, 1794–1796* (Baltimore, MD., 1907), p. 14.
2. James Monroe, *Writings* (New York, N.Y., 1900), III: p. 415.
3. *Ibid.*, II: pp. 13–15.
4. Bond, *op. cit.*, p. 22.
5. Cited in Leary, *op. cit.*, p. 258.
6. See *e.g.*, [Uriah Tracy], *Scipio's Reflections on Monroe's View of the Conduct of the Executive on the Foreign Affairs of the United States* (Boston, Mass., 1798), p. 45.
7. Monroe, *op. cit.*, II: pp. 302–303. See also *The Aurora*, January 10 and 12, 1796.
8. Allen Johnson, *Union and Democracy* (Boston, 1915), p. 86; *Annual Report of the American Historical Association for the Year 1903* (Washington, D.C., 1904), II: pp. 674–675, 754–756; Henry Adams, *The Life of Albert Gallatin* (Philadelphia, PA., 1879), pp. 164–166.
9. Monroe, *op. cit.*, II: p. 302.
10. Daniel C. Gilman, *James Monroe in his Relations to the Public Service during Half a Century* (Boston, Mass., 1883), p. 70.
11. Address and signatures cited by Monroe in *A View of the Conduct of the Executive, in the Foreign Affairs of the United States, as Connected with the Mission to the French Republic, during the Years 1794–96* (Philadelphia, PA., 1797), pp. 399–401.
12. See previous note.
13. Bond, *op. cit.*, pp. 93–96.
14. For the title of Tracy's pamphlet see note 6.
15. *Observations on the Dispute between the United States and France Addressed to His Constituents in May 1797*. It was popular in England where it had several editions.
16. [Uriah Tracy], *op. cit.*, p. 52.
17. George Gibbs, *Memoirs of the Administrations of Washington and John Adams, Edited from the Papers of Oliver Wolcott, Secretary of the Treasury* (New York, N.Y., 1846), I: p. 533; II: pp. 44, 54.
18. Adams, *Works* (Boston, Mass., 1809), pp. 374–375.
19. *Ibid.*, pp. 241–245.
20. *Ibid.*, pp. 147, 425–426.
21. *The Jersey Chronicle*, April 30, 1796.
22. See *e.g.*, *The Weekly Advertiser of Reading* (Pa.), December 17, 1796.
23. Curti, *op. cit.*, pp. 191–192.
24. Gary B. Nash, "The American Clergy and the French Revolution," *The William and Mary Quarterly*, 1965, 3RD series, XXII: pp. 197–211.
25. The titles of many answers are given in Anson Ely Morse, *The Federalist Party in Massachusetts to the Year 1800*, Appendix I.
26. Reverend Mortimer Blake, *A Centurial History of the Mendon Association of Congregational Ministers* (Boston, Mass., 1853).
27. Adolf G. Koch, *Republican Religion. The American Revolution and the Cult of Reason* (New York, N.Y., 1933), p. 79.
28. *Proofs of a Conspiracy against the Religions and Governments of Europe, Carried on in secret Meetings of Free Masons, Illuminati and Reading Societies*.
29. *Mémoires pour servir à l'histoire du jacobinisme* (London, England, 1797–1798). On Barruel and his *Mémoires*, see Bernard N. Schilling, *Conservative England and the case against Voltaire* (New York, 1950), ch. xiii; also J. M. Roberts, *The Mythology of the Secret Societies* (New York, N.Y., 1972), pp. 188–202.
30. The case against Freemasonry was presented in such works as *Le Voile levé pour les curieux* (1791), *Conjuration contre la religion catholique et les souverains* (1792), *and Les causes de la Révolution de France* (1795).
31. *The Analytical Review, or History of Literature, Domestic and Foreign*, October 1797, XXVI: p. 402.
32. Significantly, the *Massachusetts Mercury* and the *Connecticut Courant*, two leading Federalist papers, serialized an abridged version of Barruel's work. Among the toasts given on Independence Day at Newgloucester, Maine, the one to Jefferson faithfully expressed Federalist sentiment: "May he, like Saul, be struck with lightning from Heaven, and the sedition scales fall from his eyes, and he be converted from Gallic malevolence." *Jenks's Portland Gazette*, July 15, 1799.
33. For an account of the effect of Robison's work in New England see Vernon Stauffer, *New England and the Bavarian Illuminati* (New York, 1918), ch. iv. See also John C. Miller, *Crisis in Freedom: The Alien and Sedition Acts* (Boston, Mass., 1951), pp. 132–133.
34. See letter from a Mason to the Rev. Morse, *The Gazette* (Portland, Maine), January 14, 1799.
35. The best refutation of Barruel was by J. J. Mounier, *De l'influence attribuée aux philosophes, aux Francs-Maçons et aux Illuminés sur la Révolution Française* (Tübingen, 1801).
36. William A. Robinson, *Jeffersonian Democracy in New England* (New Haven, CT., 1916), p. 130.
37. *The Independent Chronicle*, April 11, 1799.
38. Gibbs, *op. cit.*, I: pp. 484–485, 489–490.
39. See Arthur Burr Darling, *Our Rising Empire* (New Haven, CT., 1940), pp. 250–261, 295–298.
40. Johnson, *op. cit.*, pp. 100–101, 102.
41. *Correspondence between the Honorable John Adams and the Late William Cunningham* (Boston, Mass., 1823), p. 107.
42. John C. Miller, *Crisis in Freedom*, p. 150. The Laws were reprinted in James Morton Smith, *Freedom's Fetters. The Alien and Sedition Laws and American Civil Liberties* (Ithaca, N.Y., 1956), Appendix.
43. James T. Austin, *The Life of Elbridge Gerry* (Boston, Mass., 1829), II: pp. 274–275.
44. Gilbert Chinard, *op. cit.*, pp. 65–66.
45. Gilbert Chinard, ed., *Considérations sur la conduité du gouvernement américain envers la France, depuis le commencement de la Révolution jusqu'en 1797 par Louis Guillaume Otto* (Princeton, N.J., 1945).
46. Samuel E. Morison included Du Pont's report as well as other documents in his communication, "Du Pont, Talleyrand and the French Spoliations," to the Massachusetts Historical Society, *Proceedings*, 1915–1916, XLIX: pp. 63–79.
47. Gibbs, *op. cit.*, II, p. 140.
48. *Ibid.*, pp. 145–147.

Chapter XIII

1. See *e.g.*, [John Lowell], *The Antigallican* (Philadelphia, PA., 1797), Nos. i–iv, *passim*.
2. James Thomson Callender, *Sketches of the History of America* (Philadelphia, 1798), pp. 163–164.
3. John C. Miller, *Crisis in Freedom: The Alien and Sedition Acts* (Boston, Mass., 1951), pp. 185–186. See also Smith, *op. cit.*, pp. 187, 189–222 and chs. xiii–xv.
4. The most detailed biography of Lyon is by J. Fairfax McLaughlin, *Matthew Lyon, the Hampden of Congress* (New York, N.Y., 1900).

5 Miller, *op. cit.*, pp. 193, 221–222. See also Smith, *op. cit.*, ch. xi.
6 See his *An Address on the Natural and Social Order of the World, as Intended to Produce Universal Good, Delivered before Tammany Society at their Anniversary on the 12th of May 1798* (Philadelphia, 1798). The best account of Logan's ideas and activities is by Frederic B. Tolles, *George Logan of Philadelphia* (New York, N.Y., 1953).
7 Tolles, *op. cit.*, p. 167. On Logan's mission, see by the same author "Unofficial Ambassador: George Logan's Mission to France, 1798," *The William and Mary Quarterly*, 1950, 3rd series, VII: pp. 3–25.
8 *Correspondence between the Honorable John Adams and the Late William Cunningham*, p. 105.
9 George Gibbs, *Memoirs of the Administrations of Washington and John Adams, Edited from the Papers of Oliver Wolcott, Secretary of the Treasury* (New York, N.Y., 1846), II: p. 193. For Logan's answer to his maligners see *The Aurora and General Advertiser*, January 3, 1799.
10 *Ibid.*, p. 192. Cutting had had some diplomatic experience as secretary to Colonel Humphreys in the mission to North Africa, 1793–1794. See his travel diaries in *The Historical Magazine, and Notes and Queries Concerning the Antiquities, History and Biography of America*, 1860, IV: pp. 262–265, 359–362.
11 Samuel Eliot Morison, *The Life and Letters of Harrison Gray Otis, Federalist, 1765–1848* (Boston, Mass., 1913), I: pp. 168–170. On the memorial to Talleyrand, attributed to Codman, see Tolles, "Unofficial Ambassador"etc., *op. cit.*, VII: pp. 13–14.
12 Skipwith's letter of March 17, 1798, appears in Gibbs, *op. cit.*, II: pp. 158–161.
13 The memorial appeared in Joel Barlow, *To His Fellow Citizens of the United States* (Paris, France, 1799), pp. 50–55.
14 Gibbs, *op. cit.*, II: p. 160.
15 Barlow Papers, Harvard, Box 2.
16 The correct text of the letter was published by John Dos Passos, *The Ground We Stand On* (New York, N.Y., 1941), pp. 346–358.
17 A copy of the pamphlet is in the Massachusetts Historical Society. It was reprinted by Federalist papers. A comparison of the correct text with the edited version shows only slight differences.
18 Charles R. King, ed., *The Life and Correspondence of Rufus King* (New York, N.Y., 1895), II: p. 467.
19 Reprinted in the Portland *Gazette*, December 3 and 10, 1798; *The Eastern Herald*, December 3 and 10, 1798; and *The Spectator*, November 14, 1798.
20 November 10, 1798.
21 Published in *The Spectator*, November 17, 1798. It was reprinted by other Federalist sheets.
22 Barlow Papers, Harvard, letter of July 26, 1798.
23 Gibbs, *op. cit.*, II: pp. 111–115; see also Ralph W. Hidy, *The House of Baring in American Trade and Finance* (Cambridge, Mass., 1949), p. 32.
24 Barlow Papers, Harvard, Box 2.
25 The letter to Washington was reprinted several times. We have relied on the text in Barlow's *Two Letters to the Citizens of the United States* (New Haven, CT., 1806), pp. 33–43.
26 Adams, *Works*, VIII: pp. 624–626.
27 *Correspondence between the Honorable John Adams and the Late William Cunningham*, pp. 105–106; Gibbs, *op. cit.*, II, pp. 161–162.
28 *Works*, IX: p. 243.
29 Gibbs, *op. cit.*, II: pp. 109–110.

30 Cited from "The Centinel of Freedom" by James Thomson Callender, *op. cit.*, p. 69.
31 The *Letters* had many editions abroad and in the United States. Four editions appeared in Paris under different headings; two, in London; and at least four in the U.S. Here we have followed the New Haven edition of 1806.
32 Pickering Papers, letters from correspondents, July–December 1799, Massachusetts Historical Society.
33 The draft, bearing the title, "Memoir on Certain Principles on Public Maritime Law," was published as an Appendix in Joel Barlow, *To His Fellow Citizens of the United States* (Philadelphia, PA., 1801).
34 "On the Commerce of the United States," *Le publiciste*, 25 Nivôse, an 8 (January 14, 1801), of which there is a rough draft in French in the Pequot Library. See also Barlow Papers, Harvard, Box 4.
35 Barlow Papers, Harvard, Box 2.

Chapter XIV

1 See Charles O. Lorche, "Jefferson and the Election of 1800: A Case Study in the Political Smear," *The William and Mary Quarterly*, 3rd series, 1948, V: pp. 468–488.
2 Barlow Papers, Harvard, Box 2, letter to Abraham Baldwin, October 3, 1798.
3 *Ibid.*, Box 2.
4 *Ibid.*, letter of July 19, 1802.
5 *Ibid.*, letter of October 1, 1800.
6 *Ibid.*, letter to Ruth, August 14, 1802.
7 *Ibid.*, letter to Ruth, May, 24, 1802.
8 *Ibid.*, letter of July 28, 1803.
9 Henry Redhead Yorke, *Letters from France in 1802* (London, England, 1804), II: pp. 370–375.
10 Cited in Gilbert Chinard, *Volney et l'Amérique*, p. 128.
11 The first was published in London in 1792; the second, in Philadelphia in 1799.
12 See his *Observations on the Increase of Infidelity* (London, England, 1796), pp. 62–65; also *A History of the Corruptions of Christianity* (London, England, 1871), pp. 304–306.
13 *Observations on the Increase of Infidelity*, pp. 65–66.
14 *Oeuvres choisies* (Paris, France, 1833), pp. 565–579.
15 Barlow Papers, Harvard, Box 2, Jefferson to Barlow, May 3, 1802.
16 New York Historical Society, Misc. MSS., Jefferson to Barlow. A copy is in the Barlow Papers, Harvard, Box 2.
17 MS. letter, Barlow to Skipwith, July 4, 1800, New York Historical Society.
18 Barlow Papers, Harvard, Box 2, Barlow to Abraham Baldwin, January 3, 1801.
19 A fair statement of Jefferson's principles can be read in his letter to Elbridge Gerry, January 26, 1799, *Writings* (Washington, D.C., 1907), X: pp. 76–79.
20 Barlow Papers, Harvard, Box 2, letter of May 15, 1802.
21 *Ibid.*, letter of May 19, 1802.
22 January 19, 1799.
23 Barlow Papers, Harvard, letter dated October 6, 1800.
24 *Ibid.*, letter to Ruth, July 19, 1802.
25 Aldridge, *op. cit.*, p. 267.
26 Barlow Papers, Harvard, Box 4, letter of May 1, 1802.
27 Jefferson, *Writings*, III: p. 457.
28 Some idea of the large sums Barlow disbursed for the experiments, begun in Paris, was indicated in letters to Ruth and in a notebook in the Barlow Papers, Harvard, Boxes 2 and 4.

29 Ibid., Box 2, letter of August 12, 1802.
30 Yorke op. cit., II: pp. 337–343.
31 Barlow Papers, Harvard, Box 4.
32 Ibid., Box 2.
33 Ibid., letters of June 30, July 5 and 11, 1802.
34 See Barlow's letter to Bishop, May 16, 1808, Yale University Library.
35 Barlow Papers, Pequot Library, letter to William Lee, March 20, 1805.

Chapter XV

1 Chester Whitney Wright, *Economic History of the United States* (New York, N.Y., 1949), p. 223–224.
2 James Clarke Welling, *Addresses, Lectures and Other Papers* (Cambridge, Mass., 1904), pp. 272–309.
3 For documents relating to the secession movement, see Henry Adams, ed., *Documents Relating to New England Federalism, 1800–1815* (Boston, Mass., 1877), passim.
4 Morison, op. cit., I: pp. 261–263.
5 Barlow Papers, Pequot Library.
6 MS. letter, October 3, 1805, Boston Public Library.
7 An account of the meeting was published in the *American Mercury*, November 7, 1805. See also Barlow Papers, Harvard, Box 2.
8 The memorandum is among Barlow's manuscripts in The Historical Society of Pennsylvania.
9 MS. letter, Barlow to Logan, September 25, 1805, The Histtorical Society of Pennsylvania.
10 See Maclure's *Opinions on Various Subjects, Dedicated to the Industrious Producers* (New Harmony, Ind., 1831–1837), II: pp. 273–274, 548.
11 Barlow Papers, Harvard, Box 4, Barlow to Maclure, September 25, 1801.
12 Barlow Papers, Pequot Library, Maclure to Barlow, May 16, 1806. For Maclure's educational ideas, see Arthur Eugene Bestor, *Backwoods Utopias* (Philadelphia, 1950), pp. 146–148, 150–153. 182–183, 191–192, 199–200.
13 Barlow's MS. letter to John Vaughan, July 21, 1806, The Historical Society of Pennsylvania.
14 Barlow's MS. letter, February 10, 1806, Indiana University.
15 Cited by G. Brown Goode, *The Origin of the National Scientific and Educational Institutions of the United States* (New York, N.Y., 1890), pp. 27–28.
16 Bernstein, op. cit., p. 103.
17 *Prospectus of a National Institution* (Washington City, 1806), p. 7.
18 Ibid., pp. 12, 17, 26.
19 Ibid., p. 13.
20 Goode, op. cit., p. 28.
21 *The Columbiad: or a Poem on the American War in Thirteen Cantos* (Philadelphia, 1795). Snowden was also the author of *The American Revolution; Written in the Style of Ancient History* (Philadelphia, PA., 1793).
22 Leary, op. cit., pp. 215, 397. The poem was published serially in several New York newspapers, for example, the New York *Journal*, the *Argus*, the New York *Gazette* and the *Time-Piece*.
23 Preface to the *Columbiad*.
24 Maria dell'Isola, "Joel Barlow, précurseur de la société des nations," *Revue de littérature comparée*, 1934, XIV: pp. 283–296.
25 The *Columbiad* (Philadelphia, PA., 1807), notes, pp. 443–444.
26 Moses Coit Tyler, *Three Men of Letters* (New York, N.Y., 1895), p. 168.
27 1809, XV: pp. 24–40.
28 Barlow Papers, Harvard, Box 2.
29 Ibid.
30 1809, VII: p. 114.
31 Both the critic's letter and the answer were published in the Raleigh (N.C.) *Register*. A clipping is in the Barlow Papers, Harvard, Box 3.
32 The full letter to Cheetham is in Charles Burr Todd, *Life and Letters of Joel Barlow* (New York, N.Y., 1866), pp. 236–239.
33 An English translation was published under the title, *Critical Observations on the Poem of Mr. Joel Barlow, the Columbiad* (Washington City, 1809).
34 Jefferson called it "a sugary answer" and liked it for that reason. *Writings*, XII: p. 321.
35 MS. letter, October 1, 1809, New York Historical Society.
36 Barlow Papers, Harvard, Box 4.
37 1809, VII: pp. 289–290.
38 L. H. Butterfield, ed., *Letters of Benjamin Rush* (Princeton, N.J., 1951), II: p. 1019.
39 These letters are in the Barlow Papers, Pequot Library.
40 Barlow Papers, Harvard, Box 2.
41 MS. letter to Bishop, May 16, 1808, Yale Univ. Library.
42 MS. letter to Gideon Granger, May 3, 1809, Pequot Library.
43 The poem was printed by Ernest A. and George L. Duyckinck, *Cyclopedia of American Literature* (New York, N.Y., 1855), I: 394. The original manuscript, corrected by Barlow, except for the final stanza, is in Barlow MSS., Henley-Smith Papers, Library of Congress.
44 The parody was included by Duyckinck, op. cit., I: p. 395.
45 *Oration Delivered in Washington, July Fourth 1809*. (Washington City, 1809).
46 *Writings*, XII: p. 321.

Chapter XVI

1 Cited by Carra Bacon-Foster, "The Story of Kalorama," *Records of the Columbia History Society*, (Washington, D.C.), XIII: pp. 98–99.
2 Cited in Charles Burr Todd, *Life and Letters of Joel Barlow* (New York, N.Y., 1866), p. 216.
3 Bacon-Foster, op. cit., p. 104.
4 Ibid., p. 105.
5 James Madison, *Letters and Other Writings* (Philadelphia, PA., 1867), II: pp. 428–429.
6 Barlow's reply to Smith's pamphlet was published anonymously under the title, *A Review of Robert Smith's Address to the People of the United States* (Philadelphia, PA., 1811).
7 John Marshall, *The Life of George Washington* (Fredericksburg, VA., 1926), V: pp. 138–139, 195.
8 For a summation of Jefferson's opinion of Marshall's work, see Albert J. Beveridge, *The Life of John Marshall* (Boston-New York, 1919), III: pp. 265–269; see also Lester J. Cappon, ed., *The Adams-Jefferson Letters* (Chapel Hill, N.C., 1959), pp. 452–453.
9 H. A. Washington, ed., *Jefferson's Writings* (New York, N.Y., 1861), IV: pp. 438–439.
10 Barlow Papers, Harvard, Box 2.
11 Barlow Papers, Pequot Library, letter to Barlow, New York, N.Y., April 10, 1806.

225

12 *Bulletin of the Bureau of Rolls and Library of the Department of State* (Washington, D.C., 1895), November 1894, VIII: p. 40.
13 Several are in the Barlow Papers, Pequot Library.
14 *Writings*, XII: p. 351.
15 Cited in Beveridge, *op. cit.*, III: p. 266.
16 *Bulletin of the Bureau of Rolls and Library of the Department of State*, VIII: p. 40.
17 Barlow Papers, Harvard, Box 2.
18 Barlow Papers, The Henry Huntington Library, Fulton to Barlow, March 1, 1809.
19 See Barlow Papers, Harvard, Box 2.
20 *The National Intelligencer*, March 11, 1807.
21 *Revue de littérature comparée*, 1922, II: 630. Jefferson's letter, dated May 28, 1813, was a reply to Mme. de Staël's of November 10, 1812, in which she argued that a war between the United States and England would be but an advantage to the military conqueror of the Continent, that if he succeeded in subduing England, America would be at his mercy. Mme. de Staël's letter is on pp. 626–628.
22 For the orders and decrees we have relied on A. C. Clauder, *American Commerce as Affected by the Wars of the French Revolution and Napoleon, 1793–1812* (Philadelphia, PA., 1932), *passim*.
23 *History of the United States of America during the Administrations of Thomas Jefferson and James Madison* (New York, N.Y., 1890), IV: p. 169.
24 *Ibid.*, p. 274.
25 *State Papers and Public Documents of the United States from the Accession of George Washington to the Presidency* (Boston, Mass., 1819), IX, p. 253; Clauder, *op. cit.*, pp. 213–216.
26 Irving Brant, *James Madison, Commander in Chief* (New York, N.Y., 1961), p. 16.
27 A good account may be read in the Pickering Papers, Massachusetts Historical Society., XIV: 328; see also Irving Brant, *James Madison, the President, 1809–1812* (New York, N.Y., 1956), pp. 278–281.
28 Barlow Papers, Pequot Library.
29 *American State Papers* (Washington, D.C., 1832), III: 509–512; Brant, *Madison the President*, p. 338.
30 Adams, *op. cit.*, VI: p. 58.
31 MS. letter, Miscellaneous MSS. B., New York Historical Society.
32 Barlow Papers, Harvard, Box 2, folder 17, and Box 4, folder 39.
33 *American State Papers*, III: 513–516.
34 It had been advanced by Richard Hildreth in his *History of the United States of America* (New York, N.Y., 1863), VI: pp. 378–379, and by Henry Adams in *op. cit.*, VI: pp. 255–259.
35 Irving Brant, "Joel Barlow, Madison's Stubborn Minister," *The William and Mary Quarterly*, 3rd series, 1958, XV: pp. 438–451.
36 *Ibid.*, p. 441.
37 *Ibid.*, p. 443.
38 Madison, *op. cit.*, pp. 527–528.
39 Brant, *James Madison, Commander in Chief*, p. 64.
40 *Ibid.*, p. 65.
41 *American State Papers*, III: pp. 603–604.

Chapter XVII

1 Letter to Ruth, No. 15, Vilna, Nov. 18, 1812, Henley-Smith Papers, Library of Congress.
2 Letter No. 7, Berlin, Nov., 5, 1812, *ibid*.
3 Letter No. 11, Königsberg, Nov. 11, 1812, *ibid*.
4 Letter No. 15, Vilna, Nov. 18, 1812, *ibid*.
5 Barlow Papers, Box 3, folder 31, Harvard.
6 *Ibid.*, Box 3, folder 32.
7 *Ibid.*, Box 3.
8 Eugene Tarlé, *Napoleon's Invasion of Russia 1812* (New York, N.Y., 1942), pp. 391–393.
9 Letter No. 26, Warsaw, December 13, 1812, Henley-Smith Papers, Library of Congress.
10 Letter No. 27, Warsaw, December 13, 1812, *ibid*.
11 Letter No. 28, Warsaw, December 16, 1812, *ibid*.
12 Same date, continued, *ibid*.
13 Tarlé, *op. cit.*, p. 390.
14 Letter No. 26, Warsaw, December 13, 1812, Henley-Smith Papers, Library of Congress.
15 Barlow Papers, Box 3, folder 33, Harvard.
16 *The Alexandria Gazette,* March 8, 1813, cited by Brant in "Joel Barlow, Madison's Stubborn Minister," 1958, 3rd series, XV: p. 438.
17 *The Proceedings of The American Antiquarian Society*, 1930, new series, XL: p. 360.
18 Cited in Dos Passos, *op. cit.*, p. 380.
19 *Notice sur la vie de M. Barlow* ([Paris], 1813), extrait des Registres de la Société d'encouragement.
20 *Notice sur la vie et les écrits de M. Joel Barlow, ministre plénipotentiaire des Etats-Unis d'Amérique auprès de S.M. l'Empéreur des Français* (Paris, France, 1813). On Oelsner see Jacques Droz, *L'Allemagne et la révolution française* (Paris, France, 1949), pp. 63–78, and the communication by Marcelle Adler-Bresse in *Annales historiques de la révolution française*, 1966, No. 4: pp. 556–560.
21 Barlow Papers, Box 3, folder, 33, Harvard.
22 The original, in Barlow's hand, dated from Vilna, December 1812, is in the Henley-Smith Papers. An incomplete copy in The Huntington Library is dated from Zarnowiec, December 1812. The poem was published for the first time in the *Erie Chronicle*, October 10, 1843. Another printing was in Evert A. and George L. Duyckinck, *op. cit.*, I: 397–398. Leon Howard published it in full, with corrections, from the MS in the Henley-Smith Papers, in *The Huntington Library Quarterly*, 1938–1939, II: pp. 49–50.
23 The last two lines are missing in the copy in The Huntington Library.

Index

A

Adams, Henry, 99
Adams, John, 64, 152-155, 158-159, 161-162, 166, 168, 190-191, 195
Adams, Samuel, 4
"Advice to a Raven in Russia," 2, 210
"Advice to the Privileged Orders," 58, 62, 65, 67, 78-79, 91, 114, 162
Aeneid, 174, 186
Age of Reason, 100, 123, 150
Albany Convention, 1754, 8
Algiers, 121, 125-128, 131, 158
Alicante, Spain, 125
Alien and Sedition Acts, 154, 156, 161, 171
Alien Bill, 87
Allen, General Ira, 175
Alsop, Richard, 113
Altona, Denmark, 100; Jacobin Club, 101
American Antiquarian Society, The, 2
American Constitutional Convention, The, 1787, 33
American Embargo Act, The, 198-199. See also Bayonne, Milan and Rambouillet Decrees, 198
American Mercury, The, 29
"American Patriot's Prayer, The," 5
American Philosophical Society, The, 3, 190
American Revolution, 1, 59, 103, 115-116, 118, 122, 156, 172, 174, 180, 182, 186, 195
Ames, Fisher, 149, 194
Analytical Review, The, 151
Anarch, 41
Anarchiad: a Poem on the Restoration of Chaos and Substantial Night, The, 40-42
Ancien Régime, 135
André, Major, 26
Anglicans, 11
Anti-Jacobin: or Weekly Examiner, The, 104
Antiquity Unveiled, 135
Appleton, Thomas, 57
"Archimedes" (of America), 140
Arnold, Benedict, 26
Articles of Confederation, 19, 29
Assembly, National (France), 58, 60
Assembly of Notables (France, 1787), 33, 119
"Association for Preserving Liberty and Property Against Republicans and Levellers," 74
Association of Ministers of New Haven, Connecticut, 24
Atheism, 114
Atlas, 187
Aurora, The, 173
Austerlitz (Battle of), 181

B

Babcock, Elisha, 29
Babeuf, 117
Babouvists, 10
Babylon (Seige of), 22
Baccri, Micaiah Cohen, 127, 130
Backman, Elias, 99
Bacon, Francis, 37, 134-135, 138

Baldwin, Aaron, 169
Baldwin, Abraham, 19, 23, 52, 57-59, 150, 158-159, 161-162, 166, 172, 174, 176, 193, 197, 200
Baldwin, Clara, 197, 201, 206, 209
Baldwin, Dudley, 47
Baldwin, Henry, 201
Baldwin, Ruth (see Barlow, Ruth)
"Ban of Commerce," 166
Baptists, 11
Barbary Powers (States), 121, 132-133
Barbauld, Anna, 35
Baring Bros., 125
Barlow, Joel, 1, 19, 34, 36, 38-40, 51-52, 55-60, 63, 65, 75, 77-78, 86, 89, 94-96, 98-100, 107-108, 113-119, 121, 123-139, 141-143, 145, 155, 158-166, 168-198, 200-210; Translation of Brissot's *New Travels in the United States of America*, from French, 80
Barlow, Ruth Baldwin, 23-24, 52, 56, 76, 81, 86-89, 100-101, 121, 126-127, 129, 132, 139, 169-170, 172-173, 175, 177-178, 196-198, 201 205-210
Barlow, Thomas, 201, 204-205, 209
Barras, 153
Barruel, Abbé Augustin, 110, 150-151
Bassano, the Duke of, 202, 206-207
Bartram, John, 3
Bastille, 51
Bastille Day, 60, 101, 111, 120
Bayle, Pierre, 134; *Dictionnaire historique et critique*, 135-137; *Oeuvres diverses*, 138-139
Beaupolis, General, 94-95
Beccaria, 5, 31, 83
Bayonne Decree, 198. See also American Embargo Acts
Belknap, Reverend Jeremy, 101
Bentham, Jeremy, 115
Bentley, Thomas, 142, 151
Berkeley, George, 184
Berlin Decree, 199, 201, 203
Berthier, The Marshall Louis Alexandre, 207
Bey of Tripoli, 131-132, 153
Bey of Tunis, 132, 152
Bill if Rights, 179
Blackden, Colonel, 57, 94, 99, 101
Blackstone, William, 6, 31, 184
Blake, William, 5, 77-78
Blue Laws, 11
Boissel, François, 70
Bolingbroke, 6
Bonald, Viscount Louis de, 61, 151
Boston Federalists, 199
Bossuet, 6
"Boston Patriotic Song, The," 5
Boston Tea Party, The, 80
Botanical Gardens, 89
Botta, Carlo, 34
Bowles, John, 105
Brant, Irving, 201
Brazen Trumpet, The, 106-107

227

Bretonne, Rétif de la, 69
Brindley, James, 142
Brissot, J. P. de Warville, 13, 47, 53, 83, 93, 95, 102, 169
British East India Company, 97
British Orders in Council, 198, 200, 203
British Reform Societies, 1
Bromfield, Henry, 56
Buckminster, Reverend Joseph, 18
Buffon, 8, 41, 50
Bunker Hill (Battle of), 51
Burdett, Sir Francis, 174, 177
Bureau des Longitudes, 89
Burgoyne, 20, 186
Burigny, Jean Levesque, 135
Burk, John Daly; *Vision of Columbus*, 185
Burke, Edmund; "Reflections on the Revolution in France," 1, 60, 63-64, 68, 78, 104-105, 120, 149, 164, 171, 176
Burlamaqui, Jean Jacques, 6
Burns, Robert, 75, 78
Burr, Aaron, 39, 180
Bushnell, Davis, 142
Butler, Samuel, 35

C

Cabot, George, 149, 162
Cahiers, 120
Calonne, Charles Alexandre de, 60
Calvin, John, 173
Calvinism, 5
Camoëns, 34
Campo Formio, Treaty of, 119
"Canal: a Poem of the Application of Physical Science To Political Economy, The," 141-142, 197
Canning, George, 61
Capac, Manco, 36
Carthage, 103
Catéchisme du genre humain, 70
Catchart, James Leander, 122, 126, 128, 133
Catherine II of Russia, 63
Chain of Being (Creator's), 63
Chais's (sic) Rebellion (Shays' Rebellion), 196
Channing, William Ellery, 150
Charleston, The Burning of, 27
Charleston, South Carolina Library Society, 3
Cheetham, James, 188
Chenevert, Edward V., 2
Chinard, Gilbert, 137
Christ, 189
Christianity Unmasked by Baron d'Holbach, 135
Chrisite, Thomas, 65
Churchill, Winston, 5
Cincinnati, The Connecticut Society of the, 42
Clark, General George Rogers, 94
Clarke, James Stanier, 77-78
Clavière, Etienne, 47
Clay, Henry, 200
Clermont, The, 197
Cloots, Anarchasis, 75, 82
Cobbett, William (also known as Peter Porcupine), 115
Code de la nature (Morelly), 69
Copley, John, 65
Codman, Richard, 157
Colden, Cadwallader, 3
Columbiad, The, 170, 185-190, 200
Columbian Centinel (Boston), 64
Columbian Institute for the Promotion of Arts and Sciences, 185

Columbus, 186
Commercial Advertiser, The (New York), 160
Commission of Commerce and Provisions (U.S.), 99
Committees of Correspondence, 17
Committee of Public Saftey, 96, 98
Common Council (Hartford, Connecticut), 31
Condorcet, 8, 50, 101, 105, 117, 169; *Esquisse d'un tableau historique des progrès de l'esprit humain*, 82
Confederacy, The, 180
Congregational Church, 15
Congregationalism, 11
Congressional Journal, 29
Connecticut Courant, 113, 152, 160
Connecticut Magazine, 40
Connecticut Wits, The, 40
Consent, Doctrine of, 108
Conservatoire des Arts-et-Metiers, 89
Conspiracy of Kings, The, 77, 79, 87
Constitutional Convention (France), 6, 87, 120, 196
Consulate (French), 169
Continental Congress (First American), 6, 17, 117
Cook, Captain (Voyages of), 29
Copernicus, 103
Cordelier Club, 59
Cornwallis, 28, 186
Cortez, 36
Court Party, The (France), 79
Cowper, William; *A Pilgrim's Progress*, 15; Translation of the *Odyssey*, 33
Craigie, Andrew, 46
Crassus, 22
Cromwell, Oliver, 156
Crown Point, 18
Crusoe, Robinson, 63
Cunningham, Timothy, 68
Cutler, Reverend Manasseh, 44, 46
Cutting, Nathaniel, 157
Cyrus, 22

D

Dalberg, Baron van, 203, 207
D'Aalembert, 6, 105, 135, 151
Daily Advertiser, 64
Dalton, John, 141
Daniel (Bible), 22
Dantonists, 100-101
Daumier, Honoré, 208
Dawson, John, 174
Day, Thomas, 40
Dean, 113
Dearborn, Henry, 202
Declaration of Independence, 4, 17
Decline and Fall of The Roman Empire, 53, 66
Defoe, Daniel, 5
Deism, 38, 39, 114
Deistical Society of the State of New York, 150
Democratic Republicanism, 10
De Paw, Cornelius, 8, 41
Descartes, 103, 139
Dey of Algiers, 122, 125-128, 130-133, 153
Dictionnaire historique et critique, 137
Dickinson, John, 4
Diderot, Dennis, 6, 34, 134, 151, 175
Dido, 34
Diggers, 10
Directory, The Executive (France), 143, 148, 152-156, 158-159, 161-162

Divan, The, 125
Donaldson, Joseph, 123-128, 133
Dryden, 14; Translation of the *Aeneid*, 33
Duer, Colonel William, 45-46, 52, 54-55
Du Marsais, César-Chesneau, 67, 135
Dunciad, 42
Du Pont de Nemours, Pierre Samuel, 210
Du Pont, Victor Marie de Nemours, 154, 155
Dupuis, Charles François, 136-137
Dwight, Theodore, 113
Dwight, Timothy, 19, 30, 34, 47, 151, 173, 181
Dwight, Mrs. Timothy, 56

E

Ebeling, Christoph Daniel, 101-102, 151
Edinburgh Review, 188
Edwards, Jonathan, 5; *The Freedom of the Will*, 16
"Elegy on the Late Honorable Titus Hosmer, An," 27
"Elegy Written in a Country Churchyard," 28
Eliot, Reverend John, 101
Ellsworth, Oliver, 18
Emigrants, The, 94
Emile, 6
Encyclopédie, 134-136
Encyclopédie méthodique, 134
Encyclopedists, 151
Enlightenment (French), 4, 60, 134
Entails, 10
Epic Poetry (Portugal, Spain), 33-34
Erskine, John, 193
Essay Concerning Human Understanding, 16
Essay on Prejudices, 67
Estates General in 1789 (France), 33, 51, 117, 120
Ethic, The Protestant, 53
Ethics, (Spinoza), 136
Evidence of Divine Revelation with Some Strictures upon Deistical Writings, 150

F

Falmouth, 18
Farrington, 42
Fayettists, 79
Federal Bank, 113
Federalsists, 107, 113, 115, 148-151, 153-154, 156, 160-164, 166, 168, 172-173, 180-181, 194-195
Feuillant Club, 59
First Congregational Church–Portsmouth, New Hampshire, 19
First Republic, The (France), 82
Fitzgerald, Lord Edward, 74
Flanders Ghent, Bruges, Brussels, Ostend, 49
Flint, Royal, 46
Fontenelle, 6
Food Commisssion (*Commission des subsistences*), 98
Fourier, Charles, 25
Fourth Massachusetts Brigade, 24
Fox, Charles James, 49, 87
Francis II of Austria, 79
Franco-American Alliance, 150
Franklin, Benjamin, 3, 39, 113
Freemasons, 151
French Convention, 1, 12, 67, 83, 146, 180, 184
French and Indian War, 9
French Revolution, 78, 86, 90-91, 94, 97, 107, 111-121, 141, 149-150, 156, 159, 174, 182, 185, 189, 195
Freneau, Philip, 5, 34, 75, 78, 140, 146, 149, 185
Fréret, Nicholas, 135
Fréron; *L'Oratuer du peuple*, 117

Frost, John, 13, 86
Fulton, Robert "Toot," 140-145, 168-170, 173-174, 177, 185, 189, 192, 196-197, 202, 209

G

Gage, General, 17
Galileo, 103
Gallatin, Albert, 193
Galloway, Joseph, 17
General Association of the State of Connecticut, 30
Génet, Edmund , 92, 94-95, 113, 116, 150
Gentz, Friedrich von, 61
Georgics, 174
Gerry, Elbridge, 153-156, 158, 161
Gibbon, Edward, 34, 53, 61, 66, 118, 137, 171, 184
Girondins, 79, 85, 88-90, 93-96, 110-111
Godwin, William, 62, 69, 111
Goldsmith, Oliver, 14
Goodrich, Chauncey, 31
Gospel, 190
Gravis, Samuel, 129-130
Gray, 14
Greene, General, 24, 26
Greenfield (Connecticut), 57
Grégoire, Abbé Henri, 12, 75, 88, 124, 189, 190
Grenville, 106
Grotius, 6

H

Hamburg; First Masonic Lodge, 100, 116
Hamilton, Alexander, 5, 39, 148-149, 152-154, 163, 168, 180, 194
Hampden, 12
Hardy, Thomas (Shoemaker), 65, 87
Harlem Heights, 18
Harper, Robert Goodloe, 149
Harrington, James, 5
"Hartford Wits, The," 40
Harvard, 3
"The Hasty Pudding," 91
Hayley, William, 65, 76-77, 84
Hays, Mary, 62, 65
Hébertists, 100
Helen, 34
Helvetius, 6, 134, 138, 175
Henry IV, 165
Herodotus, 103
Hesper, 41, 186-187
Hichborn, Benjamin, 98-99, 102, 123
History of the French Revolution, 108
History of Jacobinism, The, 111
Hobbes, Thomas, 5
"Hog's Wash or a Salmagundy for Swine," 74
Holbach Baron, 6, 67, 134-135
Holcroft, Thomas, 64, 73
Homer, 34, 188
Hooker, 6
Hopkins, Dr. Lemuel, 29, 40, 163
Hosmer, Judge Titus, 23, 27
Houghton Library–Harvard University, 2
House of Solomon, 184
Hubbard, William, 33
Hume, David, 184
Humphreys, David, 24, 29, 34, 40, 113, 121-126, 128, 130-132
"Husks for Swine," 74
Huygens, 135

I

Iliad, 186
Illuminati, 151
Imlay, Gilbert, 94, 96, 99, 101
Independent Chronicle, 115-116, 152
Inquisition, Spanish, 66
Institute of France, 182

J

Jacob, Judge Stephen, 180, 189
Jacobin, 104, 113-115, 149
Jacobin Club, 59, 112
Jacobinism, 107, 111, 150, 160
Jacobins, 156
Jacquerie, 81
Jansenists, 135
Jarvis, Benjamin, 98
Jarvis, James, 46
Jay, 45
Jay, John 146-148
Jay Treaty, 102, 108, 113, 123, 132, 152-153, 158-159, 165, 194
Jefferson, Thomas, 1, 39, 48, 50-51, 57, 82, 93, 103, 108, 121, 146-147, 151, 156-159, 168-169, 171-174, 176, 180-181, 183, 191-192, 194-196, 198-199, 2:-196, 198-199, 202
Jenyns, Soam, 70
Jesuits, 135
Jews, (Defense of), 89
Johnson, Joseph, 65, 177
Johnson, Dr. Samuel, 34
Jones, Howard Mumford, 5, 39
Jones, John Paul, 57
Jordan, J. S., 65
Josephine, 174
Josephus, 15
Journal des hommes libres, 117
Juvenal, 5

K

"Kalorama," 192-193, 197, 209
Kant, Immanuel; *Perpetual Peace*, 76
Karamzin, Nickolai, 61
Kemble, John Philip, 174
Klopstock, Friedrich, 102
Knox, General, 39, 99
Knox, John, 173
Kosciusko, Thaddeus, 170, 173

L

La Bruyère, 75
Lafayette, Marquis de, 14, 39, 51, 57, 80, 208
La Mettrie, Julien Offray de, 135
La Rochefoucauld, 50
Lathrop, Joseph Reverend (of Massachusetts), 150
Latrobe, Benjamin, 192
Lavoisier, 50
League of Nations, 187
Leavenworth, Mark, 96, 98-99, 101-102
Lefébvre, Georges, 98
Legion of Honor, 169
Leonard, Daniel, 17
Leopold of Austria, 79
Lequinio, Joseph Marie, 142
Les crimes de Joseph Le Bon, 117
Letter Addressed To The People of Piedmont, on the Advantages of the French Revolution, and the Necessity of Adopting its Principles in Italy, 89
Letter to Henry Grégoire in Reply to His Letter on the Columbiad, 189

Letter To the National Convention of France, A, 77, 82
Letter of a Genevan, 183
Letters from France, 110
Letters from Paris, 191
Lewis, Captain, 191
Lexington (Battle of), 51
"The Liberty Tree," 5
Life of Washington, 194-195
Lincoln, General, 26, 39
L'Institut de France, 89
Livingston, Harriet, 197
Livingston, Robert R. (First Governor of New York), 31, 39, 173-174
Locke, John, 5, 16, 105, 108, 135, 184
Lofft, Capell, 65
Logan, George, 156, 182-183, 185::n, George, 156, 182-183, 185
Logan, James, 3
London Corresponding Society for the Reform of Parliamentary Representation, The, 65, 73, 103
London Tower, 48
Long Island, 18
Louis XVI, 39, 58
Louis, The Coachman, 208
Louisiana, 93-97
Lucan; *Pharsalia*, 174
Lucretius, 134
Luserne, Marquis de la, 48
Lycurgus, 36
Lyle, Peter, 131
Lyon, Matthew (Congressman from Vermont), 156, 160-161
Lyonnet, Pierre, 94-95
Lyons, 111

M

Mably, 8, 41
Macaulay, Catherine, 62
Mackintosh, Sir James, 61-62
Maclure, William, 171, 182-183
Madison, Dolly, 207
Madison, James, 1, 159, 171, 180, 183, 190, 192, 196-196, 198-201, 203-204
Maecenas, 23
Maistre, Joseph de, 61, 151
Malthus, Robert, 63
Manning, William; "The Key of Liberty," 10
Marat; *Plan de législation criminelle*, 83
Marmontel; *Incas*, 6
Marseilles, 121, 129-130, 132
Marshall, John, 153, 158, 162, 194-196
Massachusetts Historical Society, 2, 101-102
Massillon, 6
Materialism, 114
Mather(s), 5
Mazzei, Philip, 50
Meigs, Josiah, 19, 188
Mémoires pour servir à l'histoire du Jacobinisme, 110, 150-151
Mendon Association of Congregational Pastors, 150
Meslier, Jean, 70
Middletown Cloth Manufactory, 197
Milan Decree, The, 198, 201, 203. See also American Embargo Act
Military Academy, 184
Military Philosophical Society, The, 190
Millar, John, 34
Milton, John, 14, 34, 36, 42, 102
Minerva, The, 152

230

Mint, 184
Mirabaud, Jean-Baptiste de, 135
Miranda, General Francisco de, 95
Mississippi River, 97
Mohammed, 36
Mohawks, 177
Monroe, James, 1, 100, 123-125, 146-149, 153, 159, 174, 201
Montagnard Régime, 100
Montesquieu, 5, 31, 109
Montgomery, General, 18, 186
Monthly Anthology and Boston Review, The, 188, 190
Monticello, 196
More, Hannah, 106
More, Thomas, 69
Morellet, Abbé André, 50
Morelly, 69
Morris, Gouverneur, 54, 57, 99-100, 159, 194
Morris, Robert, 41, 47
Morse, Reverend Jedidiah (Charlestown, Massachusetts), 151
Moses, 36
Mountainists, 85, 89, 91, 110-111, 120, 194
Murray, G. W., 78
Murray, William Vans, 155, 163

Mc
McKean, Professor Joseph, 102

N
Napoleon, Bonaparte, 2, 142-143, 153, 168-170, 173-175, 180, 182, 186, 198-199, 201-202, 207-208, 210-212
National Assembly, 79, 111
National Convention, 81, 87, 93, 115
National Gazette, 64
National Institution, 182-184
National Intelligencer, The, 183, 198
Nautilus, The, 142, 145
Naval Academy, 184
Necker, Jacques, 68
Neef, Joseph, 183
Negroes; Defense of by Abbé Henri Grégoire, 89
Nemours, Dupont de, Pierre Samuel, 210
New Harmony, Indiana, 182
New Haven Gazette, 40
New Orleans, 95, 97
Newton, Isaac, 103, 135
Nemours, Victor Marie Du Pont de, 154-155
New York City, 18
New York Dairy, 152
New York Historical Society, The, 2
Non-Importation Act, 194
Non Intercourse Act, 199-200
North, Lord, 27
North African States, 12, 125, 200
Notre Dame, Paris, 48

O
O'Brien, Captain Richard, 122, 125, 130-131, 133
Oelsner, Konrad Engelbert, 210
Oeuvres diverses, 137
O'Fallon, Dr. James, 94
Opie, John, 174
Ohio Land Company, 94
Order of Malta, The, 125
Origine de tous les cultes ou Religion universelle, 136
Osgood, Reverend David, 112
Oswald, John, 65
Otto, Louis Guillaume, 95, 154
Owen, Robert, 151, 182

P
Paine, Thomas, 4, 39, 49, 62-65, 68, 74-75, 100, 102-103, 107-108, 123, 150, 162, 169-170, 173, 175, 188-189
Pan, Mallet du, 110
Panckouke, Charles Joseph, 134
Paradise, John, 56-57
Paradise Lost, 36, 42
Parker, Daniel, 46, 48, 99
Parrington, Vernon, 4
Parsons, General Samuel, 46
Pastorals, 174
Patent Office, 184
Penelope, 174
Pequot, The Library–Southport, Connecticut, 2
Perry, Sampson, 111-112, 116
Pestalozzi, 183
Petry, Jean Baptiste, 203-204
Petty, 5
Pharsalia, 174
Philadelphia, 3
Philadelphia Library Company, 3
Philosophes (French), 4, 37, 39, 60, 117-118, 134, 139, 186
Philosophical Society in Philadelphia, 210
Physiocrats, 7, 50, 118
Pickering, Timothy, 200
Pig's Meat, 73-74
Pilgrim's Progress, 63
Pillnitz, The Declaration of, 79
Pinckney, Charles, 148, 152-154, 158-159, 162
Pinel, Nicolas, 83
Pitt, William, 87, 106, 143, 145, 154, 170
"Plan for Taking Louisiana," 96
Playfair, William, 53-55, 83, 110
Pluche, 6
"Poem at the Public Commencement, A, 28
"Poet of the American Revolution," 5
Pope, Alexander, 14, 33-34, 42, 184
Porcupine, Peter (William Cobbett), 115
Portland, Maine Public Library, 2
Portrait de Robespierre, 117
Prescription, Doctrine of, 63-64
Price, Dr. Richard, 29, 40
Priestley, John (Scientist), 61
Priestley, Joseph; *History of the Corruptions of Christianity,* 66, 171
Priests Unmasked, The, 67
Prior, Sir James, 61
Proclamation of Rebellion, 17
"Prospect of Peace, The," 2, 20
Proofs of a Conspiracy Against The Religions and Governents of Europe Carried on in Secret Meetings of Freemasons, Illuminati and Reading Societies, 150-151
Prospectus of a National Institution, 176, 183, 185, 192
Proteus, 139
Publicola, (John Quincy Adams), 64
Puffendorf, 96
Puritan, 189
Putnam, General Rufus, 23, 46, 55
Pym, 12

Q
Quesnay, 8, 50

R
Rambouillet Decree, 198. See also American Embargo Act
Raynal, 8, 41, 50
"Renovation of Society, or an Essay on the Necessity &

231

Propriety of a Revolution in the Governments of Europe, The," 58
Republican Party, 109, 113, 149, 153, 156, 160, 173, 180, 181
Review of the Constitution of Great Britain, 65
Revolution, French, 52-53, 55, 58, 60, 68, 110, 112
Richelieu, Cardinal; *Political Testament*, 68
Rights of Man, 64
"Rights of Swine, The," 74
Rittenhouse, David, 3
Rivarol, Antoine, 60
Rivière, Mercier de la, 50
Robertson, William, 33, 39, 41, 118, 184
Robespierre, 60, 76, 93, 108, 112, 116-117, 126, 156:6-117, 126, 156
Rochambeau, 14
Roland, 101
Roland, Mme., 13, 121
Rolliad, 42
Rollin; *Ancient History*, 15
Romilly, Sir Samuel, 61
Romney, George, 64
Rouen Cathedral (France), 48
Rousseau, Jean Jacques, 5, 105, 108, 134, 165, 175
Roux, Jacques, 100
Royal Proclamation against Seditious Writings, The, 76
Ruins, or Meditations on the Revolutions of Empires, 134
Rumsey; Steamboat, 49
Rush, Benjamin, 190

S

Saint-Simon, Henri de, 140, 183
St. André, Jean Bon, 132
St. Cloud Decree, 203
Saint-Etienne, Rabaut, 101
Saint-Germain, Pallier de, 75
St. Paul's Cathedral (London), 48
Saint Pierre, Abbé de, 75
Sans-culottes, 203
Sargent, Winthrop, 45, 52
Satan, 42
Savoy, 89, 92, 95
Savoyards, 85
Sayre, Stephen, 94-96
Schimmelpenick, Rutger Jan, 173
Scioto Land Company, 44, 52-57, 99, 110
Scotch, Jacobins, 182
Second Continental Congress 1775, 17
Shays, Daniel, 10, 40-41, 80
Sheridan, Richard Brinsley, 61
Sidney, Philip, 6
Sinclair, Sir John, 68
Skipwith, Fulwar, 157-159
Smirke, Robert, 177, 189
Smith, Adam, 7, 53, 68, 118, 184
Smith, Mrs. Barbara D., 2
Smith, Charlotte, 65, 84
Smith, Robert, 193
Smith, General Samuel, 200
Snowden Richard *(The Vision of Columbus)*, 185
Social Contract, The, 6
Société d'encouragement de l'industrie nationale (Paris), 210
Society of the Twenty-Four, 54
Society for Promoting Constitutional Information, The, 12-13, 65, 86
Society for the Relief of Free Negroes Unlawfully Held in Bondage, The, 1775, 9
Soisson, 54-55

Sons of Liberty, The, 80, 108
Spence, Thomas, 73
Spinoza; *Ethics*, 136
Spirit of the Clergy, The, 67
Spirit of Laws, 6
Springfield, Massachusetts, 29
Staël, Madame de, 102, 198
Stamp Act, The, 9
Stanhope, Earl, 177
Stiles, Betsy, 24
Stiles, Ezra, 16, 39, 101-102, 114-115
Stone, J. H., 172
Strong, Nathaniel, 17
Submarine (Robert Fulton), 140
Sullivan, James, 112
Sully, Peace Project, 75
Swan, James, 57, 80, 98-99, 102, 173
"Swinish Multitude," 62
Swift, Zaphaniah, 18
System of Nature, 134

T

Taine, Hippolyte, 151
Talleyrand, 153-155, 157, 162-163
Tarlé, Eugene, 207
Telemachus (Fenelon), 6
Terror, The (France), 110, 114-115
Testament, Le, 70
Thelwall, John, 65, 73
Thomson, James, 14, 36
Thucydides, 103
Ticonderoga, 18
Tooke, Horne, 49, 177
"Toot," 140. See also Robert Fulton
Topographical Description of the Western Territory of North America, A, 94
Tories, 190, 195
Tracy, Uriah, 18, 149
Trafalgar, Battle of, 181
Treaty of Amiens, 170
Treatises on Civil Government, 105
"The Tree of Liberty," 75
Tripoli, 122, 131-133
Trumbull, John, (painter), 65
Trumbull, John (poet), 29, 34-35, 40, 80
Tunis, 122, 131
Tupper, Benjamin, 46
Turgot, 8, 41, 50
Two Letters to the Citizens of the United States 163, 171

U

Ulysses, 174
Union, The, 180
United States, The, 196
University of France, 182
University of Georgia, The, 198
Utopia, 69

V

Vanderlyn, John, 177
Vattel, 6
Vega, Garcilass de la, 36
Vergniaud, 101
Vernon, William Henry, 57
Vertot, 6
Virgil, 174, 186
Vision of Columbus, The, 23, 33, 77, 120, 138, 170, 174, 176-177, 185-186, 210
Volney, Constantin, 105, 134-135, 154, 171, 173, 202,

232

Voltaire, 5, 31, 33, 105, 134, 151
"Volunteer Boys, The," 5

W

Walker, Benjamin, 55
Wakefield, Gilbert, 106
Warner, Reverend John–Chaplain of the British Embassy in Paris, 76, 84
Washington, George, 17, 39, 93, 109, 146, 148, 154, 157, 161-162, 186, 194, 200
Watson, Dr. (Bishop of Leandaff), 106
Watson, James, 161
Watts, Dr's Psalms, 30
Weber, Max, 53
Webster, Noah, 19, 30, 113-115, 119, 160, 163, 180, 189
West, Benjamin, 65, 140-141
Westminster Confession, The, 16
Whiskey Insurrection, 115, 195. See also Whisky Rebellion
"Whisky (sic) Rebellion," 109, 115
Whitehead, Alfred, 5
Whiting, Wiliam, 10
Whitman, Elizabeth, 24
Wilkinson, General James, 94
Williams, Helen Maria, 13, 62, 65, 101, 173, 202, 209
Wilson, James, 17
Windsor Castle (London), 48
Wolcott, Alexander, 19, 169, 172
Wolcott, Oliver, 19, 39, 116, 149, 161
Wollstonecraft, Mary, 62, 65, 86-87, 94, 101 111-112
Wordsworth, William, 61

X

Xerxes, 186
X Y Z Affair, 153-154

Y

Yale, 3
"Yankee Doodle's Simplicity," 5
Yorke, Henry Redhead, 170, 175
Young, Arthur, 61, 105
Yvon, Abbé, 135

Z

Zarnowiez, Poland, 209